Bradt Travel Guides and is now a freelance travel writer. Along with researching and writing Bradt guides to the *Cayman Islands* and the *Turks and Caicos Islands*, she and Bob have co-authored their guide to *St Helena, Ascension and Tristan da Cunha*, and have helped to update several others in southern Africa.

HENRY STEDMAN updated this fourth edition. He has now completed 11 National Trails and written guides to several of them, including *Hadrian's Wall Path*, *Cleveland Way* and the three books to the *South-West Coast Path*. He is also the author of guides to two other UK long-distance paths, the *Coast to Coast Path* and *Dales Way*.

With him on this trek, as usual, was **DAISY**, his (mostly) faithful dog. An experienced long-distance walker, Daisy has completed all the trails above with Henry and her ambition is to walk all 15 National Trails.

Authors

Cotswold Way First edition: 2009; this fourth edition: 2019

Publisher Trailblazer Publications
The Old Manse, Tower Rd, Hindhead, Surrey, GU26 6SU, UK ✉ trailblazer-guides.com

British Library Cataloguing in Publication Data
A catalogue record for this book is available from the British Library

ISBN 978-1-912716-04-3

Series Editor: Anna Jacomb-Hood **Editor**: Anna Jacomb-Hood **Cartography**: Nick Hill
Proofreading: Jane Thomas **Layout and Index**: Anna Jacomb-Hood
Photographs (flora): **C1** – Row 2, left: © Bob Hayne
C1 – Row 1, middle & right; Row 2, middle & right; Rows 3 & 4, right: © Tricia Hayne
C2 – Row 2, right; Row 3, middle & right; Row 4, right: © Tricia Hayne
C3 – Row 1, middle; Row 2 left & right: © Tricia Hayne **C1-3** all others © Bryn Thomas
Other photographs: © Henry Stedman (unless otherwise indicated)

Dedication

In memory of Tricia's mum, Mollie

Acknowledgements

FROM HENRY: Thanks to Zoe for the company on the first part of the walk – and for looking after little Henry so big Henry could complete the second part. I'm also grateful to everyone who helped with the research of this new edition. Thanks also to all those readers who've emailed with comments and suggestions, in particular Mary Louise Adams, Stuart Blackburne, David Burgess, Julie Cocks, David Durrant, Hans & Liset Frijters-Pollen, Tim Fuller, Marilyn Green & Larry Jones, Andrew Guppy, Dave Howell, Pete Knox, Charlotte Langston, Brian Lynch, Doris McCormick, Yuki Mikidorikawa, Justin Morgan, Patricia Pearl, Sarah Peirce, Morten Planer, John Schnake, Philip Scriver, Ian Solomon, Andy Strickland, Ann Thomas, Linda Weatherley, Flemming & Mari-Ann Weigand, Marie Williamson and Paul Woodland (for the photo of Tricia & Bob). At Trailblazer, thanks to: Anna Jacomb-Hood for her usual forensic approach to editing the text, Nick Hill for the maps, Jane Thomas for proofreading and Bryn Thomas, as always, for keeping me busy.

A request

The authors and publisher have tried to ensure that this guide is as accurate as possible. Nevertheless, things change even on these well-worn routes. If you notice any changes or omissions, please write to Trailblazer (address above) or email us at ✉ info@trailblazer-guides.com. A free copy of the next edition will be sent to persons making a significant contribution.

Warning: long-distance walking can be dangerous

Please read the notes on when to go (pp13-16) and outdoor safety (p58). Every effort has been made by the authors and publisher to ensure that the information contained herein is as accurate and up to date as possible. However, they are unable to accept responsibility for any inconvenience, loss or injury sustained by anyone as a result of the advice and information given in this guide.

Printed in China; print production by D'Print (☎ +65-6581 3832), Singapore

Cotswold Way

44 large-scale maps & guides to 48 towns and villages

PLANNING – PLACES TO STAY – PLACES TO EAT

CHIPPING CAMPDEN TO BATH

TRICIA & BOB HAYNE

FOURTH EDITION RESEARCHED AND UPDATED BY

HENRY STEDMAN

TRAILBLAZER PUBLICATIONS

INTRODUCTION

Contents

PART 4: ROUTE GUIDE AND MAPS

APPENDICES & INDEX

DISTANCE CHART 194

OVERVIEW MAPS & PROFILES 197

Contents

ABOUT THIS BOOK

This guidebook contains all the information
you need. The hard work has been done for
you so you can plan your trip without having
to consult numerous websites and other books
and maps. When you're all packed and ready
to go, there's comprehensive public transport
information to get you to and from the
Cotswold Way and detailed maps (1:20,000)
to help you find your way along it.

● Where to stay – from campsites to B&Bs,
hostels and hotels
● Walking companies if you want an organised tour and baggage-carrying services if
you just want your luggage carried
● Itineraries for all levels of walkers
● Answers to all your questions: when is the
best time to walk, how hard is it, what to pack
and the approximate cost of the trip
● Walking times in both directions; GPS waypoints as a back-up to navigation
● Availability and opening times of cafés,
pubs, tea-shops, restaurants, and shops/super-
markets along the route
● Rail, bus and taxi information for the towns
and villages on or near the path
● Street maps of the main towns and villages
● Historical, cultural and geographical background information

Cotswold Way
'The Beginning and the End'
original marker post in
Chipping Campden.

❏ **MINIMUM IMPACT FOR MAXIMUM INSIGHT**

*We do not inherit the earth from our ancestors: we borrow it from our
children.* **Native American proverb**

By their very nature, walkers tend to be both interested in and concerned
about the natural environment. This book seeks to reinforce that interest
and concern. There are sections devoted to minimum-impact walking and
conservation, with ideas on how to broaden that ethos, as well as a
detailed, illustrated chapter on wildlife.
    There can be few activities as 'environmentally friendly' as walking.
By developing a deeper ecological awareness through a better understanding of nature, and by supporting rural economies, sensitive forms of
transport and low-impact methods of farming and land use, we can all do
our bit to ensure that the environment remains in safe hands for generations to come.

Photos – Front cover and pp2-3: Broadway Tower (see p84), built in 1799 as
a folly on Beacon Hill. **Previous pages**: Looking back towards Stanway.

About this book

INTRODUCTION

Asked to conjure up an image of a quintessential Cotswold scene, most people will come up with some combination of a village of honey-coloured houses set against a backdrop of sheep grazing in hillside fields, demarcated by seemingly endless dry-stone walls. For once, the reality and the picture-postcard image still coincide, at least in part. Nevertheless, to walk the Cotswold Way is to discover a far more complex – and arguably more rewarding – environment, where wide tracts of arable land unfold over the hills, and ancient beech woods line the Cotswold escarpment.

> For once, the reality and the picture-postcard image still coincide...

With the Cotswold villages of tourist brochures along the early part of the route, and the architectural glories of Georgian Bath that await the walker in the south, it's soon clear that Cotswold limestone

Stanton's golden-stone cottages encapsulate the quiet beauty of a Cotswold village.

has been hugely influential in defining the landscape. As you head south, so the stone of the houses gradually fades, from Stanton's golden cottages to the palest ivory of Painswick's villas. Simple parish churches, towering follies and stately homes make their mark, too, all constructed of the same stone. Yet it's not just the stone that hints at the region's history. You won't get far without coming across any number of humps, lumps and bumps, relics of earlier inhabitants who left their mark in burial mounds, hill forts, monasteries and even villas right across the trail. Their chosen spots were often some of those most revered by today's walkers: wide-open expanses on windy hilltops with views west to the wide River Severn and the Malvern Hills.

Almost the entire trail runs through the Cotswolds Area of Outstanding Natural Beauty

Almost the entire trail runs through the Cotswolds Area of Outstanding Natural Beauty (AONB), crossing fields still bounded by hedges and walls, and hills where sheep have grazed for centuries. In the early years, merchants grew rich on the bounty that was sheep's wool, their fortunes invested in the foundation of towns from Chipping Campden to Dursley. Where grazing has ended, human intervention has ensured that at least some of the rich grassland can remain a haven for the wild flowers, birds and insects that previous generations took for granted.

Thoughtfully, the Cotswold Way crosses all these places – and perhaps that's the greatest advantage of a man-made trail. While earlier walkers must have taken a direct route on pilgrimage to the abbey at Hailes, today's hikers on the Cotswold Way find themselves twisting and turning along a trail that effectively showcases the very best that the region can offer. That that includes historic castles, more than a passing nod to the Arts and Crafts Movement, and some excellent pubs, is to the benefit of all.

History

HISTORY OF THE TRAIL

The Cotswold Way runs for 102 miles (163km) through the Cotswold Hills from Chipping Campden in the north to the Georgian city of Bath. The route was originally devised as a long-distance footpath by members of the Ramblers' Association (now called Ramblers) and was established in conjunction with the Cotswolds AONB in 1970.

Below: The first great view on the Cotswold Way: the panorama from Drover's Hill, just outside Chipping Campden.

INTRODUCTION

INTRODUCTION

Its development as a national trail was approved in 1998, but it was not until May 2007 that the trail was formally launched, one of just 15 in England and Wales at that time. During the transition, several changes were made to the route, and others are still in the offing, although for the most part the original paths remain open.

The path is the responsibility of the National Trail Officer, under the auspices of the Cotswold Way National Trail Office (see box p44).

GEOLOGY

Look at a geological map of England and it is immediately clear that the origins of the present-day Cotswolds lie in the Jurassic period. Such maps show a con-

> **Cotswold stone is an oolitic limestone ... formed in the shallow seas of the Jurassic**

tinuous swathe of Jurassic-age rocks, formed between 199 and 145 million years ago, extending all the way from Dorset to the Yorkshire coast, with the most complete and impressive outcrop making up the Cotswold Hills. Cotswold stone is an oolitic limestone, a sedimentary rock that was formed primarily in the

© Tricia Hayne

© Tricia Hayne

❑ **Dry-stone walls**
The dry-stone walls that are so evocative of the Cotswolds are created from irregularly shaped blocks of the local limestone. Deceptive in their simplicity, they require a considerable level of skill to build, with an expert able to complete around six or seven yards (6-7m) a day.

Some beds of Cotswold stone break down naturally into layers of around two or three inches (50-75mm) thick. Typically, the wall is created from two parallel lines of stone, gradually coming together as they near the top. Stones on each side of the wall are fitted together like a jigsaw, laid sloping outwards to draw water away from the centre. Smaller pieces of stone, and offcuts, are used to fill the central cavities, adding strength and durability to the whole wall.

warm shallow seas of the Jurassic. It is comprised of a large number of almost spherical granules, or oolites, packed closely together, and its origins explain the regular occurrence in the rock of fossils, such as sea urchins. Occasional falls in sea level, however, resulted in dry land where dinosaurs roamed, leaving behind both their footprints and their bones. While most walkers will see little difference between the rocks at various places along the trail, to the geologist there are marked distinctions according to the stages at which the sediments were deposited and compressed. In addition, while the surface rock of the Cotswold range is predominantly limestone, the underlying structure is more usually of clays, silts and sands. It is the precise structure of these rocks that both determines the wildlife that populates the hillside and influences the buildings you will see in each part of the region.

Gloucestershire Geology Trust (💻 glosgeotrust.org.uk) is committed to studying and conserving the region's geological heritage, and to recording regionally important geological sites. The trust publishes a series of trail guides (£2 each) entitled *Gloucestershire Uncovered*, which include Cleeve Hill Common, Leckhampton Hill and Crickley Hill.

Finally, a layer of slats, or 'combers', is laid along the top at right angles to the wall. The whole is usually around 3ft (1m) high, and some 20in (50cm) at the base, tapering to around 16in (40cm) at the top.

It is estimated that there are some 4000 miles (6000km) of dry-stone walls across the whole of the Cotswolds AONB. Weather, vegetation and accidents take their toll, so regular maintenance is essential. As a result of a revival of interest in traditional crafts, it is possible to go on a course to learn the basics, or to take part as a volunteer to help preserve the region's existing walls. For more information, contact Cotswolds Conservation Board (who run Cotswolds AONB, see p60) or the Dry Stone Walling Association of Great Britain (💻 www.dswa.org.uk).

INTRODUCTION

How difficult is the path?

Familiarity with the Cotswolds – or at least with the tourist areas in the north – might lead to a sense that the Cotswold Way is little more than a walk in the park. While it would be unreasonable to suggest that it is seriously challenging, it would be equally wrong to underestimate the quite literal ups and downs of a route that takes you from just above sea level to 1066ft (325m) and back over a distance of more than 100 miles.

If, as is often suggested, you plan to complete the route in seven days, you're looking at an average of nearly 15 miles, or 6-7 hours' actual walking, every day. Some of those hills are steeper than you might expect from a casual glance at the landscape and poor weather can exacerbate what would otherwise be fairly straightforward. It makes sense, then, to have a reasonable level of fitness before you set off, if only to make sure that what should be an enjoyable week or so's walking doesn't turn into a test of endurance.

Below: Pausing for breath at the (almost) halfway marker outside Painswick. The route is well signposted so you shouldn't get lost; look for the acorn logo.

INTRODUCTION

How long do you need?

This is the great imponderable. Is it reasonable – as many hikers do – to walk the path from end to end in a week? Well yes, but it's a qualified yes. If you have just seven days' holiday but need two of those to get to and from the trail, you'll be faced with walking 20 miles a day, which isn't for the faint hearted. If, on the other hand, you can spend most of those seven days on the trail, a week is realistic. That said, averaging almost 15 miles a day won't leave much time for exploring the villages on the route, taking time out for a cream tea in Broadway, or a pint of Donnington's at The Mount Inn in Stanton, or exploring

So while the world reckons that this is a week's walk, give it eight days and you'll be adding in time to breathe

Selsley Common for orchids. You might find yourself casting a wistful backward glance at old churches as you march purposefully past the lych gate, or promising yourself you'll come back to do justice to Hailes Abbey, or Dyrham Park, or even to Bath. So while the world reckons that this is a week's walk, give it eight days and you'll be adding in time to breathe.

If time is really short, you could reasonably leave out the last section, perhaps south of Cold Ashton and down Lansdown Hill into Bath (pp161-5). That isn't to say this isn't worthy of walking – far from it. But Bath is a destination in its own right, so the chances are that you could justify returning on another occasion.

See p33 for some suggested itineraries covering different walking speeds

Plenty of people can't spare the time to walk from end to end in one go, but still get that sense of achievement by building up the miles over a series of day or weekend walks until they've completed the route. Alternatively, you could simply sample the highlights (though lowlights are few); see pp36-7 for some recommendations.

When to go

SEASONS

Autumn that name of creeper falling and tea-time loving,
Was once for me the thought of High Cotswold noon-air   **Ivor Gurney**, *Old Thought*

While English weather is hardly predictable, at least some generalisations can be made. Statistically, the months when the weather is least likely to be inclement are May to September, but statistics – as we all know – can be very misleading. The air temperature at this time is generally at its warmest, with frosts unlikely from the end of May. Rain, though, is another factor. Some years can see con-

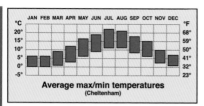

Average max/min temperatures
(Cheltenham)

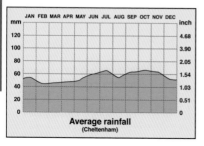

Average rainfall
(Cheltenham)

tinuous rain for several weeks and parts of the path will become impassable. While it's tempting to think that this is only likely to happen in winter, the last widespread flooding in Gloucestershire was in the summer of 2007, with 2008 running a close second. Conversely, April and October often bring days that are bright and breezy, when the walking and the surroundings are at their best.

Spring

The weather in spring is as unpredictable as the rest of the year. In **April**, it can be warm and sunny on odd days, but seldom for sustained periods. Conditions are more likely to be changeable, with blustery showers and cold spells reminding you that winter has only just passed. On the other hand, the days are long, and less rain falls on average in spring than at any other time of the year. This, coupled with the milder weather of **May** and **June**, and the proliferation of wild flowers early in the year, makes it one of the best times to tackle the trail.

Summer

July and **August** are the traditional holiday months and the conditions can be especially good for walking, with generally mild temperatures and still many hours of daylight. This, however, is also the time when the Cotswolds experience a surge in visitors, especially around the tourist honeypots of Broadway and Bath. Fortunately, most of the trippers won't be out in the fields and on the hills, so here at least you can leave the hordes behind.

Autumn

Many connoisseurs consider autumn, especially early autumn, the best time of year for walking. **September** and **October** can be lovely months to get out on the trail, especially when the leaves begin to turn. That said, although the air temperature usually remains relatively mild, October can see the first frosts and rain is an ever-present threat.

Winter

Only the very hardiest of souls will attempt the Cotswold Way in winter. There is less daylight; once the clocks have gone back at the end of October, until mid March, you will need to be at your destination by 4.30-5pm to avoid walking in the dark. Cold weather, wind and driving rain are not the best recipe for a day's walking, although a crisp winter morning takes a lot of beating.

DAYLIGHT HOURS

If you're planning to walk in autumn, winter or early spring, you'll need to take into account how far you can walk in the available daylight. It will not be possible to cover as many miles or to be out for as long as you would in the summer. The table gives the sunrise and sunset times for the middle of each month at latitude 52° North, which runs through the Cotswold Hills, giving a reason-

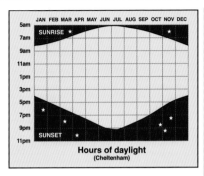

Hours of daylight
(Cheltenham)

ably accurate picture for daylight along the Cotswold Way. Depending on the weather, you should get a further 30-45 minutes of usable light before sunrise and after sunset.

❏ FESTIVALS AND ANNUAL EVENTS

The following events may need to be considered when planning your walk since all will affect the availability and sometimes price of accommodation in their area. Two with a particularly strong impact locally are The Festival in Cheltenham in March, and Badminton Horse Trials in May.

In addition to the following annual fixtures, be aware that weekend events held by the **Prescott Speed Hill Climb** (🖳 prescott-hillclimb.com) outside Winchcombe between about April and October can put a lot of pressure on the town's resources.

March
● **The Cheltenham Festival** (🖳 cheltenham.thejockeyclub.co.uk) has been rebranded as **The Festival**™. This is the best known race meeting in the National Hunt racing calendar and is held over four days in mid March. It's also one of the racing calendar's highlights – both in racing terms and socially – culminating in every jump jockey's dream, the Cheltenham Gold Cup. Tickets are hard sought after and accommodation throughout the area is often booked a year ahead. If you have no choice but to walk in this week, make sure you plan well ahead.

April/May
● **Wotton-under-Edge Arts Festival** (🖳 wottonartsfestival.org.uk) This 2-week festival takes place around the end of April and early May.
● **Cheltenham Jazz Festival** (🖳 cheltenhamfestivals.com/jazz) A week of jazz is celebrated early May.
● **Annual Cheese Rolling** Cooper's Hill There's still strong support for this wacky village event, traditionally held on the last May Bank Holiday Monday; see box p117.
● **Badminton Horse Trials** (🖳 badminton-horse.co.uk) Hugely important among the riding fraternity, this 5-day trial takes place east of the trail near Old Sodbury in early May. Accommodation is limited in this area, and guesthouses, pubs and hotels for miles around get prebooked months in advance: you've been warned!
● **The Bath Festival** (🖳 bathfestivals.org.uk/the-bath-festival) Taking place from the middle of May, this 17-day festival showcases music and literature.

(cont'd overleaf)

❏ FESTIVALS AND ANNUAL EVENTS

May (cont'd from p15)

● **Chipping Campden Music Festival** (🖥 campdenmusicfestival.co.uk) A 2-week festival of classical music, held in mid to late May and based in St James's Church.
● **Olimpick Games**, Dover's Hill, Chipping Campden (🖥 olimpickgames.co.uk) Friday after the last May Bank Holiday, followed the next day by the Scuttlebrook Wake; see box p80.
● **Winchcombe Walking Festival** (🖥 winchcombewelcomeswalkers.com) A series of graded walks and evening events taking place over the penultimate weekend in May.
● **Winchcombe Festival of Music & Arts** (🖥 winchcombefestival.co.uk) A week-long celebration of local talent held at the end of May.

June

● **Cheltenham Science Festival** (🖥 cheltenhamfestivals.com/science) Held over six days in early to mid June.
● **Cheltenham Food and Drink Festival** (🖥 garden-events.com) Three days of foodie heaven in Montpellier Gardens; mid June.
● **Cotswold Way Relay** (🖥 cotswoldwayrelay.co.uk) It might be best to avoid walking on the last Saturday in June. For details, see box p31.

July

● **Cheltenham Music Festival** (🖥 cheltenhamfestivals.com/music) Popular 2-week festival at the beginning of July with international artists playing an eclectic mix of primarily classical music.
● **Cotswold Beer Festival** (🖥 postlip.camra.org.uk) One of CAMRA's national beer festivals, usually held at Postlip Hall outside Winchcombe over the penultimate or last weekend in July.
● **Cheltenham Cricket Festival** (🖥 gloscricket.co.uk/cheltenham-cricket-festival) Founded in 1872, the 2-week festival is held in the grounds of Cheltenham College around the end of July/early August.

August

● **Artburst** (🖥 artburstpainswick.co.uk) Painswick's inaugural Art Festival in 2015 looks set to be a biennial event in late August and the next will be in 2019, then 2021.
● **Frocester Beer Festival** (🖥 frocesterbeerfestival.com) Two days of tasting, music and camaraderie, held near Stonehouse; August Bank Holiday weekend.

September

Cheltenham Comedy Festival (🖥 cheltenhamcomedy.com) A week of fun and laughter towards the end of September.

October

● **Cheltenham Literature Festival** (🖥 cheltenhamfestivals.com/literature) This 10-day festival in mid October goes from strength to strength, showcasing a range of international authors.
● **Dursley Walking Festival** (🖥 dursleywelcomeswalkers.org.uk) A 4-day festival (held early in October) focusing on walks around the little town of Dursley.

(Opposite) The Tyndale Monument (see p143) offers sweeping views across the Cotswolds landscape and it's well worth climbing the 121 steps to the top.

(Overleaf) Bath's grand Royal Crescent greets the walker on the final stretch of the walk. One of the best examples of Georgian architecture in Britain, it was completed in 1774.

PLANNING YOUR WALK

Practical information for the walker

ROUTE FINDING

Having been opened as a national trail only in 2007, it's no surprise that the Cotswold Way is clearly signposted along almost its entire length. Indeed, more than one website claims that the Cotswold Way is the most signposted of all the national trails. Be that as it may, there are a few occasions – usually in a field or a wood – where there may be some ambiguity, though in these instances the maps in this guide should quickly put you straight.

The waymark throughout your walk is the National Trails' acorn symbol, to be found on stiles, kissing gates, fingerposts and guideposts. Sometimes as an alternative you will find the standard yellow or blue footpath or bridlepath roundel overprinted with the words 'Cotswold Way', and the authorities in Bath have devised more discreet signs, sometimes a small metallic acorn on a black background, supplemented by stickers on lamp-posts and other street furniture.

Using GPS with this book

I never carried a compass, preferring to rely on a good sense of direction. I never bothered to understand how a compass works or what it is supposed to do. To me a compass is a gadget, and I don't get on well with gadgets of any sort.   **Alfred Wainwright**

While modern Wainwrights will scoff, more open-minded walkers will accept GPS technology as an inexpensive and well-established, if non-essential, navigational aid. With a clear view of the sky, GPS receivers will within a minute of being turned on establish your position and altitude anywhere on earth in a variety of formats, including the British Ordnance Survey grid system, to an accuracy of within a few metres. These days, most **smartphones** have a GPS receiver built in and **mapping software** available to run on it (see p42).

(Opposite) It's a bit of a schlep getting up there from Dowdeswell Reservoir but at least the views from Wistley Hill (see p113) are well worth the effort.

One thing must be understood, however: treating a GPS as a replacement for maps, a compass and common sense is a big mistake. Although current units are robust, it only takes the batteries to go flat or some electronic malfunction to leave you floundering, potentially in the dark. A GPS is merely a navigational aid or backup to conventional route finding and, in almost all cases, is best used in conjunction with a paper map. All a GPS does is stop you exacerbating navigational errors or save you time in correcting them.

The maps in the route guide include numbered waypoints; these correlate to the list on pp183-4, which gives the latitude/longitude position in a decimal minute format as well as a description. Typically, a waypoint has been given for most of the high spots and significant places of interest along the route, as well as for several of the towns and villages. You can download the complete list of these waypoints for free as a GPS-readable file (that doesn't include the text descriptions) from the Trailblazer website: 🖳 trailblazer-guides.com.

It's anticipated that you won't tramp along day after day, ticking off the book's waypoints as you pass them, because the route description and maps are more than adequate most of the time. Only when you're **unsure of your position**, or which way to go, might you feel the need to turn on the unit for a quick affirmation. It's also possible to buy state-of-the-art **digital mapping** to import into your GPS unit, assuming that you have sufficient memory capacity, but it's not the most reliable way of navigating and the small screen on your pocket-sized unit will invariably fail to put places into context or give you a feel for the bigger picture.

Almost everyone who has ever walked the Cotswold Way has done so without GPS, so there's certainly no need to rush out and buy one. The route is exceptionally well waymarked and with the maps in this guide there is little chance you will get lost. That said, it offers a good opportunity to try out new technology before tackling something more navigationally challenging.

ACCOMMODATION

The Cotswold Way is generally well served with bed-and-breakfast (B&B), guesthouse and pub accommodation, but there are one or two places, particularly between the Cheltenham area and Dursley, where the options are quite limited and you may be faced with up to a mile further at the end of the day's walk. That said, most places listed in this guide are either on or within easy reach of the trail. Campers, though, will find themselves with quite a challenge and may have to combine camping with the odd night at a B&B. A comprehensive selection of places to stay is given in each section of the route guide (Part 4), though do bear in mind that even the most long-standing establishments can change hands, or close, without warning.

Camping
Man is born free under the stars, yet we lock our doors and creep to bed.
Robert Louis Stevenson
There are few official campsites along the Cotswold Way, especially along the northern part of the trail between Winchcombe and the Ebley Canal area. **Wild**

camping is not permitted anywhere, which is no help to those who prefer the great outdoors to a B&B. It may be worth asking at a farm along the route if you can pitch a tent in a field, but please don't just turn up and risk it. Farmers used to be more amenable to the odd inconspicuous tent but attitudes have changed and if you were discovered you would certainly not be made welcome.

Rates for camping range from free (such as Compass Inn in Tormarton, which allows you to camp for nothing but a donation to their charity box) to £10 per person per night, so it still remains the most economical way to walk the trail – though if you're more into glamping, you're looking at around £30 a head.

Camping pods and 'glamping'
Acting as a halfway house between camping and staying in a B&B, one place (Ullenwood) has **camping pods** – basic but comfortable 'sleeping sheds', usually simply furnished with a table and sleeping platform, though you'll often have to have your own bedding/sleeping bag. Prices vary widely but the better ones are around the £30pp mark.

The current craze for **glamping** – where the campsite provides you with a luxury tent (often a bell tent or yurt) fitted out with rugs, furniture and a proper bed to sleep in. There are also a couple of **shepherd's huts** along the trail that can be used by walkers for accommodation. Smartly furnished and very cosy, these huts aren't cheap at around £40-50pp — but they're certainly novel.

Hostels
Hostel accommodation along the Cotswold Way itself is available only in Bath, where there are three hostels; two independent and a YHA hostel. The latter, where accommodation discounts are available to members of the Youth Hostels Association (YHA; ☎ 01629-592700, or tollfree ☎ 0800 019 1700, 🖳 yha.org .uk) and **Hostelling International** (🖳 hihostels.com), is a good mile east of the centre, so a fair trek for walkers. For details of membership of the YHA see the YHA website.

B&B-style accommodation
Although historically there is a distinct difference between a guesthouse and the more personal B&B, the edges are becoming increasingly blurred. Traditionally, those staying in a B&B, where overnight visitors are limited to no more than six at any one time, will find themselves very much as guests in a private house. Establishments accommodating greater numbers have to be registered as a guesthouse.

Staying in **B&Bs** brings you into contact with local people in a way that guesthouses and hotels can't. For anyone unfamiliar with the concept, you get a bedroom in someone's home along with a cooked breakfast the following morning. The accommodation is invariably clean and comfortable, traditionally with the emphasis on floral patterns and chintz – although things are changing fast and rooms in many B&Bs along the Cotswold Way compete with the best for style and elegance. If one night you find yourself in a modern bungalow, the next could be in a picture-perfect cottage, or on a working farm.

Guesthouses, which effectively bridge the gap between B&Bs and hotels, may be more structured in approach – although in reality, especially in some of the towns along the trail, you may have no idea whether you're in a B&B or a guesthouse. What matters is a warm welcome, a comfortable room, and – ideally – someone who understands that walkers tend to have muddy boots and wet clothes.

Where visitor numbers are high, such as in Bath or Broadway, you may well find that a minimum two-night stay is imposed, which can cause problems for walkers. Others simply charge a higher rate for one-nighters. Such restrictions are most likely to be the case at weekends or in the height of the tourist season.

What to expect For most long-distance walkers, tourist-board star-rating systems have little meaning. At the end of a long day you'll simply be glad of a place with hot water and a smiling welcome. It is these criteria that have been used for places included in this guide, rather than whether a room has tea- and coffee-making facilities, a shaver point or TV – though many of them do.

In the trend towards making rooms **en suite**, many places have carved out a tiny area for a shower and a loo. Yet a larger room with a bathroom across the corridor, often for your own private use, could well be preferable – and the option of a hot bath has significant appeal if you're cold and wet; establishments with at least one bath in, or for, a room are indicated in this guide with a ♥ symbol.

Finding anywhere with a **single** room isn't easy and those there are tend to be pretty small. A **double** room is supposed to have one double bed, and a **twin** room two singles, but sometimes the two are interchangeable, allowing greater flexibility. Some places have rooms that can sleep three (**triple**), four (**quad**) or more – these rooms come in a variety of arrangements (see p74) but can also always sleep just two people.

Some B&Bs and guesthouses have a **sitting room** exclusively for guests' use, a real bonus at the end of a day when retiring to your room instead of

---

❏ **Booking**

It's best to reserve your accommodation in advance, especially at peak periods and weekends, when there can be stiff competition for beds, and in winter, when several B&Bs close for the season. Very few B&B owners appreciate someone turning up on the doorstep without warning and you don't want to find yourself with nowhere to stop. The suggested itineraries on p32 should help with planning ahead.

Most hotels and some B&Bs offer online or email booking, but for some you will need to contact them by phone. In many cases you will be asked for a deposit of around 50%, rising to 100% for one-night bookings, which is generally non-refundable if you cancel at short notice. While larger places may take credit or debit cards, some via PayPal, many B&Bs accept only cheques or payments by bank transfer for the deposit, with the balance settled by cash or cheque. Do remember to take your cheque book!

If you do have to cancel, be sure to give as much notice as you can so they can offer your room to someone else.

❏ **Notes on rates**
Prices given in this guide are, unless otherwise stated, per person (based on two sharing a room) with breakfast for one night.

Few places along the Cotswold Way offer single rooms so most charge a supplement on the per person rate. However, the occasional place still charges per room, regardless of the number of people and the odd one or two charge more for a twin room than for a double – which may not seem logical to ordinary mortals.

The trend towards flexible pricing according to the time of year, the time of the week, and the occurrence of festivals, is spreading beyond hotels to pubs and even B&Bs, especially in tourist hotspots; this makes it difficult to generalise about rates so do ensure you check the rate before confirming a reservation. Booking early can make a big difference, especially out of season. Conversely, during festivals or at similar times, rates can be extortionate.

For hotels in particular, do check whether or not breakfast is included, and watch out for hidden extras such as service charge and VAT.

relaxing in a comfy chair can seem something of an anti-climax. Others will welcome guests to sit out in the **garden** on a summer's evening.

An **evening meal** is sometimes on offer at the more isolated establishments, though you should always pre-book this or you could go hungry. If you're expecting a meal, but are delayed, do ring ahead. Nobody wants to serve (or eat) dried-up lasagne and limp salad. If meals are not available, many owners will offer you a lift to the nearest pub if it's too far to walk.

Rates The image of B&B as a cheap option is no longer valid; costs have soared in recent years. Expect to pay £35-50pp per night based on two sharing a room; for single occupancy you may need to pay £50-90, and often the full room rate, though we did find one place (take a bow, Ye Olde Dursley) that charged just £25 for an en suite single – remarkable value. See box above and p30.

Transport Where places offering accommodation are not right on the Cotswold Way, B&B owners may offer to collect walkers at an agreed rendezvous point and deliver them back to the trail next day. It's a service that is usually provided free of charge, but do check first. It is important to agree lift arrangements at the time of booking and, if possible, to phone ahead to warn of your impending arrival at the pick-up point – or of any delays, of course. If the B&B doesn't offer an evening meal and is in a remote location, they may offer you a lift to a local pub or town for dinner.

Pubs Many pubs offer B&B accommodation and some supply every modern convenience – including luxuries such as four-poster beds. Obviously they tend to be less personal than B&Bs, but for some walkers that's a bonus – and you don't have far to go to the bar, either. Of greater concern for most people is that pubs can be quite noisy, especially at weekends, so bear this in mind if you fancy an early night.

In general, pub prices along the Cotswold Way are similar to those at B&Bs (see above).

PLANNING YOUR WALK

Hotels

At first glance a hotel may not seem the obvious venue for a walker. Muddy boots and a rucksack might seem at odds with the surroundings and having something suitable to change into could pose a problem, but if you can get over that hurdle, you're down to issues of cost and style.

Most hotels charge per room rather than per person, and while some will negotiate a rate for single occupancy, this is by no means the norm. (See box on p21). While you might expect to pay at least £40pp based on two sharing a room (and at least £60 for single occupancy), many hotels charge more, and during festivals or at similar times rates can be extortionate.

Airbnb

The rise and rise of Airbnb (🖳 airbnb.co.uk) has seen private homes and apartments opened up to overnight travellers on an informal basis. While accommodation is primarily based in cities, the concept has spread to tourist hotspots in more rural areas, but do check thoroughly what you are getting and the precise location. While the first couple of options listed may be in the area you're after, others may be far too far afield for walkers. At its best, this is a great way to meet local people in a relatively unstructured environment, but do be aware that these places are not registered B&Bs, so standards may vary, and prices may not necessarily be any lower than the norm.

Holiday cottages

The inclusion of holiday cottages is outside the scope of a guide dedicated to walkers on the move. However, for those who would prefer to stay at a fixed base, covering different parts of the route each day, self-catering may be the perfect option. Typically, cottages are let on a weekly or fortnightly basis, with prices starting at around £350 a week for four people in the low season. For possible places look at: 🖳 holidaycottages.co.uk or 🖳 homeaway.co.uk. If you're after something more individual, you could try one of the properties owned by the Landmark Trust (see p62).

FOOD AND DRINK

The Cotswolds area isn't known for its haute cuisine. Historically at least, this is a region of simple, farmhouse fare, based on good ingredients, rather than fine cooking.

In Bath you'll come across a few regional specialities (see box on p178), but elsewhere savvy travellers seek out the delights of Old Spot pork, Cotswold honey, or Double Gloucester cheese. Tea rooms do a fine trade in cream teas, too, though it would be stretching a point to suggest that this is typical of the region.

Breakfast and lunch

A **breakfast** fry-up of bacon, eggs and sausages is considered *de rigueur* by many walkers – and supplied by nearly all good B&B hosts. Most offer a buffet of cereals and fruit juice and toast as well, perhaps with the addition of yoghurt

❏ Real ale along the trail

Much of the beer found in pubs along the path is pasteurised and manufactured in millions of gallons for distribution throughout the UK. Known as 'keg beer', it has been reviled by real ale drinkers in its time but is invariably smooth and tastes the same wherever you are. However, traditional real ale, the product of small-scale local breweries, is always in demand. Real ale continues to ferment in the cask so can be drawn off by hand pump or a simple tap on the cask itself. Keg beer, on the other hand, has the fermentation process stopped by pasteurisation and needs the addition of gas to give it fizz and sparkle.

Keep an eye out for pubs displaying the CAMRA sticker, which shows they have been selected by the **Campaign for Real Ale** (🖳 camra.org.uk). This invaluable organisation, which publishes the annual *Good Beer Guide*, has been largely responsible for the revival of independent breweries in the UK. Their 'LocAle' initiative encourages pubs to stock at least one locally brewed ale and has been taken up by an increasing number of landlords along the trail. Many also have a selection of guest ales from surrounding counties to add variety. Some of the local brews you'll find along the Cotswold Way are those by: **Abbey Ales** (🖳 abbeyales.co.uk), **Bath Ales** (🖳 bathales.com), **Blindmans Brewery** (🖳 blindmansbrewery.co.uk), **Butcombe** (🖳 butcombe.com), **Donnington** (🖳 donnington-brewery.com), **Moles** (🖳 moles brewingco.co.uk), **Purity** (🖳 puritybrewing.com/beers), **Stanway** (🖳 stanwaybrew ery.co.uk), **Stroud** (🖳 stroudbrewery .co.uk), **Uley** (🖳 uleybrewery.com) and **Wickwar** (🖳 wickwarbrewing.com). You'll come across offerings from the Hereford-based **Wye Valley Brewery** (🖳 wyevalleybrewery.co.uk), too, while the Cornish contingent is represented by **Sharp's** (🖳 sharpsbrewery.co.uk). All create good pints, but try the brews above 4% ABV for better taste and flavour.

Whether you're after a quick half at lunch or putting your feet up in the evening, there's no shortage of pubs with good-quality beer. Scanning the pumps at the *Crown & Trumpet* (see p86) in **Broadway** you'll spot ales from the small Stanway Brewery. Broadway comes up trumps at the *Horse & Hound* (p86) too, where you could strike lucky with a pint of Purity's Mad Goose.

An evening meal at *The Mount Inn* (see p90) at **Stanton** washed down with a pint of Donnington's is hard to beat. While wandering around **Painswick**, drop into the *Royal Oak* (see p126) for a selection from the Stroud (organic beer) or Butcombe breweries. If you time it right a lunch break at *The Edgemoor Inn* (see p128), at **Edge**, offers Wickwar's BOB amongst others, or their latest bottled ale – Cotswold Way. Well worth a short detour is *The Old Crown* (see p134) at **Uley** which, as well as supporting its own local brewery, offers an ever-changing choice of other beers; if it all gets too much you can stay overnight, too.

Further south you arrive at ale-seekers' heaven, *The Old Spot* (see p140) in **Dursley**, voted CAMRA Pub of the Year in 2007, and still maintaining high standards. It offers a wonderful array of bitters, including Old Ric from Uley Brewery (named after owner Ric Sainty, who died in 2008). *Beaufort Arms* (see p152) at **Hawkesbury Upton** has an ever-changing range; continuing along the trail, *The Dog Inn* (see p154) at **Old Sodbury** has Sharp's Doom Bar.

Celebrations should be in order on reaching **Bath** (see p181), where you'll be spoiled for choice. Try *The Star Inn* or *The Old Green Tree* for a pint of Bellringer (Abbey Ales), or seek out a pint of Gem (Bath Ales) at *The Salamander*. The *Volunteer Rifleman's Arms* is another good choice, but the medal winner is arguably to be found at *The Raven*, where they have their very own brew from Blindmans Brewery, near Frome: Raven's Gold.

PLANNING YOUR WALK

and fresh fruit, so if a 'full English' isn't for you, you'll always be able to fall back on something lighter.

Unless you're planning to stop at a pub or café en route, you will probably need a **packed lunch**. Many B&B owners – indicated in this guide by the (Ⓛ) symbol – will provide one and some will also fill your flask with coffee or tea. If you don't fancy breakfast, it's worth asking if you could have a packed lunch instead. Alternatively you could pick up the makings of a picnic lunch at village shops along the trail: rolls, cheese, apples and cereal bars survive well in a ruck-sack for a couple of days. Be careful to plan ahead, though, as there are sections of the walk when you won't come across any shops at all. In any event, you should always carry some form of high-energy food in case of an emergency (see p40).

Evening meals
Perhaps more than any other national trail, the Cotswold Way is abundantly supplied with **pubs** and **inns**, not to mention some pretty exclusive **restaurants**. Where B&Bs are off the beaten track, most owners will provide an evening meal by prior arrangement, or will drive you to the nearest pub. Occasionally, however, you'll have to fend for yourself, which could involve considerable extra mileage at the end of a long day.

Aside from the ubiquitous pub grub, the choice on menus continues to widen and almost everywhere will have at least one vegetarian option. If you're keeping a strict eye on costs, stick to pubs rather than restaurants, or look for fixed-price menus – often available early in the evening before the place gets busy.

Alternatively, there are numerous **takeaways** in towns along the route, from fish & chips, pizza parlours and kebab joints to Indian and Chinese cuisine.

Self-catering
There are enough shops along the path to allow you to buy supplies reasonably frequently so, in general, you should not need to carry food for longer than a couple of days. Most supermarkets are open seven days a week, often from 8am to 8pm or even later, taking full advantage of casual trade and the sale of alco-hol. Village shops and independent places such as bakeries are open more lim-ited hours.

Fuel for camp stoves may not always be available though, and, while Camping Gaz and meths can usually be found in the towns, it makes sense not to let supplies run low.

Drinking water
Carry at least a litre of water and top it up at public toilets during the day: these are marked on the trail maps in Part 4. Alternatively, ask locally; most people are happy to fill a bottle of water, though it's only fair to buy something first in a pub or café. Drinking from streams is not advisable.

MONEY

Plan your money needs carefully. It makes sense to carry cash for day-to-day spending and to pay for campsites. Most pubs, and all but the smallest village shops, accept debit or credit cards, but in B&Bs payment in cash or (less commonly) by cheque is still the norm.

If you're planning to stick to cash start with about £200 and expect to replenish along the way. All the towns you pass through have ATMs, either in banks, post offices, or in supermarkets. Cash can also be drawn at post offices against many UK bank accounts: for details, see 🖥 postoffice.co.uk/everyday-banking. Note that you need to have your debit card with you and your PIN number. To find a post office with an ATM look at postoffice.co.uk/atm-locator.

For more on money, see p41; for budgeting, see pp29-30.

OTHER SERVICES

Many of the villages and all the towns along the trail have at least one public **telephone**, a small **shop** and a **post office**, or a post office counter. Apart from getting cash, post offices are also handy for sending home unnecessary equipment that may be weighing you down. In Part 4 mention is given to other services that may be of use to the walker such as **outdoor equipment shops**, **surgeries** (medical centres) and **pharmacies**, and **tourist information centres**. These tourist offices can help, among other things, with finding accommodation. Most pubs, cafés, hotels and B&Bs boast **wi-fi** now so you shouldn't have a problem getting connected.

TAKING DOGS ALONG THE COTSWOLD WAY

There is no reason why your dog shouldn't accompany you on the Cotswold Way, provided you act responsibly and keep it under control at all times. The deal with dog mess is the same on a national trail as it is in the local park: clear it up. In Part 4 of this guide, the symbol 🐾 indicates that dogs are usually welcome, though you should still always check ahead; some may accept only small dogs, for example. Also note that dogs may have to be on a lead especially at campsites and in pubs/cafés. Few B&Bs and campsites charge for dogs but hotels often do, with rates varying from £5 a night to £20 per stay. Hostels generally don't accept dogs at all, with the exception of assistance dogs.

For more on planning a walk with man's best friend, see pp184-6.

DISABLED ACCESS

Many areas of the trail are inaccessible to the majority of wheelchair and scooter users, and those of limited mobility, either because the terrain is unsuitable or because of the not inconsiderable number of kissing gates to be negotiated. Some sections, however, are more forgiving – particularly near country parks which also have nearby parking.

For more on countryside access for the disabled, contact Disabled Ramblers (🖥 disabledramblers.co.uk).

WALKING COMPANIES

For walkers wanting to make their holiday as easy and trouble-free as possible there are several specialist companies offering a range of services, from baggage carrying to fully guided group tours.

Baggage transfer/accommodation booking
The thought of carrying a heavy pack puts a lot of people off walking long-distance trails, but on the Cotswold Way it need not be an issue.

❑ **Information for foreign visitors**

● **Currency** The British pound (£) comes in notes of £50, £20, £10 and £5, and coins of £2 and £1. The pound is divided into 100 pence (usually referred to as 'p', pronounced 'pee') which come in silver coins of 50p, 20p 10p and 5p and copper coins of 2p and 1p.

● **Rates of exchange** Up-to-date rates can be found at 🖳 xe.com/currencyconverter and at some post offices, or at any bank or travel agent.

● **Business hours** Most **village shops** are open Monday to Friday 9am-5pm and Saturday 9am-12.30pm, though some open as early as 7.30/8am; many also open on Sundays but not usually for the whole day. Occasionally you'll come across a local shop that closes at lunchtime on one day during the week, usually a Wednesday or Thursday; this is a throwback to the days when all towns and villages had an 'early closing day'. **Supermarkets** are open Monday to Saturday 8am-8pm (often longer) and on Sunday from about 9am to 5 or 6pm, though main branches of supermarkets generally open 10am-4pm or 11am-5pm.

Main **post offices** generally open Monday to Friday 9am-5pm and Saturday 9am-12.30pm; **banks** typically open at 9.30/10am Monday to Friday and close at 3.30/4pm, though in some places both post offices and banks may open only two or three days a week and/or in the morning, or limited hours, only. **ATMs** (**cash machines**) located outside a bank, shop, post office or petrol station are open all the time, but any that are inside will be accessible only when that place is open. However, ones that charge, such as Link machines, may not accept foreign-issued cards.

Pub hours are less predictable as each pub may have different opening hours. However, most pubs on the Cotswold Way continue to follow the traditional hours (Monday to Saturday 11am to 11pm, Sunday to 10.30pm), but some still close in the afternoon especially during the week and in the winter months.

The last entry time to most **museums and galleries** is usually half an hour, or an hour, before the official closing time.

● **National (Bank) holidays** Most businesses are shut on 1 January, Good Friday (March/April), Easter Monday (March/April), the first and last Monday in May, the last Monday in August, 25 December and 26 December.

● **School holidays** School holiday periods in England are generally as follows: a one-week break late October, two weeks around Christmas, a week mid-February, two weeks around Easter, a week in late May and from late July to early September.

● **Documents** If you are a member of a National Trust organisation in your country bring your membership card as you should be entitled to free entry to National Trust properties and sites in the UK.

● **Travel/medical insurance** The **European Health Insurance Card (EHIC)** entitles EU nationals (on production of the EHIC card) to necessary medical treatment under the UK's National Health Service while on a temporary visit here. However, this is not a

Using a **baggage-transfer service** to deliver your luggage to your accommodation each night will leave you free to walk unencumbered (well, with just a day pack) during the day. Charges vary, but expect to pay from £8 for the first bag for each leg of the journey, with discounts usually offered for additional bags.

Alternatively, some of the **taxi** firms listed in Part 4 will provide a similar service on request, or you could make an arrangement with your B&B host, some of whom handle baggage transport themselves. Prices vary widely, depending on the mileage involved and the individual concerned, but generally

substitute for proper medical cover on your travel insurance for unforeseen bills and for getting you home should that be necessary. Also consider cover for loss or theft of personal belongings, especially if you're camping as there may be times when you'll have to leave your luggage unattended. If you're walking the Cotswold Way any time after March 2019 do check, too, what the latest rules are, for Britain may have left the EU that March and you can expect some changes to the legislation.

● **Weights and measures** Britain's illogical mix of metric and imperial measures is undoubtedly a source of confusion for many visitors. For example, in Britain milk can be sold in pints (1 pint = 568ml), as can beer in pubs, though most other liquid including petrol (gasoline) and diesel is sold in litres. The population remains split, too, between those (mainly the older generation) who still use inches (1 inch = 2.5cm), feet (1ft = 0.3m) and yards and those who are happy with millimetres, centimetres and metres; you'll often be told that 'it's only a hundred yards or so' to somewhere, rather than a hundred metres or so. Distances on road and path signs are also given in miles (1 mile = 1.6km) rather than kilometres, and yards (1yd = 0.9m) rather than metres.

Most food is sold in metric weights (g and kg) but the imperial weights of pounds (lb: 1lb = 453g) and ounces (oz: 1oz = 28g) are often displayed too. The weather – a frequent topic of conversation – is also an issue: while most forecasts predict temperatures in centigrade (C), many people continue to think in terms of fahrenheit (F; see temperature chart on p14 for conversions).

● **Time** During the winter the whole of Britain is on Greenwich Meantime (GMT). The clocks move one hour forward on the last Sunday in March, remaining on British Summer Time (BST) until the last Sunday in October.

● **Smoking** Smoking in enclosed public places is banned. The ban relates not only to pubs and restaurants, but also to B&Bs, hostels and hotels. These latter have the right to designate one or more bedrooms where the occupants can smoke, but the ban is in force in all enclosed areas open to the public – even in a private home such as a B&B. Should you be foolhardy enough to light up in a no-smoking area, which includes pretty well any indoor public place, you could be fined £50, but it's the owners of the premises who suffer most if they fail to stop you, with a potential fine of £2500.

● **Telephones** The international access code for Britain is +44, followed by the area code minus the first 0, and then the number you require. **Mobile phone reception** is better than you might think. If you're using a mobile phone that is registered outside Europe, consider buying a local SIM card to keep costs down.

● **Wi-fi** See p25.

● **Emergency services** For police, ambulance, fire and mountain rescue dial ☎ 999 (or the EU standard number ☎ 112).

you can expect to pay at least £20 a day, which makes a specialised baggage carrier much better value.

● **Carryabag** (☎ 01242-250642, 🖳 carryabag.co.uk; Cheltenham)   Linked to Compass Holidays (see below); can also arrange parking in Cheltenham for the duration of your walk and transfers to and from the trail.

● **Cotswold Luggage Transfers** (☎ 01386-840688, 🖳 luggage-transfers.co.uk; Volunteer Inn, Chipping Campden; see p77).

● **Sherpa Van** (☎ 01748-826917, 🖳 sherpavan.com; Richmond, N Yorks)   Also provides an **accommodation-booking** service.

Self-guided walking holidays   The following companies provide customised packages for walkers, which usually include detailed advice and notes on itineraries, maps, accommodation booking, daily baggage transfer and transport at the start and end of your walk.

● **Absolute Escapes** (☎ 0131-610 1210, 🖳 absoluteescapes.com; Edinburgh)
● **Celtic Trails** (☎ 01291-689774, 🖳 celtictrailswalkingholidays.co.uk; Chepstow)
● **Compass Holidays** (☎ 01242-250642, 🖳 compass-holidays.com; Glos)
● **Contours Walking Holidays** (☎ 01629-821900, 🖳 contours.co.uk; Derbyshire)   Trail running itineraries also offered.
● **Cotswold Journeys** (☎ 01242-254353, 🖳 cotswoldjourneys.com; Cheltenham)
● **Cotswold Walks** (☎ 01386-833799, 🖳 cotswoldwalks.com; Worcs)
● **Discovery Travel** (☎ 01983-301133, 🖳 discoverytravel.co.uk; Isle of Wight)
● **Explore Britain** (☎ 01740-650900, 🖳 explorebritain.com; Co Durham)
● **Footpath Holidays** (☎ 01985-840049, 🖳 footpath-holidays.com; Wilts)
● **Freedom Walking Holidays** (☎ 07733-885390, 🖳 freedomwalkingholidays .co.uk; Goring-on-Thames)
● **Hillwalk Tours** (☎ +353 91-763994, 🖳 hillwalktours.com; Ireland)
● **Let's Go Walking** (☎ 01837-880075 or ☎ 020-7193 1252, 🖳 letsgowalk ing.com; Devon)
● **Macs Adventure** (☎ 0141-530 8886, 🖳 macsadventure.com; Glasgow)
● **Mickledore** (☎ 017687-72335, 🖳 mickledore.co.uk; Keswick)
● **The Carter Company** (☎ 01296-631671, 🖳 the-carter-company.com; Bucks)
● **The Walking Holiday Company** (☎ 01600-713008, 🖳 thewalkingholiday company.co.uk; Monmouth)
● **Walking the Cotswolds** (☎ 01386-841966, 🖳 cotswoldwalking.co.uk; Chipping Camden)

Group/guided walking tours   Fully guided tours are ideal for individuals wanting to travel in the company of others and for groups of friends wanting the reassurance of a guide. The packages usually include meals, accommodation, transport arrangements, minibus back-up and baggage transfer, as well as a qualified guide. Companies' specialities differ widely, with varied sizes of group, standards of accommodation, age range of clients and professionalism of guides, so it's worth checking carefully before making a booking.

PLANNING YOUR WALK

● **Footpath Holidays** (see opposite)
● **HF Holidays** (☎ 020 8732 1250, 🖳 hfholidays.co.uk; Herts) Offer the whole Way from their own HF Holidays property.

For those who would like **to complete the trail in stages**, there is an annual series of guided walks run by the Cotswold Voluntary Wardens. The walks take place between May and March and each covers about 10 miles, building up over the 11 months to the full distance. There is one series of walks that heads south to north over the 11 months, and another series that heads in the opposite direction. For more information visit 🖳 nationaltrail.co.uk/cotswold-way/news/guided-warden-walks.

Budgeting

How you budget for your trip will depend largely on the type of accommodation you use and where you have your meals. If you camp and cook for yourself you will be able to keep costs to a minimum. These escalate as you go up the accommodation and dining scales and will also be affected by the extent to which you use the services offered to guests, such as transportation of luggage, packed lunches and other refinements.

CAMPING AND 'GLAMPING'

The cost of camping along the Cotswold Way varies from nothing to £10 per person (pp), sometimes plus an extra £1 or so for the use of a shower. Living frugally, you could get by on as little as £15-20pp per night, pitching your tent at official sites and cooking your own food. Most walkers, however, will indulge in the occasional cooked breakfast (around £6), the odd pint of beer (around £3.50), or a pub meal after a long hard day (£9-12), so it's probably more realistic to reckon on about £30pp per day. That said, places where you can camp along the Cotswold Way are limited, so you'll almost certainly have to budget for the occasional night in a B&B if you plan to complete the whole trail in one go, though there are a couple of **shepherd's huts** en route, and **glamping pods** at Ullenwood, if you fancy something different. However, they are not cheap.

HOSTELS

The only hostel accommodation you're going to find along the route is in Bath; Bath has a YHA, two independent hostels and a YMCA. (That said, there is also a YMCA with hostel-style accommodation in Cheltenham, which is sometimes used by Cotswold Way walkers; see p107.) A dorm bed in either of the independent hostels in Bath costs from £10pp, from £14pp a night at the YHA – less £3 with YHA membership – and from £20pp at the YMCAs.

There are self-catering facilities on-site in Bath's YHA hostel which should
help you reduce your overall expenditure, or they do offer meals there too.
Realistically therefore you'll either have to camp/glamp or B&B it for most/all
of your nights on the trail.

B&B-STYLE ACCOMMODATION

If you're sharing a room in a B&B, pub or guesthouse, allow around £35-50 per
head for an overnight stay including breakfast, perhaps more in the tourist
towns over a summer weekend and certainly more if you stay in a hotel. Add on
the cost of an evening meal at around £9-16; for a meal with a drink or two
expect to pay £15-20. Buying a packed lunch will cost an extra £5 or so. It's
therefore best to reckon on about £55-65pp per day. Those travelling alone can
anticipate at least an additional £10-20 a day for a single room, or single occupancy of a room.

EXTRAS

Don't forget to set aside some money for the inevitable extras, such as batteries,
postcards, buses and taxis, drinks, cream teas, snacks and entrance fees – or, rather
more crucially, any changes of plan. Around £100-200 should be about right.

Itineraries

All walkers are individuals. Some like to cover large distances as quickly as possible. Others are happy to amble along, stopping whenever the whim takes them.
You may want to walk the Cotswold Way in one go, tackle it in a series of days
or weekends, or use it as the basis for individual linear walks; the choice is yours.
To accommodate these different options, this guide has not been divided up into
strict daily sections, which could impose too rigid a structure on how you should
walk. Instead it has been designed to make it easy for you to plan the itinerary
that suits you.

If you need an added spur, consider signing up for the Cotswold Way Hall
of Fame, an online database that records those who have completed the entire
walk. You can download a form from the activity website of the Cotswolds
AONB (🖳 cotswoldsaonb.org.uk/visiting-and-exploring/walking).

The **planning map** opposite the inside back cover and the **table of facilities**
on pp34-7 summarise the essential information for you to make a plan of your
own, in conjunction with the **distance chart** on pp194-5. Alternatively, to make
it even easier, see the **suggested itineraries** (see p32) and simply choose your
preferred speed of walking. There are also suggestions on pp36-7 for those who
want to experience the best of the trail over a day or a weekend. The **public
transport map** (p49) may help at this stage.

PLANNING YOUR WALK

Having made a rough plan, turn to **Part 4** where you will find summaries of the route, full descriptions of accommodation, places to eat and other services in each town and village, with detailed trail maps.

WHICH DIRECTION?

Most guidebooks to the Cotswold Way assume you will walk from north to south, which is the direction that has been followed in the layout of this book. There are some compelling reasons for this. To start with, although the prevailing wind is from the west, the Cotswolds frequently experience some vicious north-easterlies, and walking into the teeth of these can be decidedly unpleasant. Then there's the fact that the north Cotswolds have more than their fair share of attractive villages and towns with plenty of places to stay and eat – so that distances can be kept shorter in the initial stages, and there's a good choice of restaurants and B&Bs at the end of a walking day. And for those in need of an incentive, what better way to celebrate the end of the walk than by relaxing in Bath's spa?

Of course, starting from Bath has its advantages, too. Some walkers prefer not to have the sun in their eyes, which can be a deciding factor (although less so than you might think, since the route takes a considerable number of twists and turns). Others may wish to explore one of the quintessential Cotswold villages at leisure once the walk is over. The maps in Part 4 give timings for both directions and, as route-finding instructions are on the maps rather than in the text, it is perfectly straightforward to walk from south to north using this guide.

❏ Cotswold Way Relay

It's been over 25 years since the first Cotswold Way Relay (🖥 cotswoldwayrelay.co .uk) and the event continues to attract a considerable number of teams each year. Today, though, improved waymarking along the trail means fewer runners take the 'scenic' route – something that gains considerably in significance when you realise there are no marshals to guide the way.

The record for the fastest ladies' team is held by the organisers, Team Bath Athletic Club, who in 2008 knocked five minutes off the previous time to clock up an impressive 14 hours, 6 minutes and 13 seconds. The senior men's record, though, has stood since 1995 at precisely 11 hours and 55 minutes, set by Stroud & District Athletic Club.

The race starts in Chipping Campden at 7am on the last Saturday in June, finishing at Bath Abbey as evening draws in. It follows the official route of the Cotswold Way, which is divided into 10 stages of varying lengths and difficulty. The shortest, between Dursley and Wotton-under-Edge, covers just 7¼ miles (11.5km), but some runners contend with distances of 12 miles (19km) or more, and one group faces an ascent of 513m into the bargain.

Each stage sees a mass start, triggered by the expected arrival time of the first runner from the previous leg. With up to 65 teams tackling the course, you might just want to step off the path and let them pass! You'll then have the one-upmanship of taking the time to savour the trail's attractions while others steam past with eyes only on the clock.

PLANNING YOUR WALK

❑ SUGGESTED ITINERARIES

B&B-style accommodation is available at all the places listed below. Few places have a **campsite**; those that do have been asterisked* below.

● Itinerary for slower walkers and those who want to linger
(**10 days**; shorter route via Middleyard)
Walking 10-11 miles (16-17.5km) a day over 10 days, with one longer day of 13 miles (21km) and two shorter days of 7 miles (11km)

Day	Daily schedule	Miles	km	B&Bs & Hotels
1	Chipping Campden to Stanton	10½	17	Stanton
2	Stanton to Winchcombe	7	11	Winchcombe*
3	Winchcombe to Dowdeswell Reservoir	11	17.5	Dowdeswell Reservoir
4	Dowdeswell to Birdlip	10½	17	Birdlip
5	Birdlip to Painswick	7	11	Painswick
6	Painswick to Middleyard	10	16	Middleyard
7	Middleyard to Wotton-under-Edge	11	17.5	Wotton-under-Edge
8	Wotton-under-Edge to Old Sodbury	13	21	Old Sodbury
9	Old Sodbury to Cold Ashton	8½	13.5	Cold Ashton
10	Cold Ashton to Bath	10	16	Bath

● Itinerary for steady walkers
(**8 days**; longer route via Selsley Common and Stinchcombe Hill)
Walking 10-14 miles (16-22.5km) a day, with 2 longer days of 15-17 miles (24-27km)

Day	Daily schedule	Miles	km	B&Bs & Hotels
1	Chipping Campden to Wood Stanway	12½	20	Wood Stanway, Hailes*
2	Wood Stanway to Prestbury Hill Reserve	13	21	Prestbury Hill Reserve*
3	Prestbury Hill Reserve to Birdlip	14	23	Birdlip
4	Birdlip to Selsley	17	27	Selsley
5	Selsley to North Nibley	13½	21.5	North Nibley*
6	North Nibley to Old Sodbury	15	24	Old Sodbury
7	Old Sodbury to Cold Ashton	8½	13.5	Cold Ashton*
8	Cold Ashton to Bath	10	16	Bath

● Itinerary for faster walkers
(**7 days**; longer route via Selsley Common and Stinchcombe Hill)
Walking 13-17½ miles (21-28km) a day, with one shorter day of 11 miles (17.5km)

Day	Daily schedule	Miles	km	B&Bs & Hotels
1	Chipping Campden to Hailes	15½	25	Hailes*, North Farmcote
2	Hailes to Dowdeswell Reservoir	13	21	Dowdeswell Reservoir
3	Dowdeswell to Painswick	17½	28	Painswick
4	Painswick to Penn Wood	11	17.5	Middleyard
5	Penn Wood to Wotton-under-Edge	14½	23	Wotton-under-Edge
6	Wotton-under-Edge to Tormarton	15	24	Tormarton*
7	Tormarton to Bath	16½	26.5	Bath

* campsite/camping facilities also available here

PLANNING YOUR WALK

SUGGESTED ITINERARIES

The itineraries in the box opposite are suggestions only, based on the location of places to stay as well as the attendant distances. How you plan your walk will depend on several factors, from the availability of accommodation to personal interests, as well as the distance you choose to walk each day. Don't forget to add travelling time before and after the walk, and to allow additional time for photography and breaks – or simply to stop and stare.

SIDE TRIPS

Most people embarking on the Cotswold Way do so with the express aim of completing the walk from A to B, and there's certainly enough of interest to justify spending at least a week along the trail. Yet it's always tempting to take off the blinkers occasionally and consider what happens to left and right.

With over 3000 miles (4800km) of footpaths in the Cotswolds AONB alone, and several long-distance trails crossing the region, there's a tantalising number of **side routes** you could follow.

Winchcombe is a great place to get sidetracked, for as well as the Cotswold Way, the town is a junction for several trails. Prime among these is **Winchcombe Way**, a 42-mile (67km) figure-of-eight route with the focus firmly on the town. Offering the option of an interesting 2-day loop are **Warden's Way** and **Windrush Way**, which run over different routes between Winchcombe and Bourton-on-the-Water, covering 13 and 14 miles (21km and 22.5km) respectively. Others include **Gloucestershire Way**, which meanders for 100 miles (160km) between Chepstow and Tewkesbury, taking in the Forest of Dean and the River Severn.

If the idea of joining up the dots appeals, you could hardly do better than look at the 55-mile (88km) **Wysis Way**. As it crosses the Cotswold Way north of Painswick, it forms a link with two other national trails: Offa's Dyke Path and the Thames Path.

Further south, around Lower Kilcott, **Monarch's Way** runs alongside the Cotswold Way for a short distance before continuing along its 615-mile (984km) journey between Worcester and Shoreham in West Sussex. The route mirrors that taken by Charles II during his escape to France after the Battle of Worcester in 1651. The journey took the king six weeks to complete – with Parliamentary forces in hot pursuit. It's certainly food for thought.

❏ **Important note – walking times**
Unless otherwise specified, **all times in this book refer only to the time spent walking**. You will need to add 20-30% to allow for rests, photography, checking the map, drinking water etc, not to mention time simply to stop and stare.

When planning the day's hike count on 5-7 hours' actual walking.

PLANNING YOUR WALK

Place name (Places in brackets are a short walk off the Cotswold Way)	Distance from previous place approx miles	approx km (via Selsley & Stinchcombe)	ATM (cash machine)	Post Office	VILLAGE AND Tourist Information Centre (TIC) or point (TIP)
Chipping Campden	Start of Cotswold Way		✔	✔	TIC
Broadway	6	9.5	✔	✔	TIC
Stanton	4½	7			
Stanway	1½	2.25			
Wood Stanway	½	0.75			
(North Farmcote	¼	0.2)			
Hailes	3½	5.5			
Winchcombe	2	3	✔	✔	TIC
Postlip	4	6.5			
Cleeve Hill	2	3			
(Cheltenham	5*	8*)	✔	✔	TIC
Prestbury Hill Reserve	1½	2.5			
(Ham Hill	¾	1.25)			
(Charlton Kings	¾	1.25)	✔		
Dowdeswell Reservoir	3½	5.5			
Seven Springs	3	5			
Ullenwood	3½	5.5			
Crickley Hill	1½	2.5			
Birdlip	2½	4			
(Little Witcombe)					
Cranham Corner	4	7			
(Painswick Hill)					
Painswick	2½	4	✔	✔	TIC
(Edge)					
(Randwick & Westrip)					
Stonehouse	7½	13.5			
Ebley (scenic route)	1	1.5 (from Stonehouse)			
Selsley (scenic route)	1½	2.5 (from Ebley)			
(King's Stanley – shorter route)	½	1 (from Stonehouse)	✔	✔	
Middleyard (shorter route)	½	1 (from King's Stanley)			
(Nympsfield	½	1)			
(Uley	½	1)		✔	
Dursley (scenic route)	7½	12		✔	✔ TIP
Dursley (direct route)	6	9.5			
Stinchcombe Hill	½	1			
North Nibley	3½	5.5			
Wotton-under-Edge	2	3	✔	✔	TIP
(Hillesley	½	1)			
Hawkesbury Upton	7½	12.5		✔	
Horton	2½	4			
(cont'd on p36)		*5 miles/8km from Cleeve Hill to the centre of Cheltenham			

TOWN FACILITIES

Eating place ✔=one; ✔✔=two; ✔✔✔=three +	Food store	Campsite (inc camping pod & shepherd's hut)	Hostel	B&B-style accommodation ✔=one ✔✔=two; ✔✔✔=three +	Place name (Places in brackets are a short walk off the Cotswold Way; see opposite for distances)
✔✔✔	✔			✔✔✔	**Chipping Campden**
✔✔✔	✔			✔✔✔	**Broadway**
✔				✔✔✔	**Stanton**
					Stanway
				✔	**Wood Stanway**
				✔	(North Farmcote)
✔		✔		✔	**Hailes**
✔✔✔	✔	✔		✔✔✔	**Winchcombe**
				✔	**Postlip**
✔✔				✔✔✔	**Cleeve Hill**
✔✔✔	✔		✔	✔✔✔	(Cheltenham)
		✔		✔	**Prestbury Hill Reserve**
		✔		✔✔	(Ham Hill)
✔	✔			✔✔	(Charlton Kings)
✔				✔	**Dowdeswell Reservoir**
✔✔					**Seven Springs**
✔		✔			**Ullenwood**
✔✔					**Crickley Hill**
✔				✔	**Birdlip**
✔				✔	(Little Witcombe)
					Cranham Corner
✔✔					(Painswick Hill)
✔✔✔	✔			✔✔✔	**Painswick**
✔					(Edge)
✔✔					(Randwick/Westrip)
					Stonehouse
✔	✔(½ mile)				**Ebley**
✔				✔	**Selsley**
✔✔	✔			✔	(King's Stanley)
				✔	**Middleyard**
✔					(Nympsfield)
✔✔	✔			✔	(Uley)
✔✔✔	✔			✔✔	**Dursley** (scenic route)
					Dursley (direct route)
					Stinchcombe Hill
✔		✔		✔✔	**North Nibley**
✔✔✔	✔			✔✔✔	**Wotton-under-Edge**
✔					(Hillesley)
✔✔	✔			✔	**Hawkesbury Upton**
					Horton

*5 miles/8km from Cleeve Hill to the centre of Cheltenham

(cont'd on p37)

PLANNING YOUR WALK

Place name (Places in brackets are a short walk off the Cotswold Way)	Distance from previous place (via Selsley & Stinchcombe) approx miles	approx km	ATM (cash machine)	Post Office	VILLAGE AND Tourist Information Centre (TIC) or point (TIP)
(cont'd from p34)					
Little Sodbury	1	1.5			
Old Sodbury	2	3			
Coomb's End	½	1			
Tormarton	1½	2.5			
(Tolldown; south of M4	550yds	500m)			
Pennsylvania	6	10			
Cold Ashton	½	1			
Bath	10	16	✔	✔	TIC

HIGHLIGHTS: THE BEST DAY AND WEEKEND WALKS

Day walks

The suggestions below take in various stretches of the Cotswold Way. In addition, the trail authorities have implemented a series of **circular walks**, ranging from 1½ to 6½ miles and varying in difficulty.

Although these walks are in part waymarked with a green roundel stating 'Cotswold Way Circular Walk', these signs are designed merely to complement the detailed and regularly updated route directions that can be downloaded from 🖳 nationaltrail.co.uk/cotswold-way/additional-walks.

● **Chipping Campden to Broadway** (see pp80-3) A good **6-mile (9.5km)** introduction to the Cotswold Way, taking in two of the trail's most attractive towns as well as some superb views from Dover's Hill and Broadway Tower. If you don't want to retrace your steps, there are buses between the two towns.

● **Broadway to Winchcombe** (see pp88-95) From one of the Cotswolds' most popular villages, this **12-mile (22km)** stretch leads to one of the prettiest at Stanton – where there's an excellent pub to break up the day. The route drops down alongside the ruins of Hailes Abbey before continuing to the attractive wool town of Winchcombe. Marchants No 606 bus service links the two towns.

● **Dowdeswell Reservoir to Crickley Hill** (see pp111-116) This **8-mile (12.5km)** walk is ideal for nature lovers, taking in both ancient beechwoods and areas of unimproved limestone grassland, as well as the Devil's Chimney at Leckhampton and some prehistoric sites. Finish at the Air Balloon pub. There are bus services to both ends of the walk.

● **Crickley Hill to Painswick** (see pp116-23) More woods characterise this lovely 9-mile (14.5km) walk along the Cotswold escarpment, broken up by Cooper's Hill and Painswick Beacon, and finishing in the attractive town of

TOWN FACILITIES

Eating place ✔=one; ✔✔=two; ✔✔✔=three +	Food store * = limited	Campsite	Hostel	B&B-style accommodation ✔=one; ✔✔=two; ✔✔✔=three +	Place name (Places in brackets are a short walk off the Cotswold Way; see opposite for distances)
					(cont'd from p35)
		✔			**Little Sodbury**
✔✔	✔*			✔✔✔	**Old Sodbury**
					Coomb's End
✔✔		✔		✔✔✔	**Tormarton**
✔	✔			✔	**(Tolldown; south of M4)**
	✔*			✔✔	**Pennsylvania**
✔		✔		✔✔	**Cold Ashton**
✔✔✔	✔		✔	✔✔✔	**Bath**

(Side text: PLANNING YOUR WALK)

Painswick. Buses serve both ends of the route and can be connected via Gloucester and Cheltenham.
● **Circular walk around Selsley Common** (see pp131-3) Start in King's Stanley and link up with the Cotswold Way as it runs along the Stroudwater (Ebley) Canal, and thence to Selsley Common and Middleyard. It's a **5-mile (8km)** round trip that takes in some spectacular views, a fascinating Arts and Crafts church, and the two alternative routes along this stretch of the Cotswold Way. Stagecoach's 66S between Gloucester and Stroud is the most frequent bus service to King's Stanley.
● **Bath to Dyrham Park** (see pp158-67: ie reverse of the route description) Climb out of Bath towards the racecourse and the battlefields near Freezing Hill, then continue on to Dyrham Park. It's about **12½ miles (20km)**, so you might have enough time to explore the house or grounds before getting a taxi back to Bath (there are no buses to Dyrham Park).

Weekend walks
● **Chipping Campden to Cleeve Hill** (see pp80-103) If there's one walk along the trail that showcases the quintessential Cotswolds, this is it. Villages of Cotswold stone, rolling hills, woodland and some excellent views: they're all in this **24-mile (38.5km)** route. Stagecoach's No 606 and 606S buses serve both ends of the walk.
● **Dursley to Tormarton** (see pp141-56) Most of this **22-mile (35km)** walk follows the edge of the Cotswold escarpment, sometimes wooded, at others more open, with numerous small villages and the final stretch through Dodington Park. Stagecoach and Cotswold Green operate bus services to Dursley and Coachstyle (No 41) to Tormarton.

What to take

How much you take with you is a very personal decision which takes experience to get right. For those new to long-distance walking the suggestions below will help you strike a sensible balance between comfort, safety and minimal weight.

KEEP YOUR LUGGAGE LIGHT

If there's one maxim that is crucial to long-distance walking, it's 'keep it light'. It is all too easy to take things along 'just in case' but such items can soon mount up. If you are in any doubt about anything on your packing list, be ruthless and leave it at home. You're rarely far from a shop on the Cotswold Way, so if you find you've left out something that turns out to be essential, the chances are you'll be able to pick up an equivalent easily enough.

HOW TO CARRY IT

The size of your rucksack depends on how you plan to walk. If you are staying in B&B-style accommodation, you should be able to get all you need into a 40- to 50-litre pack: large enough for a change of clothes, waterproofs, essential toiletries and first-aid kit, a water bottle, a packed lunch, and ideally a change of shoes. Pack similar things in different-coloured stuff sacks or plastic bags so they are easier to pull out of the dark recesses of your pack, then put these inside a waterproof rucksack liner, or tough plastic sack, to protect everything if it rains. Those camping will also need space for a tent, sleeping bag, cooking equipment, towel and food: 65-75 litres' capacity should be about right.

Whatever its size, make sure before you set off that your rucksack is comfortable. Ideally it should have a stiffened back system and either be fully adjustable or exactly the right size for your back. Carrying the main part of the load high and close to your body with a large proportion of the weight on your hips (rather than on your shoulders) by means of the padded waist belt should allow you to walk in comfort for days on end. Play around with different ways of packing your gear and adjust all those straps until you get it just right. A useful extra is a bum/waist bag or a very light daypack to carry a camera, wallet and other essentials if you go off sightseeing.

Of course, if you decide to use a baggage-transfer service (see pp27-8) you can pack most of your things separately and simply carry a daypack with the essentials for a day's walking.

FOOTWEAR

A comfortable, well-fitting pair of leather or Gore-Tex-lined **boots** is the best footwear you can take and essential if you're carrying a heavy rucksack. In addition to offering proper ankle support, which is particularly important on rough ground, they are most likely to keep your feet dry. Make sure they are properly waxed or waterproofed, both before you set out and during your walk.

Traditionally walkers wear two pairs of **socks**, one thin pair, with a thicker pair on top. Aside from adding warmth, this is a good blister-avoidance strategy, though modern walking socks with two inbuilt layers can do the job just as well. Taking three pairs of socks should be ample.

In summer you could get by with a light pair of trail **shoes** if you're carrying only a small pack, though it's not generally advisable. A second pair of shoes to wear in the evening is well worth taking – they can be useful in case of injury, too. Lightweight trainers are best for the cooler months; in summer sports sandals are equally suitable.

CLOTHES

Wet and cold weather can catch you out even in summer, so go prepared for the unexpected. Most walkers pick their clothes according to the versatile layering system, which consists of: a base layer to transport sweat away from your skin; a mid layer or two to keep you warm; and an outer layer or 'shell' to protect you from the wind and rain.

Thermal material is ideal for **base layers** as it draws moisture away from skin, keeping you drier (and thus warmer when you stop for a break) than a conventional cotton T-shirt. A **mid layer** of micro-fleece is ideal, being both warm and light, with an additional sweater or fleece useful for colder days or when you stop as you can get cold very quickly. Both thermal tops and fleeces have the added advantage that they dry relatively quickly.

All this pales into insignificance when it comes to **waterproofs**. A waterproof jacket is essential year-round and will be much more comfortable (but also more expensive) if it's also 'breathable' to prevent the build-up of condensation on the inside. It can also be worn to protect you against the wind. Waterproof trousers are important most of the year but in summer could be left behind if your main pair of trousers is reasonably windproof and quick-drying. Gaiters are rarely necessary, though they come into their own if you're walking through wet crops.

Trousers and **shorts** should be light and quick-drying: trousers with zipped legs that convert into shorts can be ideal, especially in summer when the weather can change rapidly. Never wear denim jeans for walking: if they get wet they become heavy, cold and very uncomfortable. In winter, or if you're camping, consider a pair of thermal **longjohns** or thick tights.

What you take in the way of **underwear** is very much a personal preference, but if you want to change every day, you'll need three sets to ensure you always have one dry. Women may find a **sports bra** more comfortable because pack straps can cause bra straps to dig into your shoulders.

A **warm hat** is important at any time of the year, and **gloves**, too, except perhaps in the height of summer. It's surprising how quickly you can get cold if it's raining. In summer a **sunhat** will help to keep you cool and prevent sunburn;

PLANNING YOUR WALK

swimming gear would be useful if you plan to take advantage of one of the pools en route. Finally, don't forget a change of clothes for the evenings. While wearing the same kit all week suits some, putting on clean clothes after a shower is a great morale boost – and will probably make you feel more comfortable if you're eating out.

TOILETRIES

Take only the minimum. In addition to toothpaste and a toothbrush, sunscreen is invaluable; you'll need a small bar of soap if you're camping. Also take a suitable supply of any medication and, for women tampons/sanitary towels. A roll of loo paper in a plastic bag is handy, as is a lightweight trowel if you get caught out far from a toilet (see p53). What you pack in the line of deodorants, razors, hairbrushes etc is a matter of personal preference.

FIRST-AID KIT

Medical facilities in Britain are good so you only need the essentials to cover basic problems and emergencies. Ideally, take a waterproof bag containing the following: plasters/Band Aids for minor cuts; Compeed, Moleskin or Second Skin for blisters; a selection of different-sized sterile dressings for wounds; porous adhesive tape; a stretch bandage for holding dressings or splints in place and for supporting a sprained ankle; a triangular bandage to make a sling for a broken or sprained arm; elastic knee support for a weak knee; antiseptic wipes; antiseptic cream; safety pins, tweezers and scissors; and aspirin or paracetamol for mild to moderate pain and fever.

Most importantly, do make sure you have a modicum of first-aid knowledge, or much of your kit will be rendered useless.

GENERAL ITEMS
Essential

Essential items you should carry are a whistle to attract attention if you get lost or find yourself in trouble; a torch (flashlight) with spare bulb and batteries in case you end up walking after dark; a one- or two-litre water bottle/pouch; emergency food such as chocolate, cereal bars, or dried fruit; a penknife and a watch. If you're not carrying a sleeping bag or tent you could also consider carrying an emergency plastic bivvy-bag – although at no stage on the route are you far from civilisation. A compass can be invaluable, especially in poor visibility, but do make sure you know how to use it.

Useful

Many would list a mobile phone or smartphone as essential and also a camera (with a spare memory card or film and batteries/charger) but a notebook or sketchbook are other good ways of recording your impressions, and binoculars mean you can observe wildlife more easily. A pair of sunglasses is useful, as is a vacuum flask for hot drinks. A walking stick or pole helps to take the shock off your knees (some walkers use two poles but this leaves no free hand).

A **GPS** (see pp17-18) device could also be useful in an emergency, but not as an alternative to a compass: batteries could just fail when most needed.

Note that while a mobile phone/smartphone is useful, there are areas without any signal. For this reason, make sure that you always have the wherewithal to call from a public phone box in case you have no signal at the crucial moment. Calls to the emergency services (☎ 999, or ☎ 112) are free of charge, but those urgent calls to book a night's accommodation can catch you out. Calls cost a minimum of 60p (thereafter 10p a minute), but increasingly you will need a credit, debit, BT or prepaid phone card instead.

CAMPING GEAR

If you're camping you will need a decent **tent** able to withstand wet and windy weather; a two- or three-season **sleeping bag**; a **sleeping mat**; a **stove** and **fuel**; **cooking equipment** (a pan with frying pan that can double as a lid/plate is fine for two people); a **bowl**, **mug** and **cutlery** (don't forget a can/bottle opener); and a **scourer** for washing up.

MONEY

The best way to carry your money is as **cash**. There are banks and/or post offices in most of the towns along the path, and ATMs in some others, so withdrawing money along the route with a **debit (or credit) card** (and PIN number) is fairly straightforward. Cards are also the easiest way to pay in restaurants, hotels and supermarkets, many of which offer a cash-back facility. For most B&Bs you'll need to pay in cash or – for those with a British bank account – by **cheque**. For more details, see p25.

TRAVEL INSURANCE

Do consider insurance cover for loss or theft of personal belongings, especially if you are camping or staying in hostels, as there may be times when you'll have to leave your belongings unattended. Many British walkers will be covered under their home insurance policy, but it's worth checking this.

For health insurance for visitors from overseas, see box pp26-7.

MAPS

The hand-drawn maps in this book cover the trail at a scale of just under 1:20,000, with plenty of detail and information to keep you on the right track. The **Ordnance Survey** (🖳 ordnancesurvey.co.uk) covers the whole route at a scale of 1:25,000 on four maps within their Explorer series: Nos 179, 168, 167, 155 and 45, each costing £8.99, or £14.99 for the 'weatherproof active' version. Fortunately, none of these is strictly necessary if you pay careful attention to the maps in this guide, which should help to lighten your load somewhat. That said, it's a good idea for safety's sake to carry the map covering the highest point of the walk, Cleeve Hill Common (Explorer 179). Although the area is not particularly isolated, visibility up there can be seriously compromised when the mist

❏ Digital mapping

Most modern smartphones have a GPS chip so you will be able to see your position overlaid onto the digital map on your phone. Almost every device with built-in GPS functionality now has some mapping software available for it. If you want a dedicated GPS unit, Garmin are the best known and have devices from £100.

There are numerous software packages now available that provide Ordnance Survey (OS) maps for a PC, smartphone, tablet or GPS. Maps are supplied by direct download over the Internet. The maps are then loaded into an application, also available by download, from where you can view them, print them and create routes on them.

Memory Map (🖥 memory-map.co.uk) currently sell OS 1:25,000 mapping covering the whole of Britain for £75.

Anquet (🖥 anquet.com) has the Cotswold Way available for £12.60 using OS 1:25,000 mapping but they also offer subscriptions to all their mapping including OS 1:25,000 maps from £24 per year.

For a subscription of from £2.99 for one month or £19.99 for a year (on their current offer) **Ordnance Survey** (🖥 ordnancesurvey.co.uk) will let you download and then use their UK maps (1:25,000 scale) on a mobile or tablet without a data connection for a specific period.

Harvey (🖥 harveymaps.co.uk) sell their Cotswold Way map (1:40,000 scale) as a download for £20.49 for use on any device.

Smartphones and GPS devices should complement, not replace, the traditional method of navigation (a map and compass) as any electronic device can break or, if nothing else, run out of battery. Remember that the battery life of your phone will be significantly reduced, compared to normal usage, when you are using the built-in GPS and running the screen for long periods.   **Stuart Greig**

comes down, making it easy to become disorientated and wander dangerously close to the edge of the escarpment. In such conditions a map from which you can take compass bearings is essential.

Also worth considering is **AZ**'s (🖥 az.co.uk) *Cotswold Way A-Z Adventure Atlas* (£8.95); this contains OS maps at a scale of 1:25,000 as well as an index, though it does arrange the maps as if walking from Bath to Chipping Campden.

Another useful option is the **Harvey** map (🖥 harveymaps.co.uk) which covers the whole route at 1:40,000 on a single, waterproof sheet and costs £13.95. It's also available as a digital download at £20.49.

To save on expense, it's worth noting that members of Ramblers (see box on p44) can borrow maps from their library free of charge.

RECOMMENDED READING

Field guides

There are plenty of good field guides on the market, though deciding which, if any, will justify space in a rucksack is a tough decision. The series published by Collins is unfailingly practical, if a little dated, though for visual appeal – and particularly bird identification – the RSPB's guides come out ahead.

• *British Insects: A photographic guide to every common species* by Michael Chinery (Collins, 2009)
• *The Mammals of Britain and Europe* by David Macdonald and Priscilla Barrett (Collins, 2005)
• *RSPB Pocket Birds of Britain and Europe* (Dorling Kindersley, 2017)
• *RSPB What's that Tree?* (Dorling Kindersley, 2013)
• *RSPB What's that Flower?* (Dorling Kindersley, 2013)

General reading
• *The Hidden Landscape: A Journey into the Geological Past* by Richard Fortey (Bodley Head, 2010) brings vividly and clearly to life the evolution of a landscape which most of us take for granted.
• *The Arts and Crafts Movement* by Elizabeth Cumming and Wendy Kaplan (Thames & Hudson, 1991) is an accessible introduction to the complexities of the movement (see box p76), from its roots in Britain to continental Europe and the United States. A more recent book on the subject, *The Arts and Crafts Movement in Britain* by Mary Greensted (Shire History, 2010) is also worth looking at.

Biography
No journey through the Cotswolds is complete without Laurie Lee's classic childhood autobiography, *Cider with Rosie* (Vintage Classics, 2002).

Fiction
The novelist Jane Austen lived in Bath for five years and set two of her novels, *Northanger Abbey* and *Persuasion*, in the city. Both can be found in several editions, including Penguin Classics, and afford a rather different perspective on the city and society to that seen by today's visitors.

More recently, JK Rowling of *Harry Potter* fame hails from the Cotswolds; indeed, the town of Dursley is evoked in the surname of Harry's unpleasant uncle and aunt – though there the connection ends.

If you're into crime fiction, the Cotswold Mysteries by Rebecca Tope, with titles such as *A Grave in the Cotswolds* (Allison and Busby, 2011), should give you something to ponder as you walk along the trail.

Poetry
Most prolific among the poets whose work has been influenced by the Cotswolds is the war poet Ivor Gurney (1890-1937), who was born in Gloucester and served in World War I, before suffering severe mental problems and being confined to an institution.

Others include James Elroy Flecker (1884-1915), who was buried in Cheltenham; and WH Davies (1871-1940), known the world over for his poem, *Leisure* (see p53), who made his home in Gloucestershire. Their work can be found in numerous poetry anthologies.

❏ **SOURCES OF FURTHER INFORMATION**

Trail information
● **Cotswold Way National Trail Office** (🖳 nationaltrail.co.uk/cotswold-way) The website includes news of diversions and the occasional route change as well as details of events and other trail information.
● **Cotswold Way Association** (🖳 cotswoldwayassociation.org.uk) Formed in 2016, its aim is to regularly check the condition of the path and support the continued improvement of the national trail and other walks in the area.

Tourist information offices
Tourist information offices provide all manner of locally specific information for visitors. A few – specifically in Bath and Cheltenham – have paid staff but others along the Cotswold Way are staffed by volunteers who usually have information on accommodation but may not be able to book it for you.
There are tourist information offices on or near the Way in **Chipping Campden** (see pp75-6), **Broadway** (see p85), **Winchcombe** (see p97), **Cheltenham** (see p106), **Painswick** (see p124), **Wotton-under-Edge** (see p144) and **Bath** (see p171).

Tourist boards
The Cotswolds (🖳 www.cotswolds.com) has responsibility for all matters touristic throughout the region. Bath, though, is covered by its own authority, **Visit Bath** (🖳 visitbath.co.uk). Another excellent source of information is **The Cotswolds Conservation Board** (see p60).

Organisations for walkers
● **Backpackers' Club** (🖳 backpackersclub.co.uk) A club aimed at people who are involved or interested in lightweight camping through walking, cycling, skiing and canoeing. They produce a quarterly magazine, provide members with a comprehensive advisory and information service on all aspects of backpacking, organise weekend trips and also publish a farm-pitch directory. Membership costs £15/20/8.50 per year for an individual/family/anyone under 18 or over 65.
● **The Long Distance Walkers' Association** (🖳 ldwa.org.uk) Membership includes a journal (*Strider*) three times per year with details of challenge events and local group walks as well as articles on the subject. Membership costs £18/25.50 (less for direct debit payments) a year for individuals/families.
● **Ramblers** (🖳 ramblers.org.uk) A charity that looks after the interests of walkers throughout Britain and promotes walking for health. Annual membership costs £35.85/47.85 individual/joint (concessionary rates also available) and includes their quarterly *Walk* magazine (£3.60 to non-members).

Getting to and from the Cotswold Way

While Bath at the southern end of the trail is easily reached by train, bus, National Express coach or car, getting to and from Chipping Campden is a bit more of a challenge. The nearest railway station is at Moreton-in-Marsh, from where there's a local bus, though taking a train to Stratford-upon-Avon, followed by a bus or taxi, is a viable alternative. For details see box p46, p75 in Part 4 under Chipping Campden and the local bus services table and map on pp48-50.

Although there are no other railway stations on the trail itself, trains do service Stonehouse, about half a mile (1km) west of the trail where it meets the Stroudwater (Ebley) Canal. There is also Cam & Dursley station, almost three miles (4.8km) north of Dursley, with a bus service to the town centre. Connections to Cheltenham, about 2½ miles (4km) west of the trail, are excellent. It is also possible to take the train to Stroud or Gloucester, then transfer by bus to the path from there. A network of local buses links many of the villages along the Cotswold Way, making it possible – with a bit of planning – to create a series of linear walks without having to retrace your steps.

NATIONAL TRANSPORT
By rail
The rail services of most relevance to walkers along the Cotswold Way are GWR's from London Paddington to Moreton-in-Marsh (1hr 40mins, though to get to Chipping Campden is about 3hrs in total) and from Paddington to Bath (about 1½hrs). For Chipping Campden you could also take the Chiltern

PLANNING YOUR WALK

❏ **Getting to Britain**
● **By air** Most international airlines serve London Heathrow (🖳 heathrow.com) and London Gatwick (🖳 gatwickairport.com). A number of budget airlines fly from many of Europe's major cities to the other London airports: London City Airport (🖳 london cityairport.com); Stansted (🖳 stanstedairport.com) and Luton (🖳 london-luton.co .uk). There are a few flights from mainland Europe to Bristol (🖳 bristolairport.co.uk) and Birmingham (🖳 birminghamairport.co.uk), which are closer to the Cotswold Way than London.
● **From mainland Europe by train** Eurostar (🖳 eurostar.com) operates a high-speed passenger service via the Channel Tunnel between Paris/Brussels/Amsterdam and London. Trains arrive and depart London from the international terminal at St Pancras station, which itself has connections to the London Underground and to all other main railway stations in London.
   For more information on rail travel from Europe contact your rail network, or Railteam (🖳 railteam.eu).
● **From Europe by coach** Eurolines (🖳 eurolines.eu) works with 32 long-distance coach operators across mainland Europe to provide an integrated network connecting some 500 destinations to the UK, where it links with the National Express network (see p47). Flixbus (formerly Megabus; 🖳 flixbus.com) also provides services from destinations in mainland Europe to London.
● **From Europe by car** The shortest **ferry** crossing is between Calais and Dover. An alternative point of embarkation is Dunkerque. There are also numerous other ferry services linking the major North Sea and Channel ports of mainland Europe with ports along Britain's eastern and southern coasts. Both 🖳 ferrysavers.com and 🖳 directferries.com have a full list of companies and services.
   Eurotunnel (🖳 eurotunnel.com) operates 'le shuttle' (a shuttle) train service for vehicles via the Channel Tunnel between Calais and Folkestone, taking about an hour between the motorway in France and the motorway in Britain. At peak times there are several trains an hour.

Railways' service from London Marylebone to Stratford-upon-Avon (2hrs 20mins) and catch Johnson's No 2 bus from there (40 mins). GWR also operates trains to Cheltenham Spa from Paddington (around 2hrs), with connections from there, on Mondays to Fridays only, to Cam & Dursley (30 mins).

See box below for details of the operators and an outline of the services. For the latest on train times, fares and rail information, contact **National Rail Enquiries** (☎ 03457-484950, 🖥 nationalrail.co.uk). Fares vary very widely, but significant savings can be made by booking well in advance and by travelling at off-peak times. You can buy tickets through the relevant rail operator, in person at a railway station, or online at 🖥 thetrainline.com or 🖥 qjump.co .uk. It helps to be as flexible as possible and don't forget that most discounted tickets carry some restrictions; check what they are before you buy your ticket. Travel on a Friday may be more expensive than on other days of the week.

PLANNING YOUR WALK

❑ RAIL SERVICES   (**Note**: not all stops are listed)

Chiltern Railways (☎ 0345-600 5165, 🖥 chilternrailways.co.uk)
● London Marylebone to Birmingham via Leamington Spa, daily 2/hr, Sun 5/day. Some services continue to Kidderminster.
● Leamington Spa to **Stratford-upon-Avon** via Warwick, Mon-Fri 8/day, Sat 6/day, Sun 5/day.

Cross Country (☎ 0844-811 0124, 🖥 crosscountrytrains.co.uk)
● Edinburgh to Bristol via Newcastle-upon-Tyne, York, Leeds, Birmingham New Street & **Cheltenham Spa**, daily approx 1/hr; some services continue to Exeter
● Birmingham to Plymouth via **Cheltenham Spa**, daily approx 1/hr
  Note: some services link in to destinations that include Aberdeen, Glasgow, Reading, Southampton and Bournemouth
● Nottingham to Cardiff via Derby, Birmingham & **Cheltenham Spa**, daily 1/hr
● Bristol Temple Meads to **Cheltenham Spa** via Bath Spa, daily 1-2/hr (these stops are part of the Penzance to Dundee and Exeter to Glasgow services)

Great Western Railway (☎ 0345-7000 125, 🖥 gwr.com)
● London Paddington to Bristol Temple Meads via Reading, Swindon, Chippenham & **Bath Spa**, daily 2/hr (some services continue to Weston-super-Mare)
● London Paddington to **Cheltenham Spa** via Reading, Swindon, Kemble, Stroud, **Stonehouse** & Gloucester, daily 7-8/day (additional services from Swindon)
● London Paddington to Worcester via Reading, Oxford, **Moreton-in-Marsh** & Evesham, daily approx 1/hr (some services continue to Hereford)
● Westbury to Gloucester via **Bath Spa**, Bristol, Yate & **Cam & Dursley**, Mon-Sat approx 1/hr, from Bristol Sun 6/day
● Great Malvern to Westbury via **Cheltenham Spa**, Gloucester, **Cam & Dursley**, Yate & Bristol, Mon-Fri 7/day (some services continue to Bath Spa & Westbury)
● Cardiff to Portsmouth via Bristol, **Bath Spa** & Southampton, daily 1/hr
● Bristol to Westbury via **Bath Spa**, Mon-Sat 1/hr some services continue to Frome
● Bristol to Chippenham via **Bath Spa**, daily 1-2/hr

South Western Railway (☎ 0345-6000 650, 🖥 southwesternrailway.com)
● London Waterloo to Bristol Temple Meads via Clapham Junction, Woking, Basingstoke, Andover, Salisbury & **Bath Spa**, Mon-Sat 3/day, Sun 1/day.

If you think you may need to book a taxi when you arrive, check the relevant place in the route guide; ⌨ traintaxi.co.uk *may* also be able to help. It is also possible to book train tickets that include bus travel to your ultimate destination: enquire when you book your train ticket, or look at ⌨ plusbus.info.

No discussion of the railways serving the Cotswold Way would be complete without mention of the scenic **Gloucestershire Warwickshire Steam Railway** which, although it operates a limited service, does link Broadway, Toddington and Winchcombe with Cheltenham; see p84 for more details.

By coach
National Express is the principal coach (long-distance bus) operator in Britain. Travel by coach is usually cheaper than by train but takes rather longer. Advance bookings can carry significant discounts so it makes sense to book at least a week ahead. The service of greatest use to Cotswold Way walkers is that to Bath, but coaches also run regularly to Cheltenham and Stroud. Local buses connect Cheltenham and Stroud to several points along the trail. See coach services box below.

By car
Chipping Campden lies west of Oxford, so the best access is via the M40 from London or Birmingham, leaving at junction 8 (northbound) or 9 (southbound) to link up with the A44 towards Evesham. The turning to Chipping Campden is the B4081 beyond Moreton-in-Marsh. Getting to **Bath** is infinitely more straightforward: leave the M4 at junction 18, then take the A46.

The greater problem is what to do with your car while you are tramping along the trail – and how to get back to it when you reach the end. **Parking** on the road in Bath is not an option, while the maximum stay in the city's multi-storey car parks is seven days, which is tight for all but the fastest of walkers. In Chipping Campden, the occasional B&B may allow you to park for a week or so, provided you stay with them for a night or two, and there is parking in Back Ends (see Map 1a, p79) where you can leave your car for the week. But given the logistics of returning to their starting point, many walkers choose to leave their car at home, but at least one of the baggage-transfer companies can

PLANNING YOUR WALK

❑ **COACH SERVICES**   (**Note**: not all stops are listed)

National Express (☎ 0871 781 8181, ⌨ nationalexpress.com)
327 Hull to Bristol via Nottingham, Leicester, Birmingham, Evesham, **Cheltenham**, Gloucester & Stroud, 1/day
337 Rugby to Paignton via Coventry, Warwick, Stratford-upon-Avon, Evesham, **Cheltenham**, Gloucester, Bristol & Exeter, 1/day
403 London Victoria Coach Station (VCS) to **Bath** via Chippenham, approx 1/hr (some services call at Heathrow Airport)
444 London VCS to Gloucester via **Cheltenham**, 13/day (some services call at **Charlton Kings**)
445 London VCS to Hereford via Cirencester, Stroud (1/day) & Gloucester, 2/day
460 London VCS to Stratford-upon-Avon via Coventry & Leamington Spa, 1/day

(for a fee) store your vehicle and organise transport to, or from, the start/end of the trail (see pp27-8).

LOCAL TRANSPORT

The public transport map opposite gives an overview of the most useful bus and train routes for walkers.

For contact details and the approximate frequency of rail services see the box on p46, for coach services the box on p47 and for local bus services the box below and on p50. **Timetables** are available from the operators; all timetables for bus services operating in, or through, Gloucestershire can be found on ⌨ easytraveling.org.uk/gcc. In addition to the companies listed service details can be obtained from the national public transport information line, **traveline** (⌨ traveline.info).

Although much of the trail is well served by local bus services, there is little in the way of an integrated service, particularly between the northern and southern parts of the route. Most operators issue timetables twice a year; while these vary less than in some areas, it is important to check ahead to make sure the service you want is still running.

❏ LOCAL BUS SERVICES

Note that most local bus companies have no service on a Sunday. However, if there is a Sunday service it almost always operates on a Bank Holiday Monday as well. Also, not all stops are listed.

● **Coachstyle** (☎ 01249-782224, ⌨ www.coachstyle.ltd.uk)
41   Malmesbury to Yate via Badminton, **Tormarton**, **Old Sodbury** & Chipping Sodbury, Mon-Sat 4/day

● **Community Connexions** (☎ 0345 680 5029, ⌨ communityconnexions.org.uk)
21   Brimpsfield to Gloucester via **Birdlip**, Air Balloon pub (near **Crickley Hill**) & **Little Witcombe**, Wed & Fri 1/day

● **Cotswold Green** (☎ 01453-835153)
40   Stroud to **Wotton-under-Edge** via Nailsworth, Mon-Sat 5/day
65A Uley to Coaley via **Dursley** & Upper Cam, Sat 2/day (see also Stagecoach)
230 Stroud circular route via **Ebley** & **Randwick**, Tue 2/day

● **Euro Taxis** (☎ 03336-666666, ⌨ eurotaxis.com)
202 Winterbourne to Chipping Sodbury via Yate, Mon-Fri 2/day
626 **Wotton-under-Edge** to Bristol, Mon-Fri 1/day

● **First** (☎ 0845-606 4446, ⌨ firstgroup.com/bristol-bath-and-west)
9   Upper Weston to **Bath** bus station via **Weston**, Mon-Fri 1/hr

Hedgehog Community Bus (☎ 01386-430262, ⌨ hedgehogbus.org)
H3A   Mickleton to Stratford via **Chipping Campden**, Tue 1/day
H3B, H3C & H3E Mickleton to **Chipping Campden**, Wed, Fri & Sat 1/day
H5A & H5B Mickleton to Evesham via **Chipping Campden**, Tue & Thur 1/day
(cont'd on p50)

PLANNING YOUR WALK

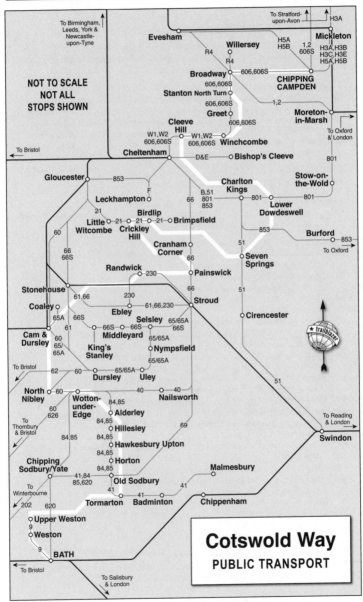

Cotswold Way
PUBLIC TRANSPORT

PLANNING YOUR WALK

❏ LOCAL BUS SERVICES (*cont'd from p48*)

● **Johnsons** (☎ 01564-797000, 🖳 johnsonscoaches.co.uk/buses)

1 & 2 Stratford-upon-Avon to Moreton-in-Marsh via **Chipping Campden,** & **Broadway** (3/day), Mon-Sat 6-7/day

● **Marchants Coaches** (☎ 01242-257714, 🖳 marchants-coaches.com)

606 Cheltenham to **Chipping Campden** via **Cleve Hill, Winchcombe**, Greet, **Stanton** North Turn & **Broadway**, Mon-Sat 3/day plus 1/day to Broadway

606S Cheltenham to Stratford-upon-Avon via **Cleve Hill, Winchcombe**, Greet, **Stanton** North Turn & **Broadway**, Sun 2/day plus 2/day to Winchcombe

W1 & W2 Cheltenham circular routes via **Winchcombe** & **Cleve Hill**, Mon-Sat 1/hr each service

● **NN Cresswell** (☎ 01386-48655, 🖳 nncresswell.co.uk)

R4 (Rural 4) Willersey to Evesham via **Broadway**, Mon-Sat 6/day

● **Pulhams Coaches** (☎ 01451-820369, 🖳 pulhamscoaches.com)

801 Cheltenham to Moreton-in-Marsh via **Charlton Kings, Lower Dowdeswell** & Stow-on-the-Wold, Mon-Sat 8/day plus Mon-Fri 1/day

● **Stagecoach** (🖳 stagecoachbus.com)

51 Swindon to **Cheltenham** via Cirencester, **Seven Springs** & **Charlton Kings**, Mon-Sat approx 1/hr, Sun 5/day

60 Gloucester to Thornbury via **Cam & Dursley** station, **Dursley, North Nibley** & **Wotton-under-Edge**, Mon-Sat 6/day, Gloucester to **Dursley**, Sun 4/day

61 Chalford to Woodmancote via Stroud, **Ebley, Stonehouse** & **Dursley**, Mon-Sat 1/hr

62 Bristol to **Dursley**, Mon-Sat 6/day

65/65A Stroud to **Cam & Dursley station** via **Selsley, Nympsfield, Uley** & **Dursley**, Mon-Fri 6/day (see also Cotswold Green)

66 Cheltenham to Gloucester via **Cranham Corner, Painswick**, Stroud, **Stonehouse** & **Ebley**, Mon-Sat 1/hr, Sun 3/day plus 2/day to Stroud

66S Stroud to Gloucester via **Selsley, Middleyard, King's Stanley**, Leonard Stanley, Bridgend & **Stonehouse,** Mon-Sat 1/hr, Sun 5/day

69 Old Sodbury to Stroud, Mon-Sat 3/day (connects with the 620)

84 Yate circular route via Chipping Sodbury, **Wotton-under-Edge, Alderley, Hillesley, Hawkesbury Upton, Horton**, Old Sodbury & Chipping Sodbury, Mon-Sat 8/day

85 Yate circular route via Chipping Sodbury, **Horton, Old Sodbury, Hawkesbury Upton, Hillesley, Alderley** & **Wotton-under-Edge**, Mon-Sat 8/day

(**Note** that the 84 and 85 do the opposite route in the return direction)

620 Old Sodbury to Bath via Chipping Sodbury & Yate, Mon-Sat 4/day plus Mon-Fri 2/day from Chipping Sodbury

B Cheltenham to Charlton Kings Mon-Sat 2/hr, Sun 1/hr

D & E Cheltenham to Bishops Cleeve via Cheltenham Racecourse, Mon-Sat 2/hr, Sun 1/hr

F Cheltenham to Leckhampton, Mon-Sat 2/hr, Sun 1/hr

● **Swanbrook** (☎ 01452-712386, 🖳 www.swanbrook.co.uk)

853 Gloucester to Oxford via **Cheltenham, Charlton Kings**, Burford & Witney, Mon-Sat 2/day plus 2/day from **Cheltenham**, Sun 1/day

Minimum-impact walking

Walk as if you are kissing the Earth with your feet
Thich Nhat Hanh, *Peace is every step*

Simply by visiting the Cotswolds you are making a positive impact on the local community – as well as on your well-being. Your presence brings money into the local economy and creates jobs for local people. It ensures that the area maintains a high profile and helps to strengthen the value of local crafts such as dry-stone walling (see box p10) that could otherwise be left to die out. So much for the positives.

On the other side, there is the risk that large numbers of tourists can unwittingly destroy the very place they have come to enjoy. If such tourists adopt a blinkered approach, damage – both environmental and social – is inevitable. But if visitors make the effort to work with local communities to protect the environment, everyone will benefit.

The following guidelines are designed to help you reduce your impact on the environment where you are a visitor, to encourage conservation and to promote sustainable tourism in the area.

ECONOMIC IMPACT

Communities along the Cotswold Way are no strangers to crises, from foot-and-mouth disease to widespread flooding. More generally, political and economic expediency threaten the closure of rural post offices and local hospitals. Yet walkers can play their part in helping to keep such communities economically viable. The watchword is 'local': buy local, support local businesses, encourage local skills, all of which bring significant social, environmental and psychological benefits.

Support local businesses

Rural businesses and communities in Britain have been hit hard in recent years by a seemingly endless series of crises. Most people are aware of the Countryside Code – not dropping litter and closing the gate behind you are still as pertinent as ever – but in light of the economic pressures there is something else you can do: **buy local**.

It's a fact of life that money spent at local level – perhaps in a market, or at the greengrocer, or in an independent pub – has a far greater impact for good on that community than the equivalent spent in a branch of a national chain store or restaurant. While no-one would advocate that walkers should boycott the larger supermarkets, which after all do provide local employment, it's worth remembering that businesses in rural communities rely heavily on visitors for their very existence.

Look and ask for local produce to buy and eat; not only does this cut down on the amount of pollution and congestion that the transportation of food creates (the so-called 'food miles'), but also ensures that you are supporting local farmers and producers; the very people who have moulded the countryside you have come to see and who are in the best position to protect it. If you can find local food which is also organic so much the better.

ENVIRONMENTAL IMPACT

By choosing to walk you have already made a positive step towards minimising your impact on the wider environment. By following these suggestions you can also tread lightly through the Cotswolds.

Use public transport whenever possible

Using public transport rather than private cars benefits both visitors and locals, as well as the environment. Local buses (see pp48-50) service many of the villages through which you'll pass and it's often possible to use them at the end of a day or several days on the trail to get back to a convenient point. Also of use are local taxi firms, which are only too happy to ferry walkers or their luggage around.

Never leave litter

Leaving litter shows a total disrespect for the natural world and others coming after you. As well as being unsightly and unhygienic, litter kills wildlife, pollutes the environment and can be dangerous to farm animals. **Please** remove your rubbish and dispose of it in a bin in the next village. It would be helpful if you were to pick up litter left by other people too.

● **The lasting impact of litter** A piece of silver foil left on the ground takes 18 months to decompose; a plastic bag 10 years; clothes 15 years; and an aluminium can 85 years. Would you want your great-grandchildren to find your discarded lemonade can next to their picnic?

● **Is it OK if it's biodegradable?** Not really. Apple cores, banana skins and the like are unsightly, encourage flies, ants and wasps, and can ruin a picnic spot for others. Orange peel left on the ground takes six months to decompose.

Erosion

● **Stay on the waymarked trail** Please. The effect of your footsteps may seem minuscule but when they are multiplied by several thousand walkers each year they become rather more significant. Avoid taking shortcuts, widening the trail or creating more than one path; your boots will be followed by many others.

● **Consider walking out of season** As the weather warms up, so plants start to grow and walkers appear on the hillsides. Thus areas of the trail subject to the greatest pressure are often prevented from recovering. Walking at less busy

times eases this pressure on the environment. It can also be more rewarding, with
fewer people on the trail and a more
relaxed atmosphere prevalent among
local communities.

Respect all wildlife

Care for all wildlife you come across on
the path; it has just as much of a right to
be there as you. Tempting as it may be to
pick wild flowers, leave them so the next
person who passes can enjoy them too.
Don't break branches off or damage trees
in any way.

What is this life if, full of care,
We have no time to stand and stare.
No time to stand beneath the boughs
And stare as long as sheep or cows.
No time to see, when woods we pass,
Where squirrels hide their nuts in grass.
No time to see, in broad daylight,
Streams full of stars, like skies at night.
No time to turn at Beauty's glance,
And watch her feet, how they can dance.
No time to wait till her mouth can
Enrich that smile her eyes began.
A poor life this if, full of care,
We have no time to stand and stare.
William Henry Davies, *Leisure*

If you come across wildlife, keep
your distance and don't watch for too long. Your presence can cause considerable stress, particularly if the adults are with young or in winter when the weather is harsh and food scarce. Young animals are rarely abandoned. Never inter-
fere if you find young deer or fledgling birds that are apparently alone; their
mother will almost certainly return as soon as you have moved on.

The code of the outdoor loo

As more and more people discover the joys of the outdoors, sorting the toilet
issue is of increasing importance. Even the least sensitive of people are offend-
ed by loo paper strewn across a path, or by the ill-disguised sight of human
excrement. Not only is it offensive to our senses but, more importantly, it can
infect water sources.

● **Where to go** Wherever possible wait until you come to a **public toilet**. These
are marked on the trail maps in this guide. If you do have to go outdoors, choose
a site at least **30m away from running water**. Use a strong stick to **dig a small
hole** about 15cm (6") deep in which to bury your excrement. It decomposes
quicker when in contact with the top layer of soil or leaf mould; using a stick to
stir loose soil into your deposit will speed up decomposition even more. Do not
squash it under rocks as this slows down the composting process. If you have
to use rocks to hide it make sure they are not in contact with your faeces.

● **Toilet paper and tampons/sanitary towels** Toilet paper takes a long time to
decompose, whether buried or not. Like tampons and sanitary towels, it is easily
dug up by animals and could end up in water sources or on the trail. The best
method for dealing with such items is to **pack them out**. Put them inside a
paper bag, then inside another bag (or two). Then simply empty the contents of
the bag at the next toilet you come across and throw it away.

ACCESS

Rights of way

As a designated national trail, the Cotswold Way is a public right of way, a path
that anyone has the right to use on foot provided they stay on the path and do

❏ The Countryside Code

The Countryside Code, originally described in the 1950s as the Country Code, was revised and relaunched in 2004, in part because of the changes brought about by the CRoW Act (see opposite); it was updated again in 2012, 2014 and also 2016. The Code seems like common sense but sadly some people still appear to have no understanding of how to treat the countryside they walk in. An adapted version of the 2016 Code, launched under the logo 'Respect. Protect. Enjoy.', is given below:

Respect other people

● **Consider the local community and other people enjoying the outdoors**
Be sensitive to the needs and wishes of those who live and work there. If, for example, farm animals are being moved or gathered keep out of the way and follow the farmer's directions. Being courteous and friendly to those you meet will ensure a healthy future for all based on partnership and co-operation.

● **Leave gates and property as you find them and follow paths unless wider access is available**
A farmer normally closes gates to keep farm animals in, but may sometimes leave them open so the animals can reach food and water. Leave gates as you find them or follow instructions on signs. When in a group, make sure the last person knows how to leave the gate. Follow paths unless wider access is available, such as on open country or registered common land (known as 'open access land'). Leave machinery and farm animals alone – if you think an animal is in distress try to alert the farmer instead. Use gates, stiles or gaps in field boundaries if you can – climbing over walls, hedges and fences can damage them and increase the risk of farm animals escaping. If you have to climb over a gate because you can't open it always do so at the hinged end. Also be careful not to disturb ruins and historic sites.

Stick to the official path across arable/pasture land. Minimise erosion by not cutting corners or widening the path.

Protect the natural environment

● **Leave no trace of your visit and take your litter home**
Take special care not to damage, destroy or remove features such as rocks, plants and trees. Take your litter with you (see p52); litter and leftover food doesn't just spoil the beauty of the countryside, it can be dangerous to wildlife and farm animals.

Fires can be as devastating to wildlife and habitats as they are to people and property – so be careful with naked flames and cigarettes at any time of the year.

● **Keep dogs under effective control**
This means that you should keep your dog on a lead or keep it in sight at all times, be aware of what it's doing and be confident it will return to you promptly on command. Across farmland dogs should always be kept on a short lead. During lambing time they should not be taken with you at all. Always clean up after your dog and get rid of the mess responsibly – 'bag it and bin it'. (See also box opposite and pp184-6).

Enjoy the outdoors

● **Plan ahead and be prepared**
You're responsible for your own safety: be prepared for natural hazards, changes in weather and other events. Wild animals, farm animals and horses can behave unpredictably if you get too close, especially if they're with their young – so give them plenty of space.

● **Follow advice and local signs**
In some areas there may be temporary diversions in place. Take notice of these and other local trail advice.

not cause damage or obstruct it in any way. The trail takes in several public rights of way which fall largely into one of three categories:

● A **footpath** (marked with a yellow arrow) is open to walkers only, not to cyclists, horse-riders or vehicles

● A **bridleway** (blue arrow) is open to walkers, horse-riders and cyclists but on bridleways cyclists have to give way to other users.

● A **restricted byway** (purple arrow) is open to walkers, horse-riders and cyclists, but not to motorised vehicles.

That said, not all footpaths are necessarily rights of way. Sometimes a landowner will allow a path across his land to be used for the convenience of walkers, although it may not be recognised as a right of way. This is known as a **permissive path**.

The maintenance of rights of way is down to the landowner in conjunction with the county council through whose area it passes, and sometimes the local authority. Farmers and land managers must ensure that: paths are not blocked by crops or other vegetation, or otherwise obstructed; the route is identifiable; and that the surface is restored soon after cultivation. If crops are growing over the path you have every right to walk through them, following the line of the right of way as closely as possible.

Should you find a path blocked or impassable, report it to the appropriate highway authority.

Right to roam

Following a concerted effort by groups such as the Ramblers (see box p44) and the British Mountaineering Council, the principle of access to open countryside and registered common land was finally allowed under the **Countryside and Rights of Way Act 2000**, affectionately known as CroW. In England, the act came into effect in full in 2005, creating a new right of access to the English countryside for recreation on foot.

There are restrictions, of course: some land (such as gardens, parks and cultivated land) is excluded, and high-impact activities such as driving a vehicle,

---

❏ **Walking through fields of cattle**

It is very rare that cows will attack walkers but it does happen. Cows get particularly nervous when dogs are about and cows with calves can be even more twitchy. Most of the time they will just watch you pass but very occasionally they will wander over out of curiosity. The following guidelines may prove helpful:

● Try not to get between cows and their calves.
● Be prepared for cattle to react to your presence, especially if you have a dog.
● Move quickly and quietly, and if possible walk around them.
● Keep your dog close and under proper control.
● Don't hang onto your dog if you are threatened by animals; let it go.
● Don't put yourself at risk. Find another way round the cows and rejoin the footpath.
● Don't panic! Most cows will stop before they reach you. If they follow just walk on quietly.
● Report any problems to the highway authority.

MINIMUM IMPACT & OUTDOOR SAFETY

cycling, and horse-riding may not be permitted. The act also: gives greater protection to SSSIs (see p61) and AONBs (see p60); lists habitats and species
important to biological diversity in England; and covers the conduct of those
walking with dogs (see p184-6). Land over which access has been granted may
be marked with a circular brown-and-white waymark, depicting a Morph-like
creature walking across a hill.

Health and outdoor safety

HEALTH

Prevention
Water and dehydration You need to drink lots of water while walking –
probably more than you think. Many health specialists recommend 2-4 litres a
day, depending on the weather and your physique. If you're feeling drained,
lethargic or just out of sorts it may well be that you haven't drunk enough.
Thirst is not always a reliable indicator of how much you should drink. The frequency and colour of your urine is a more useful guide: the clearer the better.

Sunburn Even on overcast days the sun still has the power to burn. Sunburn
can be avoided by regularly applying sunscreen, remembering your lips and
ears, and by wearing a hat to protect your face and the back of your neck. Those
with fair skin should consider wearing a light, long-sleeved top and long
trousers rather than T-shirt and shorts.

Blisters Worn-in, comfortable boots are a must, as are good, well-fitting socks.
How many people set out on a long walk in new boots and live to regret it!
   Look after your feet, too: air them at lunchtime, keep them clean and
change your socks daily. If you feel any 'hot spots' on your feet while you are
walking, stop immediately and apply a few strips of zinc oxide tape or one of
the commercially available 'blister plasters', and leave on until the area is pain
free or the tape/plaster starts to come off.
   If you have left it too late and a blister has developed, you can still protect
it from further abrasion with one of the 'blister kit' plasters. Popping it can lead
to infection. If the skin is broken, keep the area clean with antiseptic and cover
with a non-adhesive dressing material held in place with tape.

Joints and muscles If you're susceptible to joint problems – in particular
your knees and ankles – do invest in a pair of walking poles and use one or both
of them, especially during steep ascents or descents. Properly used, they can
lessen the impact of long-distance walking on your joints and thus can help to
prevent injury. Even the fittest athlete warms up before exercise and stretches
afterwards – and it's good practice for walkers. It's surprising how much easier
it is to set off in the morning without aching muscles; this, too, lessens the risk
of injury.

Hypothermia and hyperthermia

Hypothermia, or **exposure**, occurs when the body can't generate enough heat to maintain its core temperature. Since it is usually as a result of being wet, cold, unprotected from the wind, tired and hungry, it is easily avoided by wearing suitable clothing (see pp39-40), carrying and consuming enough food and drink, being aware of the weather conditions, and checking on the morale of your companions. Early signs to watch for include feeling cold and tired with involuntary shivering. If in doubt, find shelter as soon as possible and warm the person up with a hot drink and chocolate or other high-energy food. If possible, give them another warm layer of clothing and allow them to rest.

If the condition is allowed to worsen, strange behaviour, slurring of speech and poor co-ordination will become apparent and the victim can quickly progress into unconsciousness, followed by coma and death. Quickly get the victim out of the wind and rain, improvising a shelter if necessary. Rapid restoration of body warmth is essential and best achieved by bare-skin contact: someone should get into the same sleeping bag as the patient, both having stripped to their underwear, with any spare clothing laid under and over them to build up heat. This is an emergency: send for help.

At the other end of the scale, **hyperthermia** occurs when the body is allowed to overheat. **Heat exhaustion** is often caused by water depletion and is a serious condition that could eventually lead to death. Symptoms include thirst, fatigue, giddiness, a rapid pulse, raised body temperature, low urine output and, later on, delirium and coma. The only remedy is to re-establish the balance of water. If the victim is suffering severe muscle cramps it may be due to salt depletion. **Heat stroke** is caused by the failure of the body's temperature-regulating system and is extremely serious. It is associated with a very high body temperature and an absence of sweating. Early symptoms can be similar to those of hypothermia, such as aggressive behaviour, lack of co-ordination and so on. Later the victim goes into a coma or convulsions; death will follow if effective treatment is not given. Sponge the victim down or cover with wet towels, then vigorously fan them. Get help immediately.

Dealing with an accident

● Ensure both you and the casualty are out of further risk of danger, but otherwise do not move someone who may be seriously injured.

● Use basic first aid to treat the injury to the best of your ability.

● Try to attract the attention of anybody else who may be in the area: the **emergency signal** is six blasts on a whistle, or six flashes with a torch (flashlight).

● If you have to go for help, ideally leave someone with the casualty. If there is nobody else, make sure the casualty is warm, sheltered and as comfortable as possible: leave spare clothing, water and food within easy reach, as well as a whistle and/or torch for attracting attention.

● Telephone ☎ 999 (or ☎ 112) and ask for the police or other rescue service. Be sure you know exactly where you are before you call.

● Report the exact position of the casualty and his or her condition.

MINIMUM IMPACT & OUTDOOR SAFETY

❏ **Lyme disease**

Ticks are small blood-sucking creatures that live on cattle, sheep and deer and cannot fly. When you are walking with bare arms or legs through long grass or bracken, small ticks can brush off and attach themselves to you, painlessly burying their heads under your skin to feed on your blood. After a couple of days of feasting they will have grown to about 10mm and will drop off. To avoid this, wear boots, socks and trousers when walking through, or sitting on, long grass, heather and bracken.

There is a very small risk that ticks can infect you with Lyme disease, although one would normally have to be attached to you for 24-36 hours before you were affected. Check your body after a walk and remove any ticks by pinching the head as close to your skin as possible and pulling steadily away from your body, without twisting. Keep the area clean with disinfectant. If you suffer flu-like symptoms, or lasting irritation at the site of the bite for a week or more, see a doctor.

For more information see ▣ lymediseaseaction.org.uk.

OUTDOOR SAFETY

The Cotswold Way is not a hazardous undertaking and presents no greater risk than you would encounter on an average day's walk in the countryside. Nevertheless, there are some sensible precautions that can help to prevent problems.

Check the weather forecast (see below) before you set out and go properly equipped (see pp38-42). Be sure to carry plenty of food to last you through the day and at least a litre of water. Drinking from streams is not recommended since they are likely to contain traces of pesticides and other chemicals used on the land. Should the weather close in, take particular care to stay on the route, especially if you are on Cleeve Hill, or one of the other stretches of the Cotswold Way that run along the escarpment. If in doubt, stop and check – using a compass and map, and perhaps a GPS.

Weather information

Anyone familiar with the British weather will know that it can change quickly. What started out as a warm sunny day can be chilly and wet by lunchtime, so don't be fooled. Newspapers, television and radio stations all give the forecast for the day ahead and local people will have plenty of advice on the subject. Weather forecasts can be found online at ▣ metoffice.gov.uk and ▣ bbc.co .uk/weather.

Walking alone

If you enjoy walking alone you must appreciate and be prepared for the increased risk. Try to tell someone where you are going. One way of doing this is to telephone your booked accommodation and let them know you are walking alone and what time you expect to arrive. If you leave word with someone else, don't forget to let them know you have arrived safely. Carrying a mobile phone is useful, though there's no guarantee of good reception.

THE ENVIRONMENT & NATURE

Given its route within the relatively narrow range of the Cotswold Hills, the Cotswold Way runs through an unexpectedly broad range of habitats. Among these, grasslands and beechwoods stand out from the dominant farmland, where grazing land and arable farming have created their own habitats. Open moorland contrasts with long-established towns and villages; there's even a river and a canal across the trail. To do justice to the flora and fauna of such an area would take a book several times the size of this one. What follows, then, is a brief description of the animals, birds and plants you may come across – and a few that are there, but which you're unlikely to spot. To find out more, take a look at one of the field guides listed on pp42-3.

While it's interesting in itself to be able to identify individual plants and creatures, far more valuable is to understand their place within their environment and how we, as walkers, can help to protect that fragile relationship. Conservation is part of that relationship, which is why these issues are explored here.

Conserving the Cotswolds

It's the business of government to see that the countryside is preserved for the pleasure and sanity of all of us. The fatal mistake has been to imagine that the interests of the countryside are in some way different from the interests of farmers. The countryside can only be maintained by a healthy agriculture. If farming dies, a most precious part of Britain dies with it. **John Mortimer**

Perhaps John Mortimer had the Cotswolds in mind when he penned these words. He certainly could have done, for farming has been an intrinsic part of these hills for many centuries, shaping the countryside – and the towns and villages – that are seen today.

Yet for all that the Cotswolds draw tourists in their droves, the pressure for development, the economic reality of maintaining small communities, and the red tape imposed on Britain's farmers all conspire against maintaining an equable balance with nature. If it has taken just over 70 years for over 96% of the region's unimproved limestone grassland (that's permanent grassland which has not been regularly cultivated) to disappear, how long will it be before there's nothing left?

THE ENVIRONMENT & NATURE

There are plenty of organisations that are determined not to let the unthinkable happen and some are listed opposite and on p62. Environmental issues are of growing interest on the political field and thanks to the efforts of these groups, many of them voluntary, the fight-back is gaining ground. Their work relies on the active participation of everyone who cares.

GOVERNMENT AGENCIES AND SCHEMES

Primary responsibility for countryside affairs in England rests with **Natural England** (🖳 gov.uk/government/organisations/natural-england). The organisation is responsible for: enhancing biodiversity, landscape and wildlife in rural, urban, coastal and marine areas; promoting access, recreation and public well-being; and contributing to the way natural resources are managed.

One of Natural England's roles is to designate: national trails; national parks; areas of outstanding natural beauty (AONBs), which afford the second level of protection after a national park; sites of special scientific interest (SSSIs); and national nature reserves (NNRs), and to enforce regulations relating to these sites.

Cotswolds AONB

Now for some statistics. Some 95% of the Cotswold Way national trail falls within the **Cotswolds Area of Outstanding Natural Beauty** (🖳 cotswolds aonb.org.uk), the largest of the 38 AONBs in England and Wales. Established in 1966, and extended in 1990, it runs from north to south for 78 miles (126km) and covers a total of 790 square miles (2038sq km).

The area has been inhabited for around 6000 years; today over 150,000 people live within its boundaries. Despite that, around 86% of the land is still farmland, its fields demarcated by an estimated 4000 miles of dry-stone walls. A further 10% or so is woodland, especially beech, though the walker on the Cotswold Way could be forgiven for thinking that the woods accounted for a significantly higher proportion than this!

Significantly, in terms of the area's natural history, over half of the UK's total Jurassic limestone grassland is to be found here, much of it protected within SSSIs (see opposite). That figure, though, tells only a part of the story. While the region's flower-rich limestone grasslands as a whole covered 40% of the AONB in 1935, that area has shrunk to just 1.5% today. Given that such habitats can harbour almost 400 species of plants and 25 species of butterfly, it's hardly any wonder that conservation of what little remains is such a vital issue.

The **Cotswolds Conservation Board** (and a team of Cotswold Voluntary Wardens) is responsible for much of the work involved in running the AONB, including the Cotswold Way, from footpath maintenance and hedge-laying to publicity and fundraising. Others lead walks, including an annual series along the Cotswold Way (see p29). A bi-annual newspaper, *Cotswold Lion*, ensures that both local people and visitors are kept informed of what's going on across the region. (Editions can be downloaded from the AONB website).

Sites of special scientific interest (SSSIs) and national nature reserves (NNRs)

The designation **SSSI** affords protection to specific areas against anything that threatens their unique habitat or environment. There are currently 89 SSSIs across the Cotswolds, including parts of Cleve Hill & Cleve Common (🖥 cleevecommon.org.uk), Leckhampton Hill, Crickley Hill and Painswick Beacon along the Cotswold Way. 'Triple SIs' are managed in partnership with the owners and occupiers of the land who must give written notice of any operations likely to damage the site and who cannot proceed until consent is given. Many SSSIs are also designated as **national nature reserves** (NNRs), including several that combine to make up the Cotswolds Commons and Beechwoods NNR.

Geoparks

The European Geoparks initiative was originally set up to help the development and management of deprived areas which nevertheless benefit from a rich geological heritage. The concept has since moved on, with today's geoparks designed to raise awareness of an area and to educate the general public. The Cotswold Way runs through **Cotswold Hills Geopark** (🖥 cotswoldhills geopark.net); it was established by Gloucestershire Geology Trust (see p10), in partnership with the Cotswolds AONB and Natural England, and reaches as far south as Wotton-under-Edge.

VOLUNTARY CAMPAIGNING & CONSERVATION ORGANISATIONS

Voluntary organisations started the conservation movement back in the mid 1800s and are still at the forefront of developments. Independent of government but reliant on public support, they can concentrate their resources either on acquiring land which can then be managed purely for conservation purposes, or on influencing political decision-makers by lobbying and campaigning.

The **National Trust** (NT; 🖥 nationaltrust.org.uk) with its four million members protects about 248,000 hectares in the United Kingdom. NT properties on or close to the trail include Snowshill Manor (box p88), Horton Court (p152), Newark Park (p144) and Dyrham Park (p160), as well as significant tracts of land. Of these, some of the most interesting are Dover's Hill just outside Chipping Campden, and Haresfield Beacon, as well as several areas of woodland.

Separated in 2015 from the governmental body responsible for listed buildings and heritage research (now Historic England), **English Heritage** (🖥 english-heritage.org.uk) has gained independent charitable status. It is responsible for the care and preservation of ancient monuments in England, including Hailes Abbey (box p93), several of the long barrows along the Cotswold Way, and Sudeley Castle (box p96).

The **Royal Society for the Protection of Birds** (RSPB; 🖥 rspb.org.uk) has more than a million members and 200 nature reserves, but the nearest to the trail is at Highnam Woods, some 3¾ miles (6km) west of Gloucester.

THE ENVIRONMENT & NATURE

Rather smaller in scale is the work of **Butterfly Conservation** (🖥 butter fly-conservation.org), which owns and manages the 31-hectare Prestbury Hill Reserve, to the south of Cleeve Hill. The two-part reserve, incorporating both Masts Field and Bill Smyllie Reserve, features a diversity of habitat and is home to some 30 species of butterfly.

The **Woodland Trust** (🖥 woodlandtrust.org.uk) aims to conserve, restore and re-establish trees, particularly broadleaved species. Their properties along the Cotswold Way include Lineover Wood, Penn Wood, Stanley Wood and Coaley Wood.

In a different mould altogether is the **Landmark Trust** (booking enquiries ☎ 01628-825925, 🖥 www.landmarktrust.org.uk), which works to preserve historic, or architecturally interesting, buildings and to make them suitable for short-term holiday lets. The trust has accommodation options along the trail that include both the East and West Banqueting Houses that once flanked the grand Jacobean Old Campden House at Chipping Campden (see p75), Beckford's Tower (see box p164), and two very close to Bath Abbey.

Then there's the work of two other organisations, both important in environmental terms. Those keen on voluntary work may be interested in **The Conservation Volunteers** (TCV; 🖥 tcv.org.uk), which encourages people to value their environment and take practical action to improve it. And more broadly there's the **Campaign to Protect Rural England** (CPRE; 🖥 cpre.org .uk) – whose name speaks for itself.

Flora and fauna

TREES AND SHRUBS

While the Cotswold Hills are widely revered for their hills and steep cliffs, among their less-sung attractions are the magnificent woods of **beech** (*Fagus sylvatica*) that define the edge of the escarpment. Some veteran species are at least 150 years old, and one – in Lineover Wood south-east of Cheltenham – dates back over 600 years and is said to be the third biggest beech in England. They are seen at their best in spring, when the soft green of the new leaves adds texture rather than darkness to the woodland panorama. Time is inevitably taking its toll on these old timers, which are threatened by factors such as disease, wind damage and erosion, as well as the vigorous seedlings of other species such as **ash** (*Fraxinus excelsior*).

Also interspersed with the beech are **sycamore** or **sycamore maple** (*Acer pseudoplatanus*), and **oak** (*Quercus robur*), as well as **horse chestnut** (*Aesculus hippocastanum*), **lime** or **linden** (*Tilia vulgaris*) and **birch** (*Betula pubescens*). Another species, the **large-leaved lime** (*Tilia platyphyllos*), is one of the rarest trees in Britain, but there's a bank of them in Lineover Wood, whose name derives from the Anglo-Saxon word for 'lime bank'.

Amongst mixed woodland you will come across trees such as **rowan** or **mountain ash** (*Sorbus aucuparia*), popular with birds who seek out its bright orange berries around August, **silver birch** (*Betula pendula*), **aspen** (*Populus tremula*), **alder** (*Alnus glutinosa*), and **hazel** (*Corylus avellana*). While there are **conifers** to be found, most are incidental to the deciduous trees; there are none of the dark conifer plantations so prevalent in many woodland areas.

In the hedgerows, the white, star-like blossom of the **blackthorn** (*Prunus spinosa*) heralds the beginning of spring, giving way as the year progresses to dark-blue, almost dusty-looking sloes which make great sloe gin. Later, a mass of creamy flowers proclaims the **hawthorn** (*Crataegus monogyna*), whose fruit adds a splash of red in autumn. Then, in early summer, the glory goes to the **elder** (*Sambucus nigra*), with its sweet-smelling clusters of cream flowers which by September have formed into a purplish-black fruit, ripe for making jelly or wine.

WILD FLOWERS

Of speedwell and thistles there are indeed plenty, but Gurney – writing after World War I – does little more than hint at the rich-

On Cotswold edge there is a field and that
Grows thick with corn and speedwell and the mat
Of thistles, of the tall kind
Ivor Gurney, *Up There*

ness of the flora to be found in his native Cotswolds. While much has changed since then, and habitats have declined significantly, there are still wild flowers aplenty along the trail.

Limestone grassland
Until the 1950s, sheep grazed the limestone grasslands that are so characteristic of the Cotswolds (some say the name derived from the Saxon words *wold*, referring to high, open country, and *cod* meaning 'found', but others claim it came from the Cotswold sheep), encouraging a broad range of wild flowers and an attendant population of butterflies and other insects. With changes in agriculture, what was left of this 'unimproved' grassland became overgrown, but several areas are now managed to ensure that this unique habitat can continue to prosper. Over 200 species of wild flower have been identified at Crickley Hill alone, with other similar areas including Leckhampton Hill, Painswick Beacon, Coaley Peak, Selsley Common and Prestbury Hill Reserve, as well as a small patch of ground at Great Witcombe Roman Villa.

Many of the wild flowers that grow in this habitat, such as **cowslips** (*Primula veris*), are also to be found along hedgerows and in fields, but some are specific to this environment. In spring there's the **early purple orchid** (*Orchis mascula*), but it's in summer that the wild orchids really come into their own. Relatively easy to find among colourful patches of **birdsfoot trefoil** (*Lotus corniculatus*), purple **self-heal** (*Prunella vulgaris*) and red or white **clover** (*Trifolium* spp) are the bright pink **pyramidal orchid** (*Anacamptis pyramidalis*), and **common spotted orchids** (*Dactylorhiza fuchsii*), which can be pink, pale lilac or white. The **bee orchid** (*Ophrys apifera*), named for its close resemblance to a bee, is a rarity, and is carefully protected where it does grow. Also present are the **fly orchid** (*Ophrys insectifera*) – which does look like a fly – and the rather inconspicuous **musk orchid** (*Herminium monorchis*).

Striking in their summer glory are the tall spikes of startlingly blue **viper's bugloss** (*Echium vulgare*), and the **thistles** (*Cirsium* spp) and **knapweeds** (*Centaurea scabiosa*), their colourful purple flowers a magnet for bees. The delicate **harebell** (*Campanula rotundifolia*) is also at home here, as is the **scabious** (*Knautia arvensis*), their pale-blue flowers contrasting with bold **ox-eye daisies** (*Leucanthemum vulgare*) and the rather less flamboyant **yellow rattle** (*Rhinanthus minor*), named for the sound made by its seeds when they're ripe. Lower down is the **common rock rose** (*Helianthemum nummularium*), its bright-yellow, five-petalled flowers familiar to many gardeners. Look out, too, for the pinkish-purple flowers of wild herbs such as **basil** (*Clinopodium vulgare*), **marjoram** (*Origanum vulgare*) and the ground-hugging **thyme** (*Thymus serphyllum*).

Moorland

Up on the hills and on open spaces such as Cleeve Common you'll come across plenty of **bracken** (*Pteridium aquilinum*), its fronds turning to a crisp brown as the year progresses. Here, too, the bright-yellow flowers of **gorse** (*Ulex europaeus*) brighten up the hillside.

Hedgerows and field boundaries

As the days grow longer and the air begins to warm up, wild flowers start to appear along the hedgerows. Needing little introduction are the more common species which even the uninitiated will soon recognise, such as: **primrose** (*Primula vulgaris*); **common dog violet** (*Viola riviniana*); **common speedwell** (*Veronica officinalis*), which can cure indigestion, gout and liver complaints; **bugle** (*Ajuga repans*); **tufted vetch** (*Vicia cracca*); **lesser celandine** (*Ranunculus ficaria*), not unlike the related buttercup; and **red campion** (*Silene dioica*). Here, too, you might find the occasional **green alkanet** (*Pentaglottis sempervirens*) which, with its bright-blue flowers and soft, hairy leaves, is often mistaken for borage, and the tall, deep-purple **honesty** (*Lunaria redivia*), whose flat, translucent seedpods are sought after by flower arrangers.

Later, from May to September, these will be joined by **buttercup** (*Ranunculus acris*), the flowers of which children will use to tell you if you like butter, and the small pink-flowered **herb robert** (*Geranium robertianum*). The **dandelion** (*Taraxacum officinale*) grows almost everywhere, including on waste ground, as does the tall **rosebay willowherb** (*Epilobium angustifolium*). Equally tall is the purple **foxglove** (*Digitalis purpurea*). Its flowers are attractive to bees but the plant is poisonous to humans – although it's from the foxglove that the drug Digitalin is extracted to treat heart disease. Unmistakable is the vivid red splash of the **field poppy** (*Papaver rhoeas*). Then there are the tall white-flowering heads of members of the carrot family such as **cow parsley** (*Anthrisus sylvestris*), **yarrow** (*Achillea millefolium*) and **hedge parsley** (*Torilis japonica*).

Early Purple Orchid
Orchis mascula

Spotted Orchid
Dactylorhiza fuchsii

Pyramidal Orchid
Anacamptis pyramidalis

Honesty
Lunaria redivia

Field Scabious
Knautia arvensis

Woolly Thistle
Cirsium eriophorum

Rosebay Willowherb
Epilobium angustifolium

Herb-Robert
Geranium robertianum

Black Knapweed
Centaurea nigra

Red Campion
Silene dioica

Rowan (tree)
Sorbus aucuparia

Field Poppy
Papaver rhoeas

Common Dog Violet
Viola riviniana

Dog Rose
Rosa canina

Honeysuckle
Lonicera periclymemum

Ramsons (Wild Garlic)
Allium ursinum

Germander Speedwell
Veronica chamaedrys

Wood Spurge
Euphorbia amygdaloides

Self-heal
Prunella vulgaris

Green Alkanet
Pentaglottis sempervirens

Wood Anemone
Anemone nemorosa

Foxglove
Digitalis purpurea

Bluebell
Hyacinthoides non-scripta

Viper's Bugloss
Echium vulgare

Meadow Buttercup
Ranunculis acris

Rock Rose
Helianthemum nummularium

Gorse
Ulex europaeus

Lesser Celandine
Ranunculus ficaria

Birdsfoot-trefoil
Lotus corniculatus

Marsh Marigold
Caltha palustris

Yarrow
Achillea millefolium

Primrose
Primula vulgaris

Cowslip
Primula veris

Colour photos (following pages)

● **C4 Left, top**: Market Hall, Chipping Campden, and the circular plaque marking the start or finish of the Way. **Left, bottom**: View over Broadway from near its eponymous tower. **Right, top**: Belas Knap long barrow. **Middle**: Carry enough water because unless you're a dog it's not advisable to quaff from a trough. **Bottom**: You'll meet a lot of sheep on this walk.
● **C5** The sound of cars is often replaced by the clip-clop of horses' hooves in sleepy Stanton.
● **C6 Left**: Pausing for a breather by lovely Hailes Church. **Right, top**: Looking over Cheltenham from Charlton Kings Common. **Bottom**: Painswick Church (**left**, see p122) and its celebrated yew trees; the Devil's Chimney on Leckhampton Hill (**right**, see p115).
● **C7 Left**: Daisy takes in the views from the escarpment near Haresfield Beacon (**top**); the folly near Little Sodbury (**bottom**). **Right**: Buckholt and Rough Park Wood, on the way to Painswick. The Cotswold Way has proportionally more woods than any other National Trail.
● **C8** Paraglider making the most of the updrafts on a glorious day above Selsley (p130).
● **C9 Left:** Site of the Battle of Lansdown (**top**); private sculpture garden (**bottom, left**) with macabre works by Michael Morse, beside Lansdown Golf Course; limestone circle (**bottom, right**) by Bath Abbey, marking the end/start of the Cotswold Way. **Right**: Bath Abbey (p168).

C4

C7

C8

Peacock
Inachis io

Small Tortoiseshell
Aglais urticae

Large Blue
Maculinea arion

Large Garden/Cabbage White
Pieris brassicae

Small Heath
*Coenonympha
pamphilus*

Red
Admiral
Vanessa atalanta

Small Garden/Cabbage White
Artogeia rapae

Painted Lady
Cynthia cadui

Small Copper
Lycaena phlaeus

Silver-washed Fritillary *Argynnis paphia*

Summer is when the climbers and ramblers come into their own. Almost everyone is familiar with the common **bramble** (*Rubus fruticosus*), sought out in autumn by blackberry pickers. **Honeysuckle** (*Lonicera periclymenum*), also known as woodbine, makes its appearance growing through hedges and in woodland from June to September, the fruits ripening to red in the autumn. **Hedge bindweed** (*Calystegia sepium*), with its white trumpet-shaped flowers, and the related pink **field bindweed** (*Convolvulus arvensis*) are a common sight during the summer months, as is the pale-pink **dog rose** (*Rosa canina*), which later produces rosehips, an excellent source of vitamin C and used to make a subtle-flavoured jelly. Then there's another autumn beauty, the almost translucent scarlet berries of the **white briony** (*Bryonia cretica*) that tumble in profusion down many a hedgerow. Beware, though: they're extremely poisonous.

Woodland

Spring has to be the best time to walk through the Cotswolds' beech woods. This is when the air is pungent with the smell of densely packed white **ramsons** (*Allium ursinum*), widely known as **wild garlic**. In some places, carpets of **bluebells** (*Hyacinthoides non-scripta*) appear, while others are favoured by **dog's mercury** (*Mercurialis perennis*) – no floral beauty, this, but its bright green leaves make a splendid floor covering. Beneath the still-open tree canopy, the woodland floor is liberally sprinkled with white **wood anemones** (*Anemone nemorosa*), whose petals close up at night and in bad weather. With a similar night-time habit but with more rounded leaves is the smaller **wood sorrel** (*Oxalis acetosella*). The plant with the red stem, dark green leaves and soft green bracts is the **wood spurge** (*Euphorbia amygdaloides*). A little later you might see the occasional patch of **lily-of-the-valley** (*Convallaria majalis*), or the much taller **Solomon's seal** (*Polygonatum multiflorum*).

In darker areas, especially along rocks and walls (look out for them in Penn Wood and Coaley Wood), are **hart's tongue ferns** (*Phyllitis* or *Asplenium scolopendrium*), their long narrow leaves slightly furled; this is the only British fern whose leaves are undivided.

In summer and autumn, there's often the opportunity to supplement a packed lunch with wild **alpine strawberries** (*Fragaria vesca*) and to a lesser extent **wild raspberries** (*Rubus idaeus*). Steer well clear, though, of the poisonous purple fruits of **bittersweet** or **woody nightshade** (*Solanum dulcamara*).

Riverbanks and wet areas

You won't have much opportunity to spot plants along riverbanks as you're walking the trail, but there is the occasional stream, and the alternative route along Stroudwater (Ebley) Canal offers a few water-loving specimens. In summer, the soft cream heads of **meadowsweet** (*Filipendula ulmaria*), which has similar medicinal properties to aspirin, contrast with tall **purple loosestrife** (*Lythrum salicaria*).

On the edge of water courses bright-yellow **marsh marigolds** (*Caltha palustris*) may be seen, while on the water itself (take a look on the canal) are large **yellow waterlilies** (*Nuphar lutea*). You might also see the pink **cuckoo** flower (*Cardamine pratensis*) and **ragged robin** (*Lychnis flos-cuculi*), as well as **watermint** (*Mentha aquatica*), easily identified by its smell, and **hemp agrimony** (*Eupatorium cannabinum*), with its large pink flowers.

BUTTERFLIES   [see colour plate opposite p65]

The existence of unimproved limestone grasslands is one of the major features that make butterflies so important to the Cotswolds region. Some 34 species are found in this environment, with the area significant for both the **small blue** (*Cupido minimus*), and the **Duke of Burgundy fritillary** (*Hamearis lucina*). Part of the Cotswolds AONB near Stroud has seen the reintroduction of the **large blue** (*Maculinea arion*), which, along with the **Adonis blue** (*Lysandra bellargus*), had been declared extinct in this area.

Those with a serious interest would be well advised to spend some time at the Prestbury Hill Reserve south of Cleeve Hill, where many species are protected within a reserve managed by Butterfly Conservation (see p62). Some, such as the **large whites** (*Pieris brassicae*) and **small whites** (*Artogeia rapae*), and the nettle feeders like **red admiral** (*Vanessa atalanta*) and **painted lady** (*Cynthia cadui*), are familiar to many of us from our gardens and parks and are easily spotted in many other places. Other, rarer species, such as the **large skipper** (*Ochlodes venata*), **brown argus** (*Aricia agestis*), **chalk-hill blue** (*Lysandra coridon*), **green hairstreak** (*Callophrys rubi*), **dark green fritillary** (*Argynnis aglaja*), **marbled white** (*Melanargia galathea*), **grayling** (*Hipparchia semele*), **small copper** (*Lycaena phlaeus*), **small heath** (*Coenonympha pamphilus*), **speckled wood** (*Pararge aegeria*), **comma** (*Polygonia c-album*), **peacock** (*Inachis io*), **tortoiseshell** (*Aglais urticae*), and **meadow brown** (*Maniola jurtina*), benefit significantly from this protection. Some of these are also found in other reserves including Leckhampton Hill, or at Painswick Beacon. Elsewhere, perhaps in Buckholt Wood (see Map 18), you may be lucky enough to spot the **silver-washed fritillary** (*Argynnis paphia*), the largest of the British fritillaries with a wingspan of almost 3" (70mm).

There may be considerable difference between the male and female of a species, which can be particularly frustrating for the novice attempting to identify a creature that scarcely holds still for a moment. Many of the blue butterflies, for example, take their name from the male; the female is often a rather insignificant brown.

BIRDS
High overhead ran frenzied larks, screaming, as though the sky were tearing apart
                                                      Laurie Lee, *Cider with Rosie*

To most of us, the song of a skylark overhead is decidedly more appealing than to Laurie Lee's childhood ears. And fortunately, there are still several places along the Cotswold Way where skylarks can be seen. Of the 86 species of bird that have been identified in the region as a whole, the skylark is considered to be one of 20 that are designated as 'nationally important' – along with the linnet, starling, house sparrow and yellowhammer.

Open farmland and upland areas

Out on the hills is where you'll find the **sky-lark** (*Alauda arvensis*), which is often heard long before it is seen, its clear song delivered as it soars overhead. Look out for them on Cleeve Hill Common and Selsley Common; they even do an impressive job of drowning out the traffic noise on fields near the M4 south of Tormarton. The same environment could throw up the similarly sized **meadow pipit** (*Anthus pratensis*), while two other birds that you're likely to see are the **wheatear** (*Oenanthe oenanthe*), the male of which has a steel-grey back and crown and often bows and flicks its tail and perches on walls or rocks, and the **stonechat** (*Saxicola torquata*), much smaller and darker in plumage and identifiable by its call, a single sharp 'teck'. In autumn, flocks of **redwings** (*Turdus iliatus*) and **fieldfares** (*Turdus pilaris*) arrive from their breeding grounds in northern Europe to feed on wild fruit and berries.

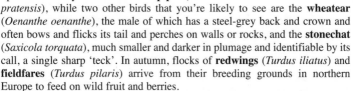

SKYLARK
L: 185MM/7.25"

Most easily spotted on hedgerows alongside farmland is the **yellowhammer** (*Emberiza citronella*), its familiar song widely translated as 'little-bit-of-bread-and-no-cheese'. This bright yellow bird with a reddish-brown back is regularly seen at Dover's Hill and Leckhampton Hill, too.

Out on the fields and across the hills is big crow country. You can't miss these gregarious birds, collectively known as corvids, whether the grey-headed **jackdaws** (*Corvus monedula*), the **rooks** (*Corvus frugilegus*), or the **carrion crows** (*Corvus corone corone*). If you doubted their community instincts, look out for jackdaws in particular at Wontley Farm, near Belas Knap, where they have taken over the derelict buildings en masse. In a similar environment you'll find **lapwings** (*Vanellus vanellus*), with their smart crests; during the breeding season the male performs a spectacular display, tumbling through the air to attract its mate.

LAPWING/PEEWIT
L: 320MM/12.5"

Increasingly seen near urban dumps, or anywhere that they can pick up scraps, are **lesser black-backed gulls** (*Larus fuscus*), usually in the company of the noisy and closely related **herring gulls** (*Larus argentatus*). Despite their prevalence, these two still seem entirely incongruous in a rural setting.

In an area where such a large proportion of land is given over to agriculture, the presence of game birds comes as no surprise. **Pheasants** (*Phasianus colchicus*) and **partridges** (*Perdix perdix*) are found practically everywhere, so don't be surprised if one suddenly flies up just in front of you, startled at your approach. You may also put up a **snipe** (*Gallinago*

gallinago), which has a zig-zag flight when flushed, or in wooded areas the nocturnal **woodcock** (*Scolopax rusticola*), easily distinguished from the snipe by its larger size and more rounded wings. Its camouflage makes it difficult to observe during the day.

Lording it over them all are the birds of prey. Both the **kestrel** (*Falco tinnunculus*) and the **sparrowhawk** (*Accipiter nisus*) can be seen, but it's the much larger **buzzard** (*Buteo buteo*), with its brown colouring and cruel yellow talons, that attracts most attention. Its mewing cry can send a shiver down the spine as it soars over fields, woods or moorland in search of its prey, anything from a beetle to a rabbit. The buzzard's fierce reputation won't stop other birds from defending their nests: rooks in particular will sometimes gang up to chase it away, although if sufficiently provoked the buzzard could well retaliate. The **red kite** (*Milvus milvus*) puts in a regular appearance, encroaching west following its successful re-introduction in the Chiltern Hills. It is easily distinguished in flight from other birds of prey by its forked tail.

Woodland

Many of the woodland residents such as the **chaffinch** (*Fringilla coelebs*), **greenfinch** (*Carduelis chloris*), **robin** (*Erithacus rubecula*), **song thrush** (*Turdus philomelos*), **blackbird** (*Turdus merula*), **blue tit** (*Parus caeruleus*) and **great tit** (*Parus major*), are familiar to us from our gardens, although less well known is the **long-tailed tit** (*Aegithalos caudatus*), which is distinguished from other tits by its very long tail: it tends to frequent woodland fringes and clearings.

Of the finches, the **goldfinch** (*Carduelis carduelis*) and **linnet** (*Acanthis cannabina*) are relatively common, too, but you might also spot the **siskin** (*Carduelis spinus*), which is smaller and more streaked than the greenfinch, and more yellow in colour. The **brambling** (*Fringilla montifringilla*), which often mixes with chaffinches in winter, is easily distinguished from them by its distinct white upper rump. The **bullfinch** (*Pyrrhula pyrrhula*) is notable for the male's brilliant red chest; the female is like a monochrome copy of her mate. They feed on berries, buds and seeds in the trees and bushes, their movements slow and deliberate. A much smaller bird is the **goldcrest** (*Regulus regulus*), which is the smallest European bird, recognised by its yellow crown with black edges.

The **willow warbler** (*Phylloscopus trochilus*) and **chiffchaff** (*Phylloscopus collybita*) will keep you guessing since distinguishing between them is quite difficult. The chiffchaff is generally rather browner than the willow warbler and its legs are blackish. More obviously, the willow warbler has the more melodic song.

Even if you're unfamiliar with the **treecreeper** (*Certhia familiaris*), it's not difficult to put a name to this small, brown bird with a curved bill that does exactly that: creeps up trees searching for insects. A similar location might also throw up the **nuthatch** (*Sitta europaea*), with its bluish-grey upper side and pinkish-cream chest, though this species tends to make its way down the trunk head first. Similar in size, although not in habit, is the **blackcap** (*Sylvia atricapilla*), quite easy to identify not just for the said black head (as well as brown back and lighter chest), but also for its pretty song. Usually a summer visitor, it nests in woods or dense shrubs. Another summer visitor is the inconspicuous **tree pipit** (*Anthus trivialis*); this one happiest on woodland fringes or any rough country, from where it delivers itself into the air, singing as it goes.

Larger and far more conspicuous are members of the woodpecker family. The **green woodpecker** (*Picus viridis*), a striking bird with a bright green body and red head, is also notable for its curious call, a kind of laughing cry that carries a long way. More often heard than seen are the **lesser spotted woodpecker** (*Dendrocopos minor*) and the much larger **great spotted woodpecker** (*Dendrocopos major*), distinctive for its striking black-and-white plumage, with a bright red patch under the tail and – in the male – similarly coloured crown. Both habitually drum on trees, usually to mark their territory and extract insects rather than to bore holes for a nest site.

GREEN WOODPECKER
L: 330mm/13"

It is highly likely that you'll see the **magpie** (*Pica pica*) in its handsome black, white and blue plumage, and the colourful **jay** (*Garrulus glandarius*) is becoming more common everywhere; both are highly efficient at cleaning eggs out of birds' nests and even taking young birds. Rarely seen, although its distinctive call is known even to children as the first harbinger of summer, the **cuckoo** (*Cuculus canorus*) is grey or occasionally brown in colour, not unlike a heavy male sparrowhawk. From the dove family, **wood pigeons** (*Columba palumbus*) and **collared doves** (*Streptopelia decaocto*) can be seen – and heard – everywhere.

Finally, there are the birds of the night, of which the one you're most likely to see – even occasionally in the daytime – is the **tawny owl** (*Strix aluco*). It can be quite unnerving to look up from a lunchtime picnic to find you're being observed from on high.

Streams, canals, rivers and reservoirs

Large tracts of open water are not something you'd associate with the Cotswolds, with the notable exceptions of the canal near Ebley, and the parallel River Frome, but reservoirs and the occasional stream or ornamental pond are enough to attract **swallows** (*Hirundo rustica*), **house martins** (*Delichon urbica*) and **swifts** (*Apus apus*). Watch their acrobatics in summer as they swoop low, picking up insects on the wing. You'll also spot these birds further afield, too. House martins often build their nests under the eaves of houses or churches, while swifts can often be seen rising on the currents; look out for them above Selsley Common. Distinctive in flight for its scimitar-shaped wings, the swift cannot perch like the swallow and martin, and spends almost its entire life aloft. The less-common **sand martin** (*Riparia riparia*) nests in colonies in holes in steep riverbanks and cliffs such as those in Witcombe Wood, near the reservoir.

In evidence along the canal are the familiar **mute swans** (*Cygnus olor*), **mallards** (*Anas platyrhynchos*), **coots** (*Fulica atra*) and **moorhens** (*Gallinula chloropus*), but there are other birds around too. The **grey wagtail** (*Motacilla cinerea*) in particular, with a blue-grey head and a bright-yellow underside, can be seen year-round bobbing up and down by bridges over fast-flowing rivers.

MAMMALS

You might occasionally spot a **roe deer** (*Capreolus capreolus*) in the woods along the Cotswold escarpment. Small in stature, with an average height of 60-75cm at the shoulder, they are reddish brown in summer, but grey in winter, and have a distinctive white rear end which is conspicuous when the deer is alarmed. Males have short antlers with no more than three points. They are active at dawn and dusk and can sometimes be heard barking. If you come across a young kid apparently abandoned, leave it alone and go away; it's normal behaviour for the mother to leave her kid concealed while she goes off to feed.

An enclosure of **red deer** (*Cervus elaphus*) can be seen at Broadway Tower, but these animals are not found in the wild in the Cotswolds.

Far more visible is the **rabbit** (*Oryctolagus cuniculus*). While many town-ies consider them to be cute relatives of Peter Rabbit, to the farmer they're a pest, responsible each year for damage to crops that can be counted in the millions. Despite being prey to buzzards, foxes, feral cats, stoats and man, they breed rapidly, bucks mating at four months old and does at three-and-a-half months, so their numbers are on the increase.

The **brown hare** (*Lepus europaeus*) is larger than the rabbit with large powerful hind legs and very long, black-tipped ears. They are found on upland, such as Leckhampton Hill, and rely for escape on their great acceleration, capable of attaining speeds of up to 45mph (70km/h).

Badgers (*Meles meles*) are nocturnal animals and rarely seen during the day, lying up in their underground burrows, or setts. Litters of cubs are born in February. Like rabbits, they are responsible for considerable damage on farmland, but unlike rabbits they are a protected species and cannot be destroyed. There is also some suggestion that cattle can catch the TB virus through contact with badgers.

Red foxes (*Vulpes vulpes*) are common, in spite of occasional persecution by man and the British roads. Readily identifiable by their colour and bushy tail, foxes are shy animals that come out mainly at night to hunt for food. Their supposed habit of killing all the hens in a coop and taking only one is apparently not the result of vicious rage but done to take advantage of abundance while it is available to compensate for times when food is scarce. Although the issue remains controversial, a ban on fox hunting was implemented in 2005.

The ubiquitous **grey squirrel** (*Sciurus carolinensis*) needs no introduction, having driven the native red squirrel into just one or two strongholds since the former's arrival here from North America in the 19th century.

The **weasel** (*Mustela nivalis*), one of Britain's smaller carnivores, is found in a wide range of habitats and is not a protected species. In fact, it may be trapped and killed by gamekeepers out to protect their birds from its claws. Mainly nocturnal and preferring dry areas, the weasel is smaller than the **stoat** (*Mustela erminea*), the tip of whose tail is always black.

Other small creatures that hide away in hedgerows include the nocturnal **hedgehog** (*Erinaceus europaeus*), which curls into a tight prickly ball when startled, as well as **shrews** (*Sorex sp.*), **voles** (*Microtus arvalis*) and **harvest mice** (*Micromys minutus*).

Of the 18 species of **bat** in the UK, several are found in the Cotswolds. The most obvious place to spot them is at Woodchester Mansion (see box p132)

❏ **Farm animals**

Dotted across the hills, **sheep** seem to take on the colour of Cotswold stone, rather dirty in the rain, but a soft warm cream in the sun, their lambs improbably white. In the Middle Ages, Cotswold sheep, or 'Cotswold Lions' as they were known, were bred for their long, thick fleeces, which brought immense fortunes to local merchants, enabling them to build the splendid manor houses and imposing 'wool' churches that still grace the region's towns. The animal is distinctive to the layman both for its long coat and a rather unkempt fringe.

Today, because of the widespread crossing of breeds, most of the sheep seen in the fields are cross-breeds, reared primarily for their meat. Yet some of the old breeds are still used, particularly for grazing on Cleeve Hill, so don't be surprised to see the occasional flock of Cotswold sheep.

While the majority of grazing animals in the Cotswolds are sheep, there are still **cattle** to be found, particularly further south along the trail. Many are the familiar black-and-white Friesians, but more conspicuous are the occasional belted Galloways, almost entirely black but with a broad white belt around their girth. Near Stanley Wood you may spot a herd of English longhorn cows, their downward curved horns distinctly different from the norm. The 'local' breed, Gloucester cattle, are distinctive, too, though you'll be lucky to see them. Once bred for Double Gloucester cheese, they have smart, near-black coats (occasionally spotted) enlivened by a bold white streak running from the middle of their spine through to their tail. Other distinguishing features are a black head and legs, and black-tipped horns.

No summary of farm animals in Gloucestershire would be complete without a nod to the **Gloucestershire Old Spot pig**. Named for the large black spots that dot their otherwise pink skins, these pigs once thrived in the outdoors, foraging on scraps and windfall apples. In fact, the spots are said to be bruises from falling apples in the orchards. They're immortalised at The Old Spot in Dursley!

Finally, there are **horses**. Lots of them – though nowadays they scarcely fall into the bracket of farm animals. From children's ponies to thoroughbred racehorses, you'll find plenty that point to man's passion for equines. Riding stables are much in evidence, especially in the north of the region, and many's the day when you'll come across a rider or party of riders as you walk along the trail. With this obvious local involvement, it's no accident that two of the country's biggest events in the horsey calendar, the Cheltenham Gold Cup and Badminton Horse Trials, take place in the Cotswolds.

If you want a closer look at many of these animals and more rare breeds, pay a visit to **Cotswold Farm Park** (☎ 01451-850307, 🖳 cotswoldfarmpark.co.uk; mid Feb-late Dec daily 10.30am-4pm; £14, or £9 online), east of Winchcombe, about four miles (6.4km) from the trail at Stumps Cross, off the B4077.

THE ENVIRONMENT & NATURE

72 Flora and fauna

THE ENVIRONMENT & NATURETHE ENVIRONMENT & NATURE

❏ **The smaller things in life**

While you're looking out for things at ground level, perhaps you'll spot two other grassland natives that are both now rare, but can still be found in this habitat.

© Tricia & Bob Hayne

The **glow worm** (*Lampyris noctiluca*) was once so common that people could read by the light of several found together.

And **Roman snails** (*Helix pomatia*, right) were considered a delicacy by the Romans, which is presumably how they acquired their name. Look out for them around Leckhampton and Crickley Hill; their cream-coloured shells can be up to two inches wide.

where six different species roost in the house and grounds. These include the endangered **greater horseshoe bat** (*Rhinolophus ferrumequinum*), with a wingspan of around 14" (35cm), and its cousin, the **lesser horseshoe bat** (*Rhinolophus hipposideros*), as well as the tiny **pipistrelle** (*Pipistrellus pipistrellus*), which is Britain's most common species of bat – and the smallest, with a wingspan of just 8" (20cm).

REPTILES

The **adder** (*Vipera berus*) is the only venomous snake in Britain but poses very little risk to walkers and will not bite unless provoked or unwittingly disturbed; if you're lucky enough to see one, leave it in peace. Their venom is designed to kill small mammals such as mice and shrews; human deaths are rare.

You are most likely to encounter an adder in spring when they come out of hibernation, and during the summer when pregnant females warm themselves on open ground in the sun. They are easily identified by the striking zig-zag pattern on their back and a 'V' on the top of their head behind their eyes.

Grass snakes (*Natrix natrix*) are Britain's largest reptile, growing up to a metre in length. They prefer rough ground with plentiful long grass in which to conceal themselves, laying their eggs in warm, rotting vegetation such as garden compost heaps, the young hatching in August. Its body has vertical black bars and spots running along the sides and usually has a prominent yellow collar round the neck. They are sometimes killed by people mistaking them for adders but are neither venomous nor aggressive.

The equally harmless **slow worm** (*Anguis fragilis*) looks like a snake but is actually a legless lizard. It has no identifying marks on its body, which varies in colour from coppery brown to lead grey and is usually quite shiny in appearance. Like lizards, they are able to blink; snakes have no eyelids. They love to sun themselves and are also found in old buildings under stones or discarded roofing sheets. Also present is the **common lizard** (*Lacerta vivipara*), which like other reptiles is partial to sunning itself during the day to warm up its body temperature.

Using this guide

The route guide has been divided into stages but these should not be
seen as rigid daily itineraries; people walk at different speeds and
have different interests. The **route summaries** describe the trail
between significant places and are written as if walking the path from
north to south, though there's nothing to stop you, of course, from
tackling the trail in the other direction.

To enable you to plan your own itinerary, **practical information**
is presented clearly on each of the trail maps. This includes walking
times in each direction, places to stay and eat, as well as shops where
you can buy supplies. Further **service details** are given in the text;
note that the hours stated for pubs relate, for the most part, to when
food is served; most venues serve drinks outside these hours.

For **map profiles** see the colour pages at the end of the book. For
an overview of this information see **itineraries** (p32) and the town &
village **facilities table** (pp34-7). The cumulative **distance chart** is on
pp194-5.

TRAIL MAPS

Scale and walking times
The trail maps are to a **scale** of just under 1:20,000 (1cm = 200m; $3^1/_8$
inches = one mile).

Walking times (see box below) are given along the side of each
map and the arrow shows the direction to which the time refers.
Black triangles indicate the points between which the times have
been taken. The time-bars are a tool and are not there to judge your
walking ability. There are so many variables that affect walking
speed, from the weather conditions to how many beers you drank the
previous evening. After the first hour or two of walking you will be
able to see how your speed relates to the timings on the maps.

❏ **Important note – walking times**
Unless otherwise specified, **all times in this book refer only to the time
spent walking**. You will need to add 20-30% to allow for rests, photography, checking the map, drinking water etc, not to mention time simply
to stop and stare.

    When planning the day's hike count on 5-7 hours' actual walking.

Up or down?

The trail is shown as a dotted line – – –. An arrow across the trail indicates the slope; two arrows show that it is steep. Note that the arrow points towards the higher part of the trail. If, for example, you are walking from A (at 80m) to B (at 200m) and the trail between the two is short and steep it would be shown thus: A– – – >> – – – B. Reversed arrow heads indicate a downward gradient.

Accommodation

Accommodation marked on the map is either on or within easy reach of the trail. Where accommodation is scarce, however, some of the places listed are a little further away. If that is the case, many B&B proprietors will collect walkers from the nearest point on the trail and deliver them back again the next morning, if requested in advance. They may also be happy to transfer your **luggage** to your next accommodation place. Some may make a charge for either or both of these services; check the details at the time of booking. Details of each place are given in the accompanying text.

The number of **rooms** of each type is stated, ie: **S** = Single, **T** = Twin room, **D** = Double room, **Tr** = Triple room and **Qd** = Quad. Note that most of the triple/quad rooms have a double bed and one/two single beds (or bunk beds); thus for a group of three or four, two people would have to share the double bed, but it also means that the room can be used as a double or twin. See also p20.

Rates quoted for B&B-style accommodation are **per person (pp) based on two people sharing a room** for a one-night stay; rates may well be discounted for longer stays and for more than two people sharing a room. Where a **single room (sgl)** is available, the rate for that is quoted if different from the rate per person. The rate for **single occupancy (sgl occ)** of a double/twin may be higher. Unless specified, rates are for bed and breakfast. At some places the only option is a **room rate**; this will be the same whether one or two people (or more if permissible) use the room. In tourist towns, particularly, you can expect to pay extra at weekends (whereas in establishments catering for business people the rate is likely to be higher during the week). Note that several places only accept advance bookings for a two-night stay, particularly at weekends and in the main season, though nearer the time may accept a single-night stay.

Your room will either have **en suite** facilities, or a **private** or **shared** bathroom or shower room just outside the bedroom. The text indicates whether a bath (🛁) is available for, or in, at least one room – for those who prefer a relaxed soak at the end of the day. It also indicates if a **packed lunch** (Ⓛ) can be prepared, subject to prior arrangement; and if **dogs** (🐾 – see also p25 and pp184-6) are welcome, again subject to prior arrangement.

Other features

The numbered **GPS waypoints** refer to the list on pp183-4. Generally, other features are marked on the maps when they are pertinent to navigation.

In order to avoid cluttering the maps and making them unusable, not all features have been marked each time they occur.

The route guide

CHIPPING CAMPDEN [MAP 1a, p79]
It feels fitting to start the trail in Chipping Campden, a beguiling town at the most northern point of the Cotswolds Area of Outstanding Natural Beauty, where the classic Cotswold images of warm honey-coloured stone and rolling green hills are so perfectly balanced.

Chipping Campden was founded on the wool industry in the 14th and 15th centuries, largely through the efforts of one of the country's most successful wool merchants, William Grevel. His home, **Grevel House** [8], still stands on the High St, and to him and other wealthy benefactors the town owes the outstanding and, revered, **St James's Church**. Over two hundred years later, another local worthy, Sir Baptist Hicks, trumped Grevel House with his **Campden House** [3], some of the remaining parts of which are now used by the Landmark Trust (see p62). Hicks was also responsible for the **Market Hall** [17], today owned by the National Trust and still in regular use, and for the **almshouses** [5] on Church St. Fast forwarding through the centuries brings us to the **Arts and Crafts Movement** (see box on p76), which played an influential role in reversing the town's decline following years of agricultural doldrums. Now tourism is the key to the economy, with plenty of restaurants and a range of accommodation suited to walkers and sightseers alike.

For something original, don't miss the **Guild** on Sheep St in Silk Mill [33]. Home to several artisans, it boasts a good art gallery (daily 10am-5pm), but the real draw is upstairs, where Hart's **silversmith** (🖳 hartsilversmiths.co.uk; Mon-Fri 9am-5pm, Sat 9am-noon) has operated since the early 20th century. Commission your own family heirloom, or take time to watch the craftsmen at work. The designs of another silversmith, **Robert Welch** [32] (🖳 robertwelch .com; Mon-Sat 9.30am-5.30pm, Sun

10am-4pm), are displayed at the shop bearing his name on Lower High St.

Every year in May the town hosts a two-week music festival (🖳 campdenmusic festival.co.uk) and – on Dover's Hill – the Olimpick Games (see box on p80).

Getting here
Access to Chipping Campden is relatively straightforward by road, but by **public transport** is more challenging. GWR (see box p46) operate train services to the nearest railway station at Moreton-in-Marsh; from there take Johnsons' bus Nos 1 or 2.

Alternatively it's possible to get a Chiltern Railways (see box on p46) train to Stratford-upon-Avon from London Marylebone, or a National Express coach (NX337 & NX460) to Stratford (see p47). From Stratford take Hedgehog Community Bus H3A (see box p48).

If you arrived by car, staff at the tourist office recommend that you avail yourself of the free **parking** in Back Ends, north of and parallel to the main High St; see map p79.

Getting around
Johnsons' **bus** Nos 1 & 2 stop on the High St, as do Hedgehog Community Bus's various H3 & H5 buses and Marchant's No 606; see pp48-50.

Taxi firms include: Les Proctor (mob ☎ 07580-993492; see Cornerways, Where to stay); Cotswolds Angel's Taxi (mob ☎ 07766-032725); Chipping Campden Taxis (☎ 01386-840111, 🖳 chippingcampden taxis.co.uk) and Red Lion Cars (☎ 01386-840760, mob ☎ 07565-226887; see Red Lion Inn Where to stay).

Services
The good **tourist information centre** [16] (☎ 01386-841206, 🖳 chippingcampdenon line.org; mid Mar-mid Nov daily 9.30am-5.30pm, mid Nov-mid Mar Mon-Thur

9.30am-1pm, Fri-Sun 9.30am-4pm) has its base in the Old Police Station on the High St. In addition to plenty of brochures and leaflets, there is a town guide for £1.50.

Those in search of a **bank** will find a branch of Lloyds [10] on the High St, and there's an **ATM** [29] in the car park on the wall of Huxleys restaurant. The **post office** [13] stands a couple of doors down from the tourist office.

Nearby are two small **convenience stores**: Co-operative [15] (daily 7am-10pm), and One Stop [39] (daily 6am-10pm). More individual fare is to be found at **delis** such as Sara's [41] (Tue-Fri 8.30am-4pm, Sat 8am-4pm), the nearby Fillet & Bone [25] (Mon-Sat 9am-6pm, Sun 10am-4pm), and Toke's [9] (Mon-Thur 9am-6pm, Fri 9.30am-6pm, Sat 9am-5pm, Sun 10am-4pm), where bread, cheese and pork pies are lined up alongside racks of wine. Every second Saturday morning (Mar-Nov 10am-5pm) of each month there's an **indoor market** (🖳 campden-market.co.uk) with food and craft stalls in the Town Hall [22].

❏ **Arts and Crafts Movement**

The Arts and Crafts Movement was founded in late Victorian Britain, born of a backlash against the uniformity which resulted from the Industrial Revolution. Its proponents – practical architects and designers as well as theorists – were largely concerned with restoring a sense of individuality and cohesion to an increasingly fragmented workplace. There was more than a touch of the romantic in their ideals, which included spiritual harmony and a oneness with nature. These aims were to be achieved in part through reuniting the fields of art, craft and design, so that the designer would be brought back in touch with the maker. Authenticity was a key principle, for example with houses to be constructed from naturally occurring materials and fitting into their environment. If buildings and furniture were relatively simple, ornamental pieces such as books and needlework were considerably more elaborate, often drawing on influences not only from the past but from external cultures. Ironically, high-minded intentions to improve the lot of the working man proved unrealistic, since individually crafted work was expensive to produce and out of the reach of all but a privileged few.

The major founders of the movement were the writer and critic John Ruskin, and William Morris, who trained as an architect and was variously a designer, Socialist and author. Although the movement was essentially urban, many of its practitioners moved to the country, and some to the Cotswolds. One of these, the architect CR Ashbee, was the founder in 1888 of the **Guild of Handicrafts**, which he moved from London to Chipping Campden's Silk Mill [33] in 1902. When Ashbee went bankrupt eight years later, his workshop was taken over by the silversmith George Hart. The work of Ashbee and eight other craftsmen is featured at **Court Barn Museum** [4] (🖳 courtbarn.org.uk; Apr-Sep Tue-Sun & bank hol Mon 10am-5pm, Oct-Mar Tue-Sun & bank hol Mon 10am-4pm; £5), in a converted barn near the church.

Other places along the trail that are linked to the movement include **Gordon Russell Design Museum** in Broadway (see p84), **The Wilson** in Cheltenham (see p107), inspired by William Morris, **Ashton Beer Collection** in Painswick (see p122), and **All Saints' Church** in Selsley (see p130).

Arts and Crafts visionaries had an impact on gardens, too, typically using topiary hedges to create a series of 'rooms'. Such influences were important at both **Owlpen Manor** (see box on p138) and **Hidcote** (off Map 1a; ☎ 01386-438333, 🖳 nationaltrust.org.uk; Easter-Sep daily 10am-6pm, Mar-Easter & Oct-daily 10am-5pm, mid-end Feb & early Nov-mid Dec weekends only 11am-4pm; £12.70, £7.70 in winter months and garden only, NT members free), a few miles north of Chipping Campden.

Campden Surgery [19] (☎ 01386-841894, 🖳 chippingcampdensurgery.co.uk; Mon-Fri 8.30am-1.30pm & 2-6pm) is along Back Ends. The **pharmacy** [7] (Mon-Fri 9am-1pm & 2-6pm, Sat 9am-1pm) is on the corner of the High and Church streets.

There are public **toilets** behind the tourist office and opposite Silk Mill.

Where to stay

Many walkers starting at Chipping Campden will want to stay a night before setting off the following morning, if only to have a chance to see something of the town. There's plenty of choice – though accommodation does get booked up quickly, especially in the summer and at weekends.

Campers will need to ask at the tourist information centre (see p75) to find out if anywhere is available locally to pitch a tent. Otherwise, the nearest official site is at Hailes (see p93).

A few **B&Bs** are centrally located among the stone cottages of the High St itself. On Lower High St, rooms at *The Old Bakehouse* [31] (☎ 01386-840979, 🖳 the oldbakehouse.org.uk; 1T/1D, both en suite; WI-FI) cost from £45pp (sgl occ £80-95). They accept cash or cheque only.

Further up the street, two of the tea rooms offer B&B in rooms above the premises: at *Badgers Hall* [14] (☎ 01386-840839, 🖳 badgershall.co.uk; 2D/1T or D/1T, all en suite; WI-FI; ⓛ) there's a minimum stay of two nights for advance bookings but a single-night stay may be accepted at the last minute. B&B costs from £70pp (sgl occ rates available on request) including a clotted cream tea if the room booking is made online.

Bantam Tea Rooms [12] (☎ 01386-840386, 🖳 bantamtea-rooms.co.uk; 1S/2T/4D, all en suite; ☛; WI-FI; ⓛ) charges £52.50-70pp (sgl/sgl occ from £80/ £95). If you stay the night (and subject to arrangement) you can leave your car here for the duration of your walk for £5 per day.

South of the main street on George Lane sits a modern option with footpath access to the High St: *Cornerways* [24] (☎ 01386-841307, 🖳 cornerways.info; 1Tr/1Qd, both en suite; WI-FI) charges from

£50pp (sgl occ room rate) and only accepts advance bookings for at least two nights. They also offer station pick ups: contact Les Proctor (see Getting around).

Several of the town's B&Bs lie in the opposite direction, along Aston Rd: solid stone houses with gardens backing on to open countryside. The first, *Cherry Trees* [2] (☎ 01386-840873, 🖳 cherrytreescamp den.com; 1D/1Tr, both en suite; ☛; WI-FI; ⓛ), is slightly elevated along a narrow track about 150m from the road, with views to Broadway Tower. The double room has a balcony and is above the garage. B&B costs £47.50-55pp (sgl occ rates on request). They have a two-night minimum stay policy year-round.

Back on Aston Rd itself at No 5, is *Taplins* [1] (☎ 01386-840927, 🖳 cotswold stay.co.uk; 2D/1T, all en suite; ☛; WI-FI), under the same ownership as the antiques shop in the town, which perhaps accounts for the Victorian-style roll-top bath in one of the rooms. B&B costs from £42.50pp, or from £70 for single occupancy. They will operate a taxi service from 2019.

If a **pub** is more your idea of a convivial place to spend the night, Chipping Campden comes up trumps. On Lower High St, almost opposite St Catharine's Church, the 17th-century *Volunteer Inn* [34] (☎ 01386-840688, 🖳 thevolunteerinn .net; 4D/3D or T/1T/1Qd, most en suite; WI-FI) has a couple of rooms where an extra bed can be added, but some rooms are over the bar so can be noisy. B&B costs from as little as £32.50pp (sgl occ from £50), though rates may be negotiable if you turn up on spec. They also offer a luggage-transfer service (end Mar-end Oct; see p28) under the name 'Cotswold Luggage Transfers'.

B&B at the family-run *Red Lion Inn* [28] (☎ 01386-840760, 🖳 theredlioninn .org; 1T or D/4D, all en suite; ☛; WI-FI; 🐾), Lower High St, normally costs £35-57.50pp (sgl occ £70-85). They also offer a pick-up service from local railway stations, or airports such as Bristol, Heathrow and Gatwick (see Red Lion Cars, p77).

Further along the High St and not to be confused with its namesake in Broadway, is

ROUTE GUIDE AND MAPS

the *Lygon Arms* [11] (☎ 01386-840318, 💻 lygonarms.co.uk; 7D or T/3Tr, all en suite; 🍽️; WI-FI; ⓁΞ; 🐾), a 16th-century coaching inn. Featuring exposed beams and stone walls, its rooms come in at £60-80pp (sgl occ from £85) for B&B.

Continuing upmarket brings you to *Eight Bells Inn* [6] (☎ 01386-840371, 💻 eightbellsinn.co.uk; 6D, all en suite; WI-FI; 🐾 bar area), on Church St, a 14th-century hostelry where the rooms are furnished in a contemporary yet sympathetic style. Note that from May to September and at weekends throughout the year there's a minimum two-night stay for advance bookings; rates *per night* are £49.50-72.50pp (sgl occ £75-150, but full room rate from May to Sep).

Smarter still are the **hotels**, of which *The Kings* [21] (☎ 01386-840256, 💻 kings campden.co.uk; 10D/3D or T in main house and 4D/1D or T in a separate cottage; all en suite; 🍽️; WI-FI; ⓁΞ; 🐾) has B&B at around £65pp (about £120 for sgl occ), though rates can be much higher for a de luxe room. By prior arrangement it may be pos-

sible to leave your car here for the week while you walk.

Noel Arms [23] (☎ 01386-840317, 💻 bespokehotels.com/noelarmshotel; 17T or D/10D, all en suite; 🍽️; WI-FI; 🐾) charges £70-117.50pp (sgl occ £130-225). In this rather elevated sphere, and part of the same hotel chain, there's also *Cotswold House Hotel & Spa* [20] (☎ 01386-840330, 💻 bespokehotels.com/cotswoldhouse; 8D/20D or T, all en suite; 🍽️; WI-FI; ⓁΞ; 🐾), which might justify a splurge at the end of a walk. Dynamic pricing makes B&B rates – £65.50 to £178.50pp for the smaller doubles (sgl occ £75-130), including use of the hydrotherapy pool and steam rooms – something of a lottery, but come in the winter months and you could strike lucky.

Where to eat and drink

Top-quality food with prices to match is done well along Chipping Campden's High St, but there's a good range of more accessible fare as well, especially at lunchtime.

For lingering over tea, coffee or a light lunch, several places fit neatly into the

---

CHIPPING CAMPDEN – MAP KEY

Where to stay
1 Taplins
2 Cherry Trees
6 Eight Bells Inn
11 Lygon Arms
12 Bantam Tea Rooms
14 Badgers Hall
20 Cotswold House Hotel & Spa
21 The Kings Hotel
23 Noel Arms
24 Cornerways
28 Red Lion Inn
31 The Old Bakehouse
34 Volunteer Inn

Where to eat & drink
6 Eight Bells Inn
11 Lygon Arms
12 Bantam Tea Rooms
14 Badgers Hall Tea Rooms

Where to eat & drink
(cont'd)
18 Michael's Mediterranean
21 The Kings Hotel
23 Noel Arms
28 Red Lion Inn
30 Huxley's
33 Campden Coffee Co (in Silk Mill)
34 Maharaja at Volunteer Inn

What to see & do
3 Campden House
4 Court Barn Museum
5 Almshouses
8 Grevel House
17 Market Hall
33 Silk Mill
35 Graham Greene's House

Other
7 Pharmacy
9 Toke's
10 Lloyds Bank
13 Post office
15 Co-operative
16 Tourist Information Centre
19 Campden Surgery
22 Town Hall
25 Fillet & Bone
26 Sara's Deli
27 One Stop
29 ATM
32 Robert Welch

frame. For irresistible cakes, **Bantam Tea Rooms** [12] (see Where to stay; daily 10am-5pm) has an enviable selection, as does the friendly **Badgers Hall Tea Rooms** [14] (see Where to stay; Thur-Sat 10am-4.30pm).

For a serious coffee fix, head straight for the more contemporary but still welcoming **Campden Coffee Company** [33] (☎ 01386 849251; Mon 9.30am-4pm, Tue-Fri 9am-4pm, Sat & Sun 10am-4pm, lunch served noon-2.30pm), in **Silk Mill** on Sheep St, where coffee beans are freshly ground and the cakes – including gluten free – are home-made. There are smoothies, too, as well as soups, jacket potatoes, baguettes and ice-creams.

The town also has some excellent **pubs**. *Eight Bells Inn* [6] (see Where to stay; food Mon-Thur noon-2pm & 6.30-9pm, Fri-Sat noon-2.30pm & 6.30-9.30pm, Sun noon-3pm & 6-9pm), which retains the atmosphere of a traditional pub, offers plenty of options. Wherever you eat – in the bar, the restaurant or the courtyard garden – you should eat well, particularly on a Sunday with their magnificent roast dinners (£15.45). At *Lygon Arms* [11] (see Where to stay; food Mon-Fri 12.30-2.30pm & 6-9pm, Sat noon-9pm, Sun 12.30-8pm) the menu features lamb and beef from the family farm, as well as sandwiches (from £7), homemade soup (£6) and jacket potatoes (from £9.25).

The atmosphere at the *Red Lion Inn* [28] (see Where to stay; food Mon-Thur noon-2pm & 6-8.45pm, Fri noon-2.30pm & 6-9.30pm, Sat noon-3pm & 6-9.30pm, Sun

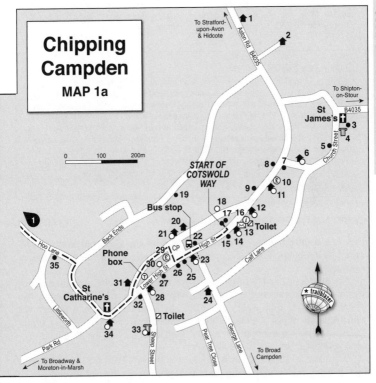

Chipping Campden

MAP 1a

To Stratford-upon-Avon & Hidcote

To Shipton-on-Stour

B4035

St James's

0   100   200m

START OF COTSWOLD WAY

Bus stop

Back Ends

Hoo Lane

Phone box

St Catharine's

Littleworth

Park Rd

To Broadway & Moreton-in-Marsh

Lower High St

High St

Church Street

Calf Lane

Toilet

Toilet

Sheep Street

Pear Tree Close

George Lane

To Broad Campden

★ trailblazer

ROUTE GUIDE AND MAPS

noon-3pm & 6-8.45pm) is relaxed and friendly, and there's a courtyard bar if you'd rather be outside with a pint of IPA. The menu is primarily traditional English, with daily specials that reflect seasonal produce: expect to pay from £11.95 for a main course, with lighter bites at lunch costing around £7.95.

The bar at *The Kings Hotel* [21] (see Where to stay; daily noon-2.30pm & 6.30-9pm) is much classier than the name would suggest, though more intimate than its formal restaurant. Its menu changes regularly, but expect dishes such as maple-glazed gammon (£16), or fried potato gnocchi (£13).

Michael's Mediterranean [18] (🖥 michaelsmediterranean.co.uk; Tue-Sat 11am-2.30pm & 7-10pm, Sun noon-3pm) does all things Greek/Mediterranean, albeit at decidedly un-Greek prices. Try *mezedakia* (nine hot/cold hors d'oeuvres for sharing) at £15.50, or moussaka with salad (£15.95).

Close to the car park in the town centre, the convivial *Huxleys* [30] (☎ 01386-849077, 🖥 huxleys.org; Mon 8.30am-5pm, Tue-Fri 8.30am-10.30pm, Sat 9am-11pm, Sun 10am-5pm, winter Mon & Tue to 5pm; WI-FI; 🐾) serves Italian treats from antipasti to seafood pasta (from £13). A terrace under willow trees makes a popular summer alternative to the restaurant.

If you fancy a curry, head for the Indian *Maharaja* [34] (🖥 www.maharaja catering.net daily 6-10.30pm) at the Volunteer Inn (see Where to stay). The pub itself sticks to the beer, which can be savoured in summer in the garden. Otherwise you might be in luck if *Noel Arms* [23] (see Where to stay; food Mon-Fri noon-3pm & 6-9.30pm, Sat & Sun noon-9.30pm) is hosting one of their regular curry nights (every last Thursday of the month).

❏ **Olimpick Games**
Chipping Campden displays its frivolous side in the form of Robert Dover's Olimpick Games (🖥 olimpickgames.co.uk), held on Dover's Hill (Map 1) every May on the Friday after the Whitsun Bank Holiday. Dating back to 1612, it's a noisy affair, with bands, cannon fire and fireworks, culminating in a torchlit procession into the town for dancing in the square. If events such as sack races, a tug of war and even shin-kicking would raise an eyebrow at the Olympics, there's also the more conventional shot put, part of the Championship of the Hill, as well as wrestling and cross-country races. The following day is the **Scuttlebrook Wake**, more of a village fête in style, with a Scuttlebrook Queen, maypole dancing and colourful floats.

CHIPPING CAMPDEN TO BROADWAY   MAPS 1-3

This first **6-mile (9.6km, 2¾-3¼hrs)** stretch of the Cotswold Way, characterised by agricultural land and open hills, is a great introduction to the trail as a whole.

The start – or finish – of the trail is marked by a circular limestone plaque set into the flagstones at the foot of the Market Hall (see p75). Designed, like its partner outside Bath Abbey (see p166), by artist Iain Cotton, it is engraved with the names of places along the trail, encircled by a line from TS Eliot's *Four Quartets*: 'Now the light falls across the open fields leaving the deep lane shuttered with branches dark in the afternoon.'

A gradual ascent leads across farmland to **Dover's Hill**, at 738ft (225m) the first of many high points along the walk, affording the first of several superb

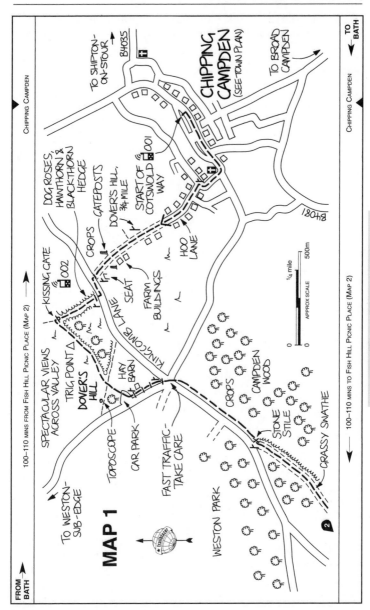

FROM BATH →

CHIPPING CAMPDEN ►

← TO BATH

CHIPPING CAMPDEN

100–110 MINS FROM FISH HILL PICNIC PLACE (MAP 2)

100–110 MINS TO FISH HILL PICNIC PLACE (MAP 2)

MAP 1

TO SHIPTON-ON-STOUR

B4035

CHIPPING CAMPDEN (SEE TOWN PLAN)

TO BROAD CAMPDEN

DOG ROSES, HAWTHORN & BLACKTHORN HEDGE

GATEPOSTS

DOVER'S HILL, ¾ MILE

START OF COTSWOLD WAY 001

CROPS

KISSING GATE 002

SEAT

FARM BUILDINGS

HOO LANE

B4081

SPECTACULAR VIEWS ACROSS VALLEY

TRIG POINT △

DOVER'S HILL

HAY BARN

KINGCOMBE LANE

TOPOSCOPE

CAR PARK

FAST TRAFFIC - TAKE CARE

TO WESTON-SUB-EDGE

WESTON PARK

CROPS

CAMPDEN WOOD

STONE STILE

GRASSY SWATHE

2

¼ mile

APPROX SCALE

0   500m

views. Get your bearings (and your breath) at **Broadway Tower** (see box on p84), the second-highest point along the trail, before the steep descent to Broadway.

BROADWAY [MAP 3a, p87]

Named for its wide central street, once the main road between Worcester and London, Broadway is to many tourists (and there are a lot of them) synonymous with the Cotswolds.

A broad green at the western end of the High St sets a somewhat bucolic tone, enhanced by trees lining the road and rows of stone cottages, giving rise to an excess of clichés and tourist shops. And yet, despite

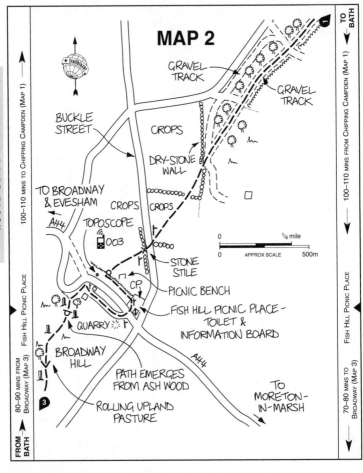

ROUTE GUIDE AND MAPS

MAP 2

100–110 MINS TO CHIPPING CAMPDEN (MAP 1)

100–110 MINS FROM CHIPPING CAMPDEN (MAP 1)

TO BATH

GRAVEL TRACK

GRAVEL TRACK

BUCKLE STREET

CROPS

DRY-STONE WALL

TO BROADWAY & EVESHAM

A44

CROPS

CROPS

TOPOSCOPE

003

STONE STILE

PICNIC BENCH

FISH HILL PICNIC PLACE – TOILET & INFORMATION BOARD

CP

QUARRY

BROADWAY HILL

PATH EMERGES FROM ASH WOOD

ROLLING UPLAND PASTURE

A44

TO MORETON-IN-MARSH

0   ¼ mile
0   APPROX SCALE   500m

Fish Hill Picnic Place

80–90 MINS FROM BROADWAY (MAP 3)

FROM BATH

3

Fish Hill Picnic Place

70–80 MINS TO BROADWAY (MAP 3)

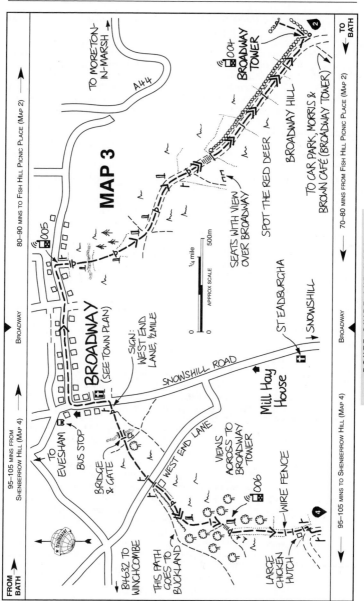

FROM BATH →

95–105 MINS FROM SHENBERROW HILL (MAP 4) →

80–90 MINS TO FISH HILL PICNIC PLACE (MAP 2) →

← TO BATH

95–105 MINS TO SHENBERROW HILL (MAP 4) →

70–80 MINS FROM FISH HILL PICNIC PLACE (MAP 2) →

BROADWAY

BROADWAY

TO MORETON-IN-MARSH

A44

004 BROADWAY TOWER

BROADWAY HILL

TO CAR PARK, MORRIS & BROWN CAFÉ (BROADWAY TOWER)

SPOT THE RED DEER

SEATS WITH VIEW OVER BROADWAY

MAP 3

005

BROADWAY (SEE TOWN PLAN)

SIGN: WEST END LANE, ½ MILE

SNOWSHILL ROAD

STEADBURGHA

SNOWSHILL

Mill Hay House

TO EVESHAM

BUS STOP

BRIDGE & GATE

WEST END LANE

VIEWS ACROSS TO BROADWAY TOWER

006

WIRE FENCE

LARGE CHICKEN HUTCH

B4632 TO WINCHCOMBE

THIS PATH GOES TO BUCKLAND

¼ mile

500m

APPROX SCALE

0

0

★ trailblazer

the high number of visitors, the town retains a considerable charm, particularly outside the summer months.

Celebrating Broadway's links with the Arts and Crafts Movement (see box on p76), **Gordon Russell Design Museum** (☎ 01386-854695, 🖥 gordonrusselldesign museum.org; Tue-Sun Mar-Oct 11am-5pm, Nov-Dec & Feb 11am-4pm; £5) pays tribute to a man who from 1918 committed his working life on this site to designing and making furniture.

Broadway Museum & Art Gallery (☎ 01386-859047, 🖥 broadwaymuseum .org.uk; Feb-Oct Tue-Sat & Bank Hol Mon 10am-5pm, Nov & Dec same but to 4pm; £5), in partnership with the Ashmolean in Oxford, harks back to an earlier period. It is housed in a beautifully preserved 17th-century house, which is no small part of its attraction. As at the main Ashmolean in Oxford, it includes a 'cabinet of curiosities', as well as a fine collection of 18th-century paintings, with an emphasis on the local area. The top floor showcases temporary exhibitions featuring artists such as Whistler.

Somewhat unusually, Broadway's original parish church of **St Eadburgha** (Map 3) is marooned in a serene location well over half a mile (1.10km) to the south, towards Snowshill. Severely damaged in the 2007 floods, it has been restored and makes an interesting detour. Today, its former role is filled by **St Michael & All Saints**, close to the town and an attractive backdrop to the trail as it leaves Broadway.

Those with a nostalgic bent might make time for a trip on the **Gloucestershire Warwickshire Steam Railway** (GWSR; ☎ 01242-621405, 🖥 gwsr.com). Axed by Beeching in the 1960s, the line – which skirts the town to the west – was bought in 1981 and restored by volunteers. In 2018 a further section of track between Toddington and Broadway was reopened, bringing the total length from Broadway to its southern terminal at Cheltenham Racecourse to 14 miles; for timetables and special events, see the website.

❑ **Broadway Tower**   **[Map 3, p83]**
With its turreted top and walls of oolitic limestone, the tall tower that looms into view as you cross the fields on the outskirts of Broadway is an unlikely sight, apparently protecting only the sheep that graze nearby. Built in 1799 as a folly for Lady Coventry by the 6th Earl of Coventry, it sits atop Broadway Hill, a beacon hill which, at 1024ft (312m), is the second highest point in the Cotswolds. In its heyday, it was a lively retreat, attracting several Pre-Raphaelite artists, among them the Socialist and artist William Morris (1834-96), who was a regular visitor from his home at Kelmscott. Rejected by the National Trust in 1949, the tower is now in private hands, but it is open to the public (☎ 01386-852390, 🖥 broadwaytower.co.uk; daily 10am-5pm; £5).

According to Morris's daughter, May, men used to bathe on the roof of the tower, which was described as 'the most inconvenient and the most delightful place ever seen'. Today's visitors can climb up to the roof, too, but only for the scenery: in good weather there are superb 360° views of up to 16 counties! Some 200m north of the tower, and somewhat incongruous in this setting, is a **Cold War nuclear bunker** (Apr-Oct weekends & bank hol Mon; 45-minute tour £4.50, or £8.50 to include entrance to the tower; no under 12s), which used to be manned by the Royal Observer Corps. Rather more in keeping with the rural surroundings is a herd of red deer, which roam peacefully within a small enclosure.

Morris & Brown Café (☎ 01386 852945; daily 9am-5pm; no WI-FI; 🐾) in the grounds is next to a small but swanky gift shop where you can also buy tickets for the tower. The décor is contemporary, the food likewise: panini and ciabatta from £6.50 are set alongside 'soup of the moment', and dishes that include sweet potato and five-bean chilli (£11). And lots of tea and cakes.

Transport

Several **bus** services (see pp48-50) stop here providing connections with Chipping Campden, Cheltenham and Evesham. The most useful for walkers is the 606/606S, run by Marchants. Other services include NN Cresswell's R4 and Johnstons' Nos 1 & 2.

The GWSR (see opposite) provides rail access to places on/near the path but services are limited.

Broadway's **taxi** firms include Blue Cabs (mob ☎ 07770-175175) and Cotswold Horizons (☎ 01386-858599).

Services

Almost everything in Broadway happens on the High St, though the smart **tourist information centre** (☎ 01386-852937, 🖳 broadway-cotswolds.co.uk; Mon-Sat Apr-Oct 10am-5pm, mid Feb-Mar & Nov to late Dec 10am-4pm, Sun mid Feb-end Oct 11am-3pm but the staff are all volunteers so the hours can be variable) is set back behind Budgens **supermarket** (Mon-Sat 7am-9pm, Sun 10am-4pm). The supermarket also plays host to the **post office** (Mon-Fri 9am-5.30pm, Sat 9am-12.30pm) and nearby is an **ATM**. Across the road on the High St itself is the more personal and very well-stocked Broadway Deli (Mon-Sat 8am-5pm, Sun 9am-3pm), with fresh fruit and veg, freshly baked bread and all sorts of goodies.

Close at hand is Blandford Books (☎ 01386-858588; hours vary but generally Mon-Sat 9.30am-5.30pm, Sun 10.30am-5.30pm; winter daily 10am-4pm) stocks a good range of **books** and is particularly strong on local titles. Those browsing for **antiques** will find plenty to delay them along the street, too.

For **medical** matters, contact Barn Close Surgery (☎ 01386-853651, 🖳 barnclose.co.uk; Mon-Fri 8am-6.30pm), or the nearby Lloyds **pharmacy** (Mon-Fri 9am-6pm, Sat to 5.30pm).

A footpath from the High St leads through to the public **toilets** in the car park on Church Close.

Where to stay

There's no shortage of places to stay in this picture-postcard village that draws American visitors in their droves. Finding something within a tight budget is much harder – and unless you're planning to walk in the depths of winter, you'd be well advised to book ahead.

A couple of **pubs** offer accommodation. At the pleasant *Horse & Hound* (☎ 01386-852287, 🖳 horseandhoundbroadway.com; 5D/1Qd, all en suite; ♥; WI-FI; 🐾 bar area only and on a lead), at the top of the High St, a room above the pub costs £42.50-70pp (sgl occ room rate). Note that in the winter the pub is closed all day on Monday.

Room-only rates at the 17th-century *Crown & Trumpet* (☎ 01386-853202, 🖳 crownandtrumpet.co.uk; 1T/4D, all en suite; ♥; WI-FI; 🐾 bar area only), on Snowshill Rd, are from £34pp (sgl occ room rate); cooked breakfast (£10pp) available if booked in advance. At weekends there is a two-night minimum stay for advance bookings.

At the other end of the High St away from any traffic but also on the Cotswold Way, is the award-winning *Olive Branch* (☎ 01386-853440, 🖳 theolivebranch-broadway.com; 1S private shower facilities, 3D/2T or D/1Tr/1Qd, all en suite; ♥; WI-FI; ⓛ), built in 1592 and offering B&B for over 50 years. Today, rooms are fitted out in an elegant but cottagey style (three with a bath) with a range of extras. Rates are £55-72pp (sgl/sgl occ £85-90/105-110). Advance bookings at weekends must be for two nights but if there is availability near the time they will accept a single-night stay.

Still very central, on Leamington Rd just off the High St, is *Hadley House* (☎ 01386-853486, 🖳 hadley.house; 2T/2D/1Tr, all en suite; WI-FI; ⓛ; small 🐾); B&B costs £42.50-47.50pp (sgl occ from £65).

The neighbouring *Windrush House* (off Map 3a; ☎ 01386-853577, 🖳 windrushhouse.com; 2D or T/3D, all en suite; WI-FI; Feb-Dec, weekends only Jan-Feb) offers a more contemporary décor in the rooms which is reflected in the higher price: £47.50-52.50pp a night (sgl occ from £80). Advance bookings at weekends must be for two nights; single nights are available depending on existing bookings.

ROUTE GUIDE AND MAPS

At **Apple Tree** (off Map 3a; ☎ 01386-853681, 🖥 appletreebroadway.co.uk; 1S private facilities, 2T/4D/1D or T, all en suite; ☞; WI-FI; Mar-Dec) there's a bath in one of the pretty double rooms and a drying cupboard for wet clothes. B&B here costs from £40pp (sgl £62-69, sgl occ £70). Walkers are welcome but note that they have a two-night minimum booking rule, which they only waive if it's out of season, the date requested is between other bookings or if you're booking at the last minute.

A similar distance further up the road is **Brook House** (off Map 3a; ☎ 01386-852313, 🖥 brookhousebandb.co.uk; 1S & 1D share bathroom, 2D/1Qd, all en suite; ☞; WI-FI; (L); 🐾), where rates start from £47.50pp (sgl £60, sgl occ rates on request).

Last of the bunch, about half a mile (0.8km) from the trail, is **The Old Stationhouse** (off Map 3a; ☎ 01386-852659, 🖥 broadwaybedandbreakfast .com; 4D, all en suite; ☞; WI-FI), occupying the old stationmaster's lodgings down a private drive between the railway bridge and the petrol station. B&B costs £50-67.50pp (sgl occ £85-120) but the minimum stay over summer weekends is two nights.

For most walkers, the renowned **Lygon Arms** (pronounced 'Ligon' not 'Liegon'; ☎ 01386-852255, 🖥 lygonarmshotel.co.uk; 7S/70D or T/9Tr, all en suite; ☞; WI-FI; 🐾) where prices start at £117.50-230pp (sgl from £230, sgl occ room rate) a night is likely to remain firmly out of reach, but at least it puts other places in perspective.

And if you fancy being truly decadent, you could swap your boots for Queen Anne-style splendour at **Mill Hay House** (see Map 3, p83; ☎ 01386-852498, 🖥 mill hay.co.uk; 3D, all en suite; ☞; WI-FI) where, from a mere £97.50-127.50pp (sgl occ £175-235), Annette Gorton offers a 'gourmet breakfast', though there is a minimum two-night stay policy throughout the year. It lies on Snowshill Rd less than half a mile (0.65km) south of the trail.

Where to eat and drink

A popular option for a meal is **The Swan** (☎ 01386-852278, 🖥 theswanbroadway.co.uk;

food Mon-Fri noon-10pm, Sat 9.30am-10pm, Sun 9.30am-9pm; WI-FI; 🐾 bar area only), opposite The Green, where comfy chairs & heavy wooden tables feel right at home in the old building. Relaxed and informal, it offers a varied menu, with the likes of wagyu burgers (£15.95) alongside pan-fried British venison (£19.75). Do book if you want to be sure of a table.

Just up the road, a welcome new addition to the restaurant scene in Broadway is **The Bakehouse** (🖥 thebakehousebroad way.co.uk; Tue-Sat 10am-6pm, Sun 10am-5pm), with tasty baguettes for £6.90 and delicious mains such as shin of beef stew with shallots in red wine (£10.50).

At the **Horse & Hound** (see Where to stay; food Tue-Fri noon-2.30pm & 6-8.30pm, Sat noon-3pm & 6-8.30pm, Sun noon-3pm), the refurbished bar has a lighter touch but still feels traditional, with at least three guest ales on tap; they may also have Purity's Mad Goose (see box p23). Their standard lunch menu includes a decent tapas selection (six plates for £11) as well as pizzas from £10.95 and more substantial fare (£10-19).

More lively is the **Crown & Trumpet** (see Where to stay; food Mon-Thur noon-2pm & 6-9pm, Fri-Sun noon-9pm) where there's jazz and blues every Thursday evening in the main season (less frequently in the winter), and contemporary live music every Friday and Saturday year-round. Their Sunday roast costs from £9.95 and they have ales such as Stanney Bitter and Broadway Artists from Stanway Brewery (see box on p23) as well as from other local breweries.

Back on the High St, **Number 32** (☎ 01386-306670, 🖥 number32broadway.co .uk; daily 9am-5pm, last orders 4.30pm), is a good choice: think sandwiches, superfood salads (£12), and tapas (£9). They even do takeaways.

Part of Lygon Arms (see Where to stay), but in a separate building, the not-inaccessible **Lygon Wine Bar** (☎ 01386-854418; food Mon-Fri 11am-3pm & 6-9pm, Sat & Sun 11am-9pm; WI-FI) spills out onto the pavement on sunny days, with pasta and pizza mains for £9-14.

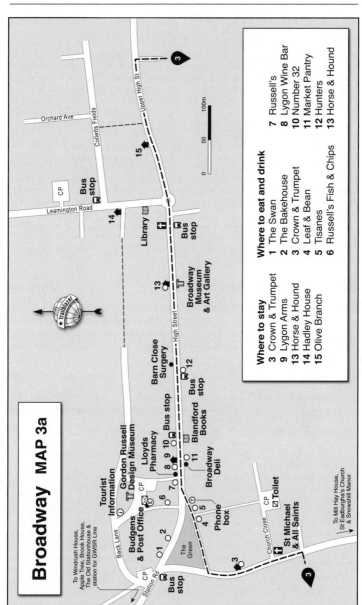

Broadway MAP 3a

Orchard Ave

Colletts Fields

Upper High St

Leamington Road

CP

Bus stop

15

Library

Bus stop

14

Broadway Museum & Art Gallery

13

High Street

Barn Close Surgery

Bus stop

12

Blandford Books

Bus stop

8 9 10

11

Broadway Deli

Lloyds Pharmacy

Gordon Russell Design Museum

Tourist Information

CP

7

6

5

4

Phone box

Budgens & Post Office

Back Lane

CP

1 2

The Green

Station Rd

Bus stop

CP

To Windrush House, Apple Tree, Brook House, The Old Stationhouse & station for GWSR Line

Church Close

CP

Toilet

St Michael & All Saints

To Mill Hay House, St Eadburgha's Church & Snowshill Manor

3

3

Trailblazer

0   50   100m

Where to stay

3 Crown & Trumpet
9 Lygon Arms
13 Horse & Hound
14 Hadley House
15 Olive Branch

Where to eat and drink

1 The Swan
2 The Bakehouse
3 Crown & Trumpet
4 Leaf & Bean
5 Tisanes
6 Russell's Fish & Chips

7 Russell's
8 Lygon Wine Bar
10 Number 32
11 Market Pantry
12 Hunters
13 Horse & Hound

ROUTE GUIDE AND MAPS

Along a passageway leading from the High St, *Russell's Fish & Chips* (☎ 01386-858435, 🖳 russellsfishandchips.co.uk; Mon-Sat noon-2.30pm & 5-8.30pm, Sun noon-6pm) does exactly what it says, either to eat in or take away and from £9.95. The relaxed sibling of Russell's (see below), it has tables both inside and out, with no traffic fumes to add to the mix.

Continuing upmarket, *Russell's* itself (☎ 01386-853555, 🖳 russellsofbroadway .co.uk/restaurant; Mon-Fri noon-2.15pm & 6-9.15pm, Sat noon-2.15pm & 6.30-9.15pm, Sun noon-2.30pm) offers a fixed-price menu at £16-24 (not available on either Sat evening or Sun). There's an à la carte menu, too, albeit best kept for very special occasions.

Not surprisingly, with so many tourists around, tea is high on the agenda here. Try *Tisanes* (☎ 01386-853296, 🖳 tisanes-tearooms.co.uk; daily 10am-5pm), on The Green, complete with waitresses in white pinnies and traditional bow window, though the option of gluten-free dishes is rather more contemporary.

Further up, on the High St, the popular *Market Pantry* (☎ 01386-858318, 🖳 marketpantry.co.uk; Mon-Fri 9am-5pm, Sat 9.30am-5pm, Sun 10am-5pm) serves breakfast, lunch and tea, to include toasted sandwiches from £6.40 and some innovative tartines (£6.90).

The nearby *Hunters* (☎ 01386-858522, 🖳 huntersofbroadway.co.uk; Mon-Fri 10am-4pm, Sat & Sun 10am-5pm) falls into a similar category, its menu including substantial takeaway sandwiches from £2.30. More modern but still cosy is *Leaf & Bean* (☎ 01386-859151, 🖳 leafbeanbroadway.com; daily 10am-5pm), whose range of fancy sandwiches (£4.50) include falafel, caramelised onion and tomato.

BROADWAY TO WINCHCOMBE   MAPS 3-8

This **12-mile (19.3km, 5½-6½hrs)** stretch should fulfil the expectations of anyone who has leafed through glossy coffee-table books on the Cotswolds. Here are the rolling hills, the fine views and the cottages of time-weathered stone. This is rural England at its best, with **Stanton** (Map 5) the quintessential Cotswold village.

❏ Snowshill Manor   [off Map 4]
Even those least interested in museums will find something appealing about a man who amassed a collection that ranged from Samurai armour to stringed instruments to boneshaker bicycles. Charles Paget Wade was just such a collector, cramming his house, 2½ miles (4km) south of Broadway, with a seemingly random range of over 22,000 items. Even the gardens, with their terraces, ponds and outdoor rooms, were the subject of his apparently boundless enthusiasm.

Today, Snowshill Manor (☎ 01386-852410, 🖳 nationaltrust.org.uk; mid Mar-Oct daily 11am-5.30pm, Manor House noon-5pm; Nov weekends only, grounds 11am-5.30pm, guided tour of house 11.15am-2.15pm; manor and gardens £11.60, gardens only £6.80, Nov £7.10, gardens only £4.50, NT members free) is in the hands of the National Trust, which struggles to keep pace with the number of visitors to what is a relatively small house.

For walkers on the Cotswold Way, the house is best approached along the tracks leading east/south-east from Shenberrow Hill; it's a distance of around three-quarters of a mile (1.2km). The *tea room* in the grounds makes a detour particularly appealing, but with timed tickets to visit the house, you may need to be flexible to avoid disappointment. Walkers (or cyclists) get a £1 voucher to be used in the shop or restaurant.

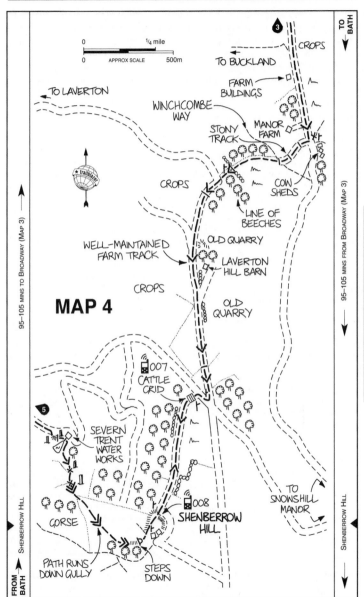

3

TO BATH

CROPS

TO BUCKLAND

FARM BUILDINGS

WINCHCOMBE WAY

STONY TRACK

MANOR FARM

COW SHEDS

LINE OF BEECHES

TO LAVERTON

CROPS

WELL-MAINTAINED FARM TRACK

OLD QUARRY

LAVERTON HILL BARN

CROPS

OLD QUARRY

MAP 4

trailblaze

0   1/4 mile
0   500m
APPROX SCALE

007
CATTLE GRID

5

SEVERN TRENT WATER WORKS

CROPS

008
SHENBERROW HILL

TO SNOWSHILL MANOR

GORSE

PATH RUNS DOWN GULLY

STEPS DOWN

95–105 MINS TO BROADWAY (MAP 3)

95–105 MINS FROM BROADWAY (MAP 3)

ROUTE GUIDE AND MAPS

SHENBERROW HILL

SHENBERROW HILL

FROM BATH

FROM BATH

Some steep ups and downs bring in several cultural highlights, too: **Stanway House** (see below); the site of the Iron-Age **Beckbury Camp** (Map 6), where a stone monument known locally as 'Cromwell's seat' is reputed to mark where Thomas Cromwell watched Hailes Abbey burn; and the ruins of **Hailes Abbey** itself (Map 7; see box on p93) – which are well worth exploring. From Hailes it's an easy and pleasant walk to the fine old wool town of **Winchcombe**.

STANTON   [MAP 5]

Broadway may attract the tourists, but for true Cotswold beauty Stanton is hard to beat. At the heart of the village is the **church of St Michael & All Angels**, its tall spire clearly visible in the valley from the surrounding hills. For general information about Stanton, visit 🖳 stantonvillage.uk.

Marchants' No 606/606S **bus** (see pp48-50) stops at Stanton North Turn – the most northerly of the junctions on the B4632, about half a mile from the village. At the time of research there was just a stop on the southern side of the road (ie for those buses heading towards Cheltenham), but if you flag the bus down from the opposite side it should stop.

There are a few **B&Bs** in the village, all on the trail, and all benefiting from an excellent **pub**, *The Mount Inn* (☎ 01386-584316, 🖳 themountinn.co.uk; **food** Easter-end Aug daily noon-2pm & 6-9pm, Sep to Easter Tue-Sat noon-2pm & 6-9pm, Sun noon-3pm; WI-FI; 🐾), but note that it closes in the afternoon. Up a steep hill, yet only a stone's throw from the trail, it boasts an inglenook fireplace, Donnington Brewery beers and superb views; evening reservations are strongly recommended. The menu ranges from baguettes to The

Mountmans: a cheese, meat & chutney variation on the ploughman's theme (£13).

Within just 200m of the pub is *Shenberrow Hill* (☎ 01386-584468, 🖳 broadway-cotswolds.co.uk/shenberrowhill bb; 1D/1Tr/1T, all en suite; ✆; WI-FI), not to be confused with the complex of buildings at the top of Shenberrow Hill (Map 4). B&B costs from £52.50pp (sgl occ rates on request).

Right in the heart of the village, *The Vine* (☎ 01386-584250, 🖳 broadway-cots wolds.co.uk/thevine; 1D en suite, 1T/1Tr private facilities but shared toilet; ✆; WI-FI; (Ⓛ); 🐴) offers B&B from £47.50pp (sgl occ £75-95). The owner specialises in horseriding.

Equally central is *The Old Post House* (☎ 01386-584398, ☎ 0700 766 0998, 🖳 jo .imeson1@gmail.com; 1T en suite, 1S/2T private facilities; ✆; WI-FI), its gate tucked behind the scarlet phone kiosk that now serves as an information post. Conversion of the old telephone exchange has resulted in a traditional but tasteful twin room, with three further rooms in the main house. Expect to pay from £47.50pp for B&B (sgl/sgl occ £85).

STANWAY   [MAP 5]

If you're passing through in June, July or August on a Tuesday or Thursday between 2pm and 5pm, do drop into the Jacobean **Stanway House** (🖳 www.stanwayfountain .co.uk; fountain £6, house & fountain £9). Set in a restored 18th-century water garden, with its own tea room, it claims to have the tallest gravity fountain in the world which, at 300ft (91m), usually 'plays' at 2.45pm and 4pm. At other times you'll have to be content with the sight of the imposing gatehouse and the neighbouring church.

Spare a glance, too, for the thatched cricket pavilion set on staddle stones nearby. It was a gift from *Peter Pan* author JM Barrie, who used to rent the house during the summer months.

A further attraction on the Stanway estate is the restored **Stanway Watermill** (🖳 www.stanwaymill.co.uk; £3), which opens to visitors at the same times as the house, plus 10am-noon on Thursday all year.

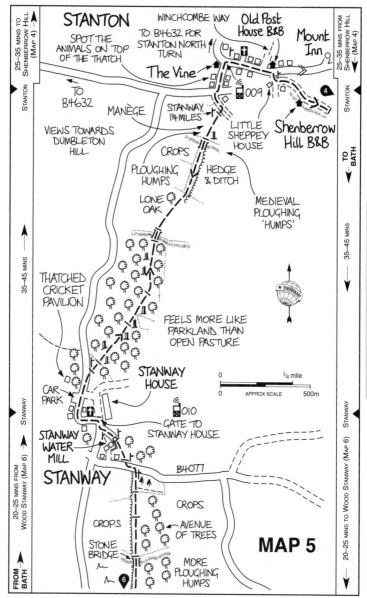

STANTON

WINCHCOMBE WAY Old Post House B&B

Mount Inn

SPOT THE ANIMALS ON TOP OF THE THATCH

TO B4632 FOR STANTON NORTH TURN

The Vine

009

TO B4632

MANÈGE

STANWAY 1¼ MILES

LITTLE SHEPPEY HOUSE

Shenberrow Hill B&B

VIEWS TOWARDS DUMBLETON HILL

CROPS

PLOUGHING HUMPS

HEDGE & DITCH

LONE OAK

MEDIEVAL PLOUGHING 'HUMPS'

THATCHED CRICKET PAVILION

FEELS MORE LIKE PARKLAND THAN OPEN PASTURE

STANWAY HOUSE

CAR PARK

010

GATE TO STANWAY HOUSE

STANWAY WATER MILL

STANWAY

B4077

CROPS

AVENUE OF TREES

MAP 5

CROPS

STONE BRIDGE

MORE PLOUGHING HUMPS

6

0   ¼ mile

APPROX SCALE   500m

STANTON

35–45 MINS

STANWAY

FROM BATH

20–25 MINS FROM WOOD STANWAY (MAP 6)

STANTON

TO BATH

35–45 MINS

STANWAY

20–25 MINS TO WOOD STANWAY (MAP 6)

ROUTE GUIDE AND MAPS

WOOD STANWAY [MAP 6]

Blink and you could miss the sleepy hamlet of Wood Stanway but it does have a **B&B**. The 17th-century *Wood Stanway Farmhouse* (☎ 01386-584318, 🖥 wood stanwayfarmhouse.co.uk; note the email address should be greensbedandbreakfast@gmail.com – it is wrong on the website; 1D/1T/1Qd, all en suite; 🛁; WI-FI; 🄻; 🐾),

30 yards down the road to the right as you come through the gate. It has open views across farmland and the hills and B&B costs from £42.50pp (sgl occ £50). The nearest pub is 1¼ miles (2km) away in Toddington, but a three-course evening meal for around £18pp can be prebooked.

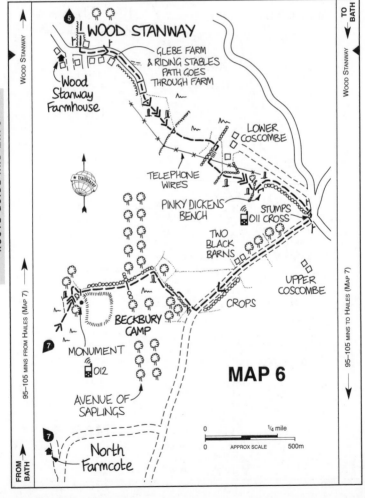

MAP 6

ROUTE GUIDE AND MAPS

NORTH FARMCOTE   [MAP 6]
One of a handful of working farms offering
B&B within reasonable reach of the
Cotswold Way is *North Farmcote* (☎
01242-602304, 🖥 northfarmcote.co.uk;
1D/1T, both en suite, 1T private bathroom;
🛋; WI-FI; 🐾; Mar-end Nov); it is in a glorious location just over quarter of a mile
(0.2km) from the trail (see Map 7 for
access, and follow the sign for **Farmcote**

Herbs). B&B costs £50-55pp (sgl occ from
£70). If the owners aren't busy they will
drive guests to the nearest pub, a couple of
miles away at Ford, for an evening meal.
An additional bed can be put in all rooms.
Also often require a minimum two-night
stay for advance booking at weekends
between May and the end of October,

HAILES   [MAP 7, p94]
Hailes (or Hayles, or Hales) – which really
does have three spellings – takes its name
from the **abbey** (see box below).

Hailes Abbey Halt is a request stop for
GWSR **train** services (see p84). If you
wish to alight here you must tell the guard
before you leave Toddington or
Winchcombe and you must travel in the
front two coaches of the train. To join the

train at Hailes Abbey you just need to hail
the train as it approaches.

The trail descends parallel to the
orchards of *Hayles Fruit Farm* (☎ 01242-
602123, 🖥 haylesfruitfarm.co.uk; WI-FI;
🐾). This has one of the few **campsites**
along the entire Cotswold Way that is actually on the trail, so make the most of it.
(cont'd on p96)

❏ Hailes Abbey   [Map 7, p94]
Hailes Abbey (☎ 01242-602398, 🖥 english-heritage.org.uk; daily late Mar-Jun &
Sep-early Nov 10am-5pm, Jul-Aug 10am-6pm; £6.50, English Heritage and National
Trust members free) dates back to the 13th century. It owes its construction to a vow
made by Richard, Earl of Cornwall (1209-72), should he survive a storm at sea during his return from a military campaign. The ship returned safely to harbour, and the
then earl, son of King John and brother of Henry III (who was responsible for the construction of Westminster Abbey), founded the abbey in 1246.

The site, that of an existing settlement, was chosen carefully. Limestone was
readily available for building, there was good grazing for sheep, and a reliable water
supply, with which the monks created a series of fishponds. The building itself was
an elaborate affair, in contrast with the traditional simplicity of the Cistercian broth-
erhood – and indeed with the austerity of the earlier parish church, which lies across
the road, and is still in use. The importance and grandeur of the abbey lay largely in
its possession of the Holy Blood relic, which was housed in its own specially
designed shrine and which brought considerable income into the abbey's coffers.

Initially, the population at the new abbey comprised a prior, 20 monks and 10 lay
brothers, who moved here from Beaulieu Abbey in Hampshire, but many of the community died in 1361 during a recurrence of the Black Death. The monastery was dis-
solved in 1539, one of the last to be closed on Henry VIII's orders, and the abbey
destroyed. The remainder of the estate was given by the king to Katherine Parr. Later,
the buildings were adapted as a country house, but by 1794 that, too, lay in ruins.
Today, it is the ruined cloisters that most vividly conjure up some sense of the ordered
life once led by the monks. All that remains of the abbey are the footings, yet these –
together with artefacts found on the site, on display in the excellent visitor centre –
give a powerful indication of the scale and drama of the original building. In the
words of St Bernard, *Bonum est nos hic esse*: 'It is good for us to be here.'

ROUTE GUIDE AND MAPS

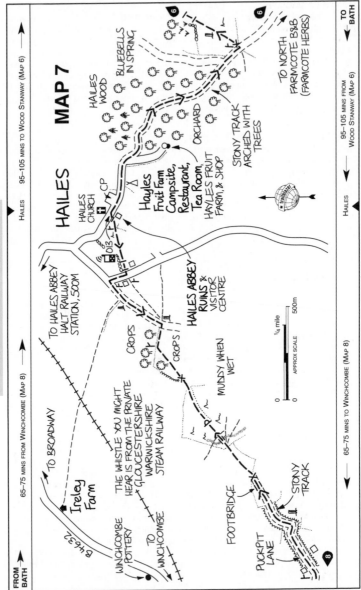

MAP 7

HAILES

95–105 MINS TO WOOD STANWAY (MAP 6)

BLUEBELLS IN SPRING

HAILES WOOD

ORCHARD

STONY TRACK ARCHED WITH TREES

TO NORTH FARMCOTE B&B (FARMCOTE HERBS)

6

6

TO BATH

HAILES CHURCH

CP

Hayles Fruit Farm Campsite, Restaurant, Tea Room, HAYLES FRUIT FARM, & SHOP

HAILES ABBEY RUINS & VISITOR CENTRE

TO HAILES ABBEY HALT RAILWAY STATION, 500M

CROPS

CROPS

MUDDY WHEN WET

FROM BATH

65–75 MINS FROM WINCHCOMBE (MAP 8)

TO BROADWAY

Ireley Farm

THE WHISTLE YOU MIGHT HEAR IS FROM THE PRIVATE GLOUCESTERSHIRE WARWICKSHIRE STEAM RAILWAY

WINCHCOMBE POTTERY

B4632

TO WINCHCOMBE

¼ mile

APPROX SCALE

0   500m

FOOTBRIDGE

PUCKPIT LANE

STONY TRACK

8

HAILES   95–105 MINS FROM WOOD STANWAY (MAP 6)

HAILES   65–75 MINS TO WINCHCOMBE (MAP 8)   TO BATH

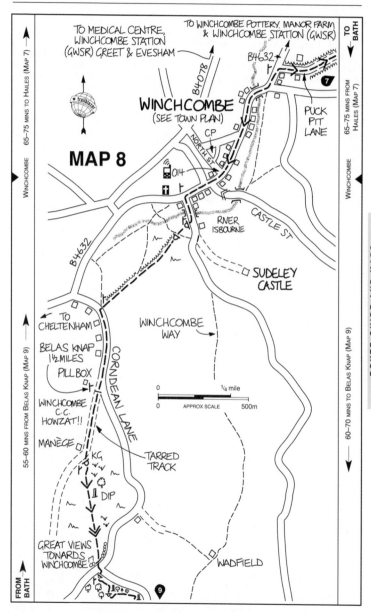

(cont'd from p93, *Hayles Fruit Farm Campsite*) It's a large, fairly level, grassy site, with shower and toilet facilities, where you can pitch a tent for £8pp per night. They also have three pre-erected **bell tents** sleeping either three (£40) or five people (£50); these should be booked in advance. Just up the hill is their excellent **farm shop** (Apr-Dec daily 9am-5pm, Nov-Mar closed Mon), where you can buy good cakes and delicious apple juice, as well as ice-cream, fresh bread and the makings for a substantial breakfast. There's also a welcoming **tea room and restaurant** (same hours as shop;

hot food served noon-3pm); sit by the window to combine your meal with a spot of birdwatching!

If you'd prefer a **B&B**, *Ireley Farm* (☎ 01242-602445, ✉ ireleyfarm.com; 1T private bathroom/2D, both en suite; ☛; WI-FI; Ⓛ; 🐾) could fit the bill. You'll pay from £32.50pp (sgl occ £32.50), with a simple meal available from about £7.50 a head. Dogs have to stay in an outside building. Access is via a footpath from Hailes of just over half a mile (0.8km); the farm is also within walking distance of Winchcombe Pottery (see below).

WINCHCOMBE   [MAP 8a, p99]

The ancient Saxon borough of Winchcombe, one-time capital of the kingdom of Mercia, later enjoyed status as a focal point for pilgrims. Its abbey has long since gone, but the town – emphatically not a village – of Winchcombe remains a significant presence in the Cotswolds. For walkers along the Way, it's an ideal place to stay or to stop for a bite to eat at one of a number of pubs, restaurants and tea rooms. Even if you're short of time, it's worth taking a look inside the wool church of **St Peter's**.

If you've longer to spare, you might want to check out **Sudeley Castle** (Map 8; see box below), or one of two small museums. At **Winchcombe Folk and Police**

Museum (✉ winchcombemuseum .org.uk; Apr-Oct Mon-Sat 10am-4pm; £2) next to the **old stocks** and the tourist information office (see opposite), exhibits about the town's history rub shoulders with a collection of police paraphernalia.

Just over half a mile (1km) north of Puck Pit Lane on the B4632, to the left just after the railway bridge, you'll find **Winchcombe Pottery** (Map 7, p94; ☎ 01242-602462, ✉ winchcombepottery.co .uk; Mon-Fri 8am-5pm, Sat & bank hols 10am-4pm, May-Sep Sun noon-4pm), where traditionally crafted pots are still turned, fired and sold on the premises. Anyone interested in a ride on the

---

❏ **Sudeley Castle**   **[Map 8, p95]**

The history of Sudeley Castle (☎ 01242-604244, ✉ sudeleycastle.co.uk; Mar-end Oct daily 10am-5pm, Nov-mid Dec to 4pm; £16.50, £11.50 in winter months, 20% discount to English Heritage members) can be traced back as far as King Ethelred, in the 10th century. Although nothing of his manor house remains, the estate's royal connections run like a thread through its chequered past, from Edward IV to Queen Elizabeth I. The buildings visible today, including the Dungeon Tower and St Mary's Church, were constructed by Baron Sudeley from the mid 15th century. It is in the church that Katherine Parr, the sixth of Henry VIII's wives, is buried, having lived at Sudeley following the king's death. A century later, the castle fell into disuse, becoming increasingly dilapidated until it was bought and restored during Victoria's reign by members of the Dent family. The castle today is the private home of their descendants.

Visitors may look round the church and tour the estate, with its beautiful rose gardens, a pheasantry, and a wonderful wooden fort that will make you wish you were 10 years old again. A number of rooms in the castle are also accessible to the public, including the library, the morning room, and Chandos bedroom. The new **visitor centre** (daily 10am-5pm) includes a shop and *café* (to 4.30pm).

Gloucestershire Warwickshire Steam Railway (see p84) should note that the actual station for this not in Winchombe but in Greet, about a mile away.

Cotswold Voluntary Wardens lead a heavily oversubscribed annual series of **11 consecutive walks** for those who would like to complete the trail in stages, one of them based from Winchcombe; for details, see p29.

See box p16 for details of the festivals held here in May.

Transport
Winchcombe is well placed on a north–south **bus** route running through the Cotswolds. The 606/606S, operated by Marchants, stops at the war memorial and North St. Marchants also operates the W1 and W2 services. For details, see pp48-50.

A reliable **taxi** service is run by Taylor's (mob ☎ 07814-570876).

Services
There's a small but helpful **tourist information centre** (☎ 01242-602925; Easter-Oct daily 10am-4pm, Nov-Easter Sat 10am-4pm, Sun 10am-3pm), in the old Town Hall, on the corner of North St. Useful websites are 🖥 winchcombewelcomeswalkers.com and 🖥 winchcombe.co.uk.

Coventry Building Society has a branch with an **ATM** on the High St; where High St morphs into Hailes St there's a **newsagent** (Mon-Sat 6am-5pm, Sun 6am-1pm) that sells drinks and snacks, but most other tourist amenities are found along North St. This lies at right angles to the trail from the tourist information centre and is where you'll find several independent shops of interest including North's **bakery** (Mon-Fri 7am-4.30pm, Sat to 4pm) for fresh rolls and sandwiches, Winchcombe **Fruit & Veg** (Mon & Thur 9am-1pm, Tue, Wed & Fri 9am-4pm, Sat 9am-2.30pm) or the excellent **delicatessen** Food Fanatics (see Where to eat), where sandwiches are made to order or to eat in. There's a **supermarket**, Co-op (daily 7am-10pm), which also plays host to the **post office** (daily 7am-10pm) and an **ATM**; and there's a second supermarket, Budgens (Mon-Sat 7am-

9pm, Sun 10am-4pm), with its own ATM, just off North St on Greet Rd.

There's a **shoe repairer** (☎ 01242-604602; Mon-Fri 8am-12.30pm) at Winchcombe Pottery (see opposite), so if your boots need some attention, it's worth going out of your way.

Winchcombe **medical centre** (☎ 01242-602307, 🖥 winchcombemedical.nhs .uk; Mon-Fri 8am-6.30pm) is about a quarter of a mile (0.4km) north of the town, along Greet Rd, and there's a branch of Lloyds **pharmacy** (Mon-Fri 9am-6pm, Sat to 5.30pm) on the High St.

Where to stay
Winchcombe has a good assortment of small pubs and inns and a few B&Bs, most of them fairly central. **Campers**, though, will need to walk some three-quarters of a mile (1.2km) from the trail to *Manor Farm* (off Map 8a; ☎ 01242-602423, 🖥 janetday 423@gmail.com; 3D, all en suite; ♥; WI-FI) where **campers** (no WI-FI; 🐾) will pay £8pp (toilet/shower facilities are available) and **B&B** costs from £47.50pp (sgl occ £60). To get there from the Cotswold Way, turn right at the end of Puck Pit Lane, go under the railway bridge and turn immediately left (past the pottery) on Becketts Lane to **Greet**. Just before you arrive at the B4078/Evesham Rd, turn right up Market Lane; the farm is about a quarter of a mile (0.4km) up that road on the left-hand side.

Blair House (☎ 01242-603626, 🖥 blairhousewinchcombe.co.uk; 1S/1T shared bathroom, 1D en suite; ♥; WI-FI), at 41 Gretton Rd, charges from £43pp (sgl/sgl occ £58-68) for B&B.

Of the **pubs** and inns, *White Hart Inn* (☎ 01242-602359, 🖥 whitehartwinchcombe .co.uk; 3T/3T or D/5D, most en suite; ♥; WI-FI; ①; 🐾), on High St, is right on the trail and ideal for walkers, with three designated 'ramblers' rooms' (2T/1D) which share a bathroom and cost £19.50-39.50pp. The other (en suite) rooms are divided into standard (£29.50-49.50pp) and superior (£29.50-59.50pp). Single occupancy of any room costs upwards of £45 and expect to pay the room rate in peak periods. Right next door is the smartly gabled *Wesley*

House (☎ 01242-602366, 🖥 wesleyhouse
.co.uk; 3D/1D or T/1T, all en suite; WI-FI;
ⓛ; 🐾), more of a restaurant with rooms,
charging £47.50-55pp (sgl occ £75-85)
from Sunday to Thursday. Single-night
bookings on a Friday and Saturday are only
accepted if dinner is also taken at £97.50-
107.50pp (sgl occ around £145). Rates may
be higher during the festival in March (see
box p15).

Set back from the main road on Abbey
Terrace, near Coventry Building Society,
The Plaisterers Arms (☎ 01242-602358, 🖥
theplaisterersarms.com; 2T/3D, all en suite;
🛁; WI-FI; ⓛ; 🐾) has B&B for around
£35pp (sgl occ from £45 though room-rate
at weekends). If you have a dog you will
need to bring bedding for it.

Close to the shops on North St is *The
Lion Inn* (☎ 01242-603300, 🖥 thelion
winchcombe.co.uk; 2D or T/6D, all en
suite; 🛁; WI-FI; 🐾), where B&B in com-
fortably refurbished rooms with a blissful
lack of TV costs £67.50-105pp (sgl occ
room rate) though the rate may drop in the
winter months. For a convivial evening,
just head downstairs to the excellent bar.

Where to eat and drink
'Winchcombe welcomes walkers' proclaims the sign, and nowhere more so than
in its wide range of places to eat. On North
St, the licensed deli *Food Fanatics* (see
Services; ☎ 01242-604466, 🖥 food-fanat
ics.co.uk; Mon-Sat 8am-6pm, Sun 10am-
5pm) serves a range of sandwiches, platters
and cakes as well as breakfasts; the pork
pies topped with apple or cranberry sauce
(£2.70) are wonderful. Those with an
acquisitive nature might be drawn to
Garden Tea Rooms at **Winchcombe
Antiques Centre** (☎ 01242-300556, 🖥
winchcombeantiquescentre.co.uk; summer
Mon-Sat 11am-5pm, Sun 11am-4pm, winter Sat & Sun only), off the High St, where

you'll pass rooms enticingly jammed with
antiques to reach the simple basement café
for tea and cakes, or a light lunch.

For more hearty fare, try one of the
pubs. On the main street is *The Plaisterers
Arms* (see Where to stay; food Mon-Fri
noon-2.30pm & 6-9pm, Sat noon-3pm & 6-
9pm, Sun noon-5pm), which does a good
range of ciabattas at lunchtime and substantial mains in the evening, not to mention
some scrumptious desserts. They've a lovely garden, too, and as a diversion, more
than 50 different gins!

Further along is *Corner Cupboard* (☎
01242-602303, 🖥 cornercupboardwinch
combe.co.uk; Mon-Fri noon-3pm & 6-9pm,
Sat noon-9pm, Sun noon-8pm), where the
Sunday lunch is particularly good and real
ales are prominent. In a class of its own is
The Lion Inn (see Where to stay; food
daily noon-3pm & 6-9pm); the atmosphere
is relaxed but the food – from a lunchtime
smoked salmon open sandwich with dill
crème fraîche (£8.25) to a Cornish plaice
with summer bean cassoulet & chorizo butter sauce at dinner (£15.50) – is taken very
seriously.

The restaurant at the *White Hart Inn*
(see Where to stay; food daily 8am-9pm,
Fri & Sat to 9.30pm), is unfussy, generous
and tasty – which is music to most trekkers'
ears. They serve breakfast, coffee and afternoon teas, too. Nearby is *Rosie's* (☎ 01242
604879, 🖥 rosiesthairestaurant.co.uk;
Mon-Sat 9am-10pm, Sun to 9pm), an
unpretentious and sometimes rowdy bar
that serves English food till 3pm and con-
verts into a Thai restaurant from 5pm with
a very good range of Thai mains from
£7.50, and nothing more than a tenner.
Food is not served between 3pm and 5pm.

For a special occasion, try *The Wesley
Restaurant* (see Where to stay; Tue-Sat
noon-2pm & 6.30-9pm, Sun noon-2pm),
where mains start at £18 for the vegetarian

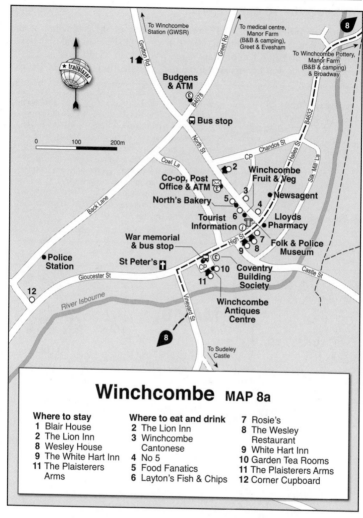

Winchcombe MAP 8a

Where to stay
1 Blair House
2 The Lion Inn
8 Wesley House
9 The White Hart Inn
11 The Plaisterers Arms

Where to eat and drink
2 The Lion Inn
3 Winchcombe Cantonese
4 No 5
5 Food Fanatics
6 Layton's Fish & Chips
7 Rosie's
8 The Wesley Restaurant
9 White Hart Inn
10 Garden Tea Rooms
11 The Plaisterers Arms
12 Corner Cupboard

grilled aubergine with chickpeas & sun-blushed tomato, or *No 5* (☎ 01242-604566, 🖳 5northstreetrestaurant.co.uk; Wed-Sun 12.30-1.30pm, Tue-Sat 7-9pm) on North St, where the set 7-course menu can be as much as a whopping £74, though a 2-course lunch can cost from £27.

If none of these appeals, Winchcombe also has a couple of takeaways, also along North St: *Layton's Fish & Chips* (Tue-Sat 11am-2pm & 4.30-9.30pm); and *Winchcombe Cantonese Chinese Takeaway* (Wed-Mon 5-11pm).

WINCHCOMBE TO CLEEVE HILL

MAPS 8-10

The next **6 miles (9.6km, 3-3½hrs)** take in one of the highlights of the Cotswold Way: **Cleeve Common** (Map 10), passing the ancient and impressive long barrow of **Belas Knap** (Map 9; see box below). Considered to be the largest single area of unimproved limestone grassland in Gloucestershire, the

---

❏ Belas Knap   [Map 9]

Sheltering in the corner of a field, at the edge of the woods, the ancient long barrow (see box on p134), or burial ground, of Belas Knap rises up from the ground rather like a beached whale, some 180ft (55m) long and 18ft (5.5m) high. Dating back to around 2500BC, it was used for successive burials, possibly over several centuries, until it was deliberately blocked. Archaeologists have uncovered the remains of 38 human skeletons, as well as animal bones, flints and pottery. At the northern end, an apparent entrance in fact leads nowhere, but the reason for this is unclear.

The grass-covered mound – for such is its appearance today – is dotted with cowslips and daisies, but you can clearly see the thin layers of stone, neatly stacked like sheaves of paper, that were used in its construction.

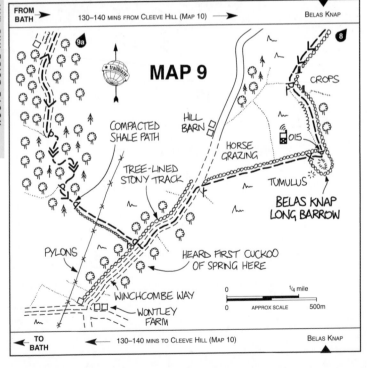

ROUTE GUIDE AND MAPS

FROM BATH →

130–140 MINS FROM CLEEVE HILL (MAP 10) →

BELAS KNAP

9a

trailblazer

MAP 9

CROPS

COMPACTED SHALE PATH

HILL BARN

HORSE GRAZING

015

TREE-LINED STONY TRACK

TUMULUS

BELAS KNAP LONG BARROW

PYLONS

HEARD FIRST CUCKOO OF SPRING HERE

0 ...... ¼ mile
0 ...... APPROX SCALE 500m

WINCHCOMBE WAY

WONTLEY FARM

← TO BATH

← 130–140 MINS TO CLEEVE HILL (MAP 10)

BELAS KNAP

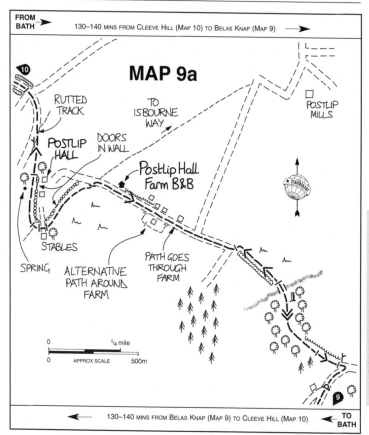

130–140 MINS FROM CLEEVE HILL (MAP 10) TO BELAS KNAP (MAP 9) →

MAP 9a

RUTTED TRACK

TO ISBOURNE WAY

POSTLIP MILLS

POSTLIP HALL

DOORS IN WALL

Postlip Hall Farm B&B

trailblazer

STABLES

SPRING

ALTERNATIVE PATH AROUND FARM

PATH GOES THROUGH FARM

0   ¼ mile

0   APPROX SCALE   500m

← 130–140 MINS FROM BELAS KNAP (MAP 9) TO CLEEVE HILL (MAP 10)   ← TO BATH

ROUTE GUIDE AND MAPS

common, an SSSI (see p61), rises to the highest point on the trail, **Cleeve Hill**, at 1066ft (325m). Wild and windswept, its closely cropped turf is shared by sheep, cattle, golfers and walkers, but it's a successful partnership; there is plenty of space for all.

Much of the trail from this point runs along the edge of the Cotswold escarpment, with a grandstand view of **Cheltenham Racecourse** (Map 11a) on the plains below. If visibility is poor, take especial care along this stretch; it would be all too easy to stray too close to the edge.

❏ **Important note – walking times**
All times in this book refer only to the time spent walking. You will need to add 20-30% to allow for rests, photography, checking the map, drinking water etc.

POSTLIP   [MAP 9a, p101]

The Cotswold Way neatly sidesteps the hamlet of Postlip, but the section between Belas Knap and Cleeve Common does skirt around the edge of the privately owned Postlip Hall; see box on p16 for details of the Cotswold Beer Festival which is usually held here.

There's a perfectly positioned **B&B** right on the trail here at *Postlip Hall Farm* (☎ 01242-603351, 🖳 cotswoldsfarmstay.co .uk/postlip-hall-farm-winchcombe; 1T or

D/1D, both en suite; WI-FI; ⓛ; Feb-Nov), but with no evening meal available you may have to walk or consider a taxi to The Rising Sun (see below) on Cleeve Hill. The house itself is built of stone and sheltered behind high hedges on a working farm. Rooms cost from £42.50pp, or £65 for single occupancy for B&B.

CLEEVE HILL   [MAP 10]

Right by the trail, and up on Cleeve Hill itself, the bar at *Cleeve Hill Golf Club* (☎ 01242-672025, 🖳 cleevehillgolfclub.co.uk; food daily 8am-7pm, winter 9am-4pm; WI-FI; 🐾) is open to non-members for tea, coffee and light lunch. You can eat in the clubhouse, on the veranda or on the grass looking up to Cleeve Hill and the golf course, choosing from a menu that includes breakfasts (full English £6.75), sandwiches and baguettes (from £3/4.40 respectively) to fish & chips at around £7.50.

All three hotels on Cleeve Common are clustered fairly close together about a quarter of a mile (0.4km) down the hill from the trail, along the busy B4632 but with views across to the Malvern Hills. To avoid walking along the road, you can take one of the footpaths that lead down from the trail, bringing you out at the back of the hotels. First up is the elegant *Cleeve Hill Hotel* (☎ 01242-672052, 🖳 cleevehill-hotel.co.uk; 7D/5D or T/1Qd, all en suite; 🍽; WI-FI; ⓛ; 🐾), where you'll need sufficient energy in reserve for the steep steps up to the front door. Under new ownership, some rooms are suites or have half-tester beds; B&B costs £49.50-69.50pp (sgl occ room rate).

Slightly further down the hill, *Malvern View* (☎ 01242-672017, 🖳 malvernview .com; 6D all en suite, 1D or T private bathroom; 🍽; WI-FI; ⓛ; 🐾) has rooms of varying styles. Rates are £45-65pp (sgl occ £80-120) for B&B; note there is a two-night minimum stay policy in the main season (Mar-end Sep) but if they have a gap they may accept a one-night stay.

Finally, just a couple of hundred yards further down, there's the rather larger *Rising Sun* (☎ 01242-676281, 🖳 oldeng lishinns.co.uk; 1S/4T/17D/2Tr, all en suite; 🍽; WI-FI; ⓛ; 🐾). B&B rates are complex but range from £29 *per room* to £60pp (sgl £55-70, sgl occ room rate). Dining (**food** daily 11am-10pm) is pretty relaxed, whether in the restaurant or bar or outside on the terrace. As well as lunchtime favourites there's an inexpensive menu with mains averaging £8-13, and a daily specials board. Sometimes they also have live music.

Marchants' **bus** Nos 606/606S and W1/W2 stop at the top of Stockwell Lane, opposite the first two hotels, and also by the Rising Sun; see pp48-50.

CLEEVE HILL TO LECKHAMPTON HILL   MAPS 10-15

The **9½-mile (15km)** section of the trail that skirts around Cheltenham takes about **4¾ to 5½ hours** to complete. If it seems from on high as though the town goes on forever, much of the walking is across open common land with exceptionally rewarding views.   *(cont'd on p106)*

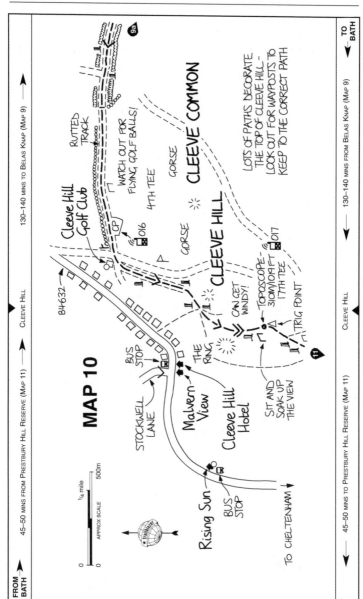

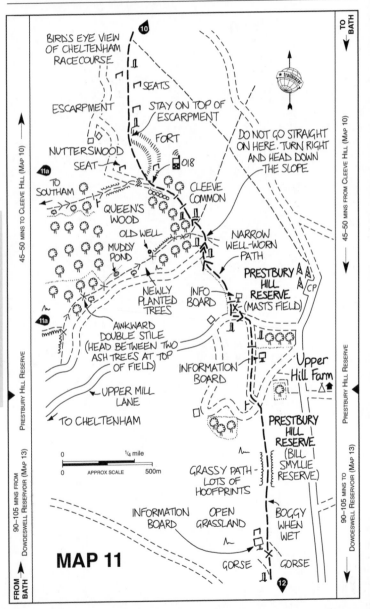

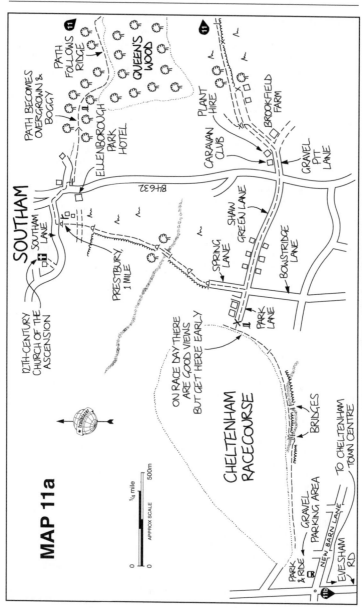

MAP 11a

¼ mile

500m

APPROX SCALE

SOUTHAM

12TH-CENTURY CHURCH OF THE ASCENSION

PRESTBURY, 1 MILE

SOUTHAM LANE

PATH BECOMES OVERGROWN & BOGGY

PATH FOLLOWS RIDGE

QUEEN'S WOOD

ELLENBOROUGH PARK HOTEL

11

B4632

CARAVAN CLUB

PLANT HIRE

BROOKFIELD FARM

GRAVEL PIT LANE

11

SPRING LANE

SHAW GREEN LANE

BOWSTRIDGE LANE

PARK LANE

ON RACE DAY THERE ARE GOOD VIEWS BUT GET HERE EARLY

CHELTENHAM RACECOURSE

BRIDGES

PARK & RIDE

GRAVEL PARKING AREA

NEW BARN LANE

TO CHELTENHAM TOWN CENTRE

EVESHAM RD

11b

(cont'd from p102) Those interested in natural history are in for a treat, with ancient beeches and large-leaved limes in **Lineover Wood** (Map 13; the word means 'lime bank'), and the protected areas of **Prestbury Hill Reserve** (Map 11; incorporating both Masts Field and Bill Smyllie Reserve), **Charlton Kings Common** (Map 14) and **Leckhampton Hill** (Map 15), each sheltering several rare flowers and butterflies.

Leckhampton Hill itself is the site of one of the many hill forts (see box on p122) that line the escarpment, and of the much-photographed **Devil's Chimney**. This tall outcrop of rock towers over a disused quarry, giving rise to a legend involving the Devil hurling stones from this spot at worshippers as they made their way to church on a Sunday. More prosaic suggestions as to its provenance include erosion (somewhat unlikely), and the attractive possibility that it was created as a bawdy joke by 18th-century quarry workers. Whatever its history, the chimney has been regularly climbed by local youngsters over the years and even survived an earthquake in the 1920s. Today, it is securely fenced to help protect it from (very real) erosion.

Walking between Cheltenham and the Cotswold Way
[Map 11a, p105]

While the most direct route from Cheltenham to the Cotswold Way is probably along the busy London Rd, this is hardly attractive walking territory. Far more interesting is to head north out of town through the park towards the racecourse, from where a network of footpaths along the edge of Queen's Wood leads up to Cleeve Common – some of it coinciding with the Gustav Holst Way (see opposite). If you fancy returning a different way, you can descend along the woodland path to Southam and thence back to the racecourse, a circular trip of just over 5 miles (8.25km).

CHELTENHAM　　[MAP 11b, p108]

Cheltenham was swept into the popular consciousness by George III, who first came to take the waters in 1788. Its Regency architecture, with whitewashed houses rather than the natural dressed stone typical of Georgian Bath, continues to attract visitors, but today the town's primary attractions are considerably broader than its architecture or spa waters. Although Cheltenham is some distance from the trail, many visitors to the town will want to sample at least a section of the Cotswold Way, while some walkers along the trail may wish to work the town into their trip in some way, so the information given here is intended as a starting point.

The town's **tourist information centre** (☎ 01242-237431 then press 1 for 'leisure', 🖳 visitcheltenham.com; Mon-Wed 9.30am-5.15pm, Thur to 7.45pm, Fri-Sat to 5.30pm, Sun 10.30am-4pm) is on the ground floor of The Wilson (see opposite) on Clarence St.

Cheltenham is also home to several festivals (see box pp15-16), and regularly hosts live concerts. For more information see 🖳 cheltenhamtownhall.org.uk.

What to see and do

Cheltenham was built with pleasure in mind, laid out with wide promenades, formal gardens and elegant houses fronted by intricate metal balconies.

The town's Regency architecture can best be viewed by walking in the **Montpellier district** then on through the central area and north alongside **Pittville Park**. Significant among the buildings is **Pittville Pump Room** which, with its distinctive columns and decorated dome, stands at the head of the park. Completed in 1830, it was restored in 1960, and remains in regular use for private-hire functions, though it's no longer open to the general public.

From the uber-modern entrance hall (housing the tourist information centre; see opposite) to a new permanent art gallery, their archive department (known as the Paper Store), and space for temporary exhibitions, **The Wilson**, Cheltenham's **Art Gallery and Museum** (☎ 01242-237431, 🖥 thewilson.org.uk; Mon-Wed & Fri-Sat 9.30am-5.15pm, Thur to 7.45pm, Sun 11am-4pm; free except for special exhibitions: £4 donation suggested), on Clarence St, is certainly a dramatic space. Of major importance is an exhibition of furniture, together with silver, textiles, ceramics and paintings, from the Arts and Crafts Movement; don't miss the remarkably intricate piano created by CR Ashbee for his wife. Other artefacts span the period from ancient Egypt to the 20th century, with a small exhibition dedicated to Edward Wilson of Antarctic fame, who was born in the town, and for whom the gallery is named.

Next door, do make time for **The Guild at 51** (☎ 01242-245215, 🖥 guild crafts.org.uk; Tue-Sat 10am-5pm, Sun 11am-4pm), which continues the Arts and Crafts theme through displays and sales of work by members of the Gloucestershire Guild of Craftsmen.

Further north, **Holst Birthplace Museum** (☎ 01242-524846, 🖥 holstmuse um.org.uk; mid Feb-mid Dec Tue-Sat 10am-4pm & Bank Hol Mon; £6), 4 Clarence Rd, is set in a small Regency townhouse, displaying a drawing room of that period and a Victorian kitchen. It celebrates the life of the composer Gustav Holst, internationally renowned for his *Planets* suite, which was first performed in London in 1918. Holst was born in this house in 1874, was educated in the town, and returned in the late 1920s, remaining until his death in 1934. The composer's love of his native countryside is celebrated in the waymarked 35-mile (56km) Gustav Holst Way, from Cranham to Wyck Rissington, which in parts runs parallel to the Cotswold Way.

Prestbury Park, just north of the town, has been home to **Cheltenham Racecourse** (☎ 01242-513014, 🖥 cheltenham.thejock eyclub.co.uk) since 1831. Before that, race meetings were held on Cleeve Common, where horses are still regularly exercised. The course hosts around 14 meetings a year between October and May, with the highlight being the Cheltenham Festival, the famous race meeting in the National Hunt racing calendar held over four days in mid March (see box p15). A footpath alongside the course affords a close-up view of the races, though be warned: it's a popular spot!

Transport
Cheltenham is well served by trains, coaches and buses.

Both GWR and Cross Country **train services** (see box p46) call at Cheltenham Spa, which is about a mile (1.6km) west of the town centre. Stagecoach's D and E bus services operate frequently between here, Clarence St (but not the bus station) and the Racecourse Park & Ride, making it ideal for walkers heading up onto the Cotswold Way. Their B service operates to Charlton Kings and the F service to Leckhampton.

All National Express **coaches** (see box p47), and most other **buses**, go to Royal Well bus station behind the Promenade. Probably of greatest use to walkers is Marchants' No 606/606S service, but Pulhams' No 801 and Swanbrook's No 853 also call here. Stagecoach's No 51 and 66 stop on the Promenade. For details, see pp48-50.

Central Taxis (☎ 01242-228877) are at the **taxi** rank at the bus station.

Where to stay
Details of accommodation in Cheltenham can be obtained from the tourist information centre (see opposite). At the budget end of the spectrum is *Cheltenham YMCA* (Map 11b; ☎ 01242-533934, 🖥 number6 cheltenham.co.uk; 19S/7T/2Tr share facilities, 1 x 6- & 1 x 8-bed dorms; ☞; WI-FI) at 6 Vittoria Walk. Breakfast is not included in the rate (single-sex dorm bed £20pp, £25-

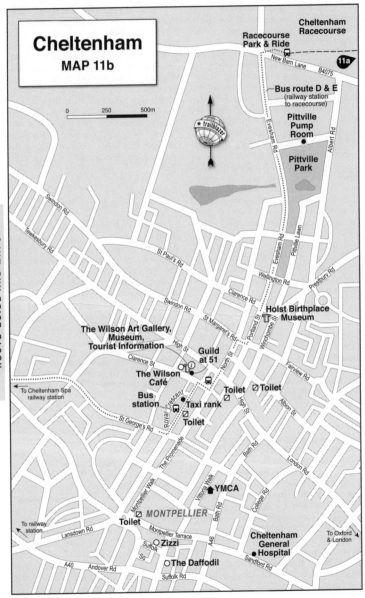

Cheltenham
MAP 11b

0   250   500m

★ trailblazer

Cheltenham Racecourse

Racecourse Park & Ride

New Barn Lane

B4075

11a

Bus route D & E
(railway station
to racecourse)

Pittville
Pump
Room

Albert Rd

Pittville
Park

Swindon Rd

Tewkesbury Rd

St Paul's Rd

Evesham Rd

Pittville Lawn

Wellington Rd

Presbury Rd

Swindon Rd

Clarence Rd

St Margaret's Rd

Holst Birthplace
Museum

Portland St

Winchcombe St

The Wilson Art Gallery,
Museum,
Tourist Information

High St

Guild
at 51

North St

Fairview Rd

Clarence St

The Wilson
Café

Bus
station

Royal Crescent

Taxi rank

Toilet

Toilet

Albion St

To Cheltenham Spa
railway station

St George's Rd

Toilet

High St

Bath Rd

London Rd

The Promenade

Montpellier Walk

YMCA

Victoria Walk

College Rd

MONTPELLIER

Bath Rd

To railway
station

Lansdown Rd

Toilet

Montpellier Terrace

Suffolk
Sq

Zizzi

A46

Cheltenham
General
Hospital

To Oxford
& London

A40

Andover Rd

The Daffodil

Suffolk Rd

Sandford Rd

27.50pp, sgl £30-35, sgl occ room rate), but there is a kitchen available where you cook your own. Note that the YMCA is in two buildings and the accommodation is in the Georgian building, not the modern one. Access is available 24hrs a day when you have checked in.

Where to eat and drink
While it is beyond the scope of this guide to cover Cheltenham's restaurants in detail, a couple of places in the attractive Montpellier district should point you in the right direction. A good start might be *Zizzi* (☎ 01242-252493, 🖳 zizzi.co.uk; daily 11.30am-10pm), 3 Suffolk Sq. It's part of the relatively predictable pizza/pasta chain, but the star is the setting: a large converted church with stained-glass windows looking down on an outsize pizza oven in place of the altar.

Another restaurant with a twist is *The Daffodil* (☎ 01242-700055, 🖳 thedaffodil .com; Mon, Wed & Thur 5-11pm, Fri & Sat noon-midnight, Sun noon-6pm), 18-20 Suffolk Parade, grandly located in the old Art Deco cinema. Where once the audience sat enthralled by the big screen, today's visitors dine in contemporary style, with live jazz on Saturday lunchtimes. They serve afternoon tea, too, on Friday and Saturday. Their two-course 'Theatre' menu at £14.95 is available for Fri & Sat lunch and early evenings Mon-Sat. Booking is advised in the evenings.

During the day, combine a visit to The Wilson (see p107) with coffee or a light lunch in the contemporary space at *The Wilson Café* (☎ 01242-257441; Mon-Sat 9am-5pm, Sun 11am-4pm; WI-FI).

PRESTBURY HILL RESERVE
[MAP 11, p104]
About half a mile (0.8km) from the trail as it heads south of Cleeve Common through Prestbury Hill Reserve is the exceptionally welcoming *Upper Hill Farm* (Map 11; ☎ 01242-235128, 🖳 upperhillfarm.co.uk; 1T/2D, all en suite; ☞; WI-FI; ⓛ; 🐾). Sympathetically restored, it has an elegant guests' lounge and spacious rooms with modern décor. These cost from £45pp (sgl occ £70). In the evening, the owner will drive walkers to a pub for dinner. If you stay for two nights they will also pick you up from where you walk to (normally around Wood Stanway/Birdlip) and drop you back the next morning. They let people *camp* (🐾; Mar-Oct) in their garden (there are six pitches; £10pp) and there is a toilet and cold water tap in the garage block.

HAM HILL
[MAP 12, p110]
Some three-quarters of a mile (1.25km) from the Cotswold Way on Ham Rd is *Glenfall Farm B&B* (☎ 01242-520302, 🖳 glenfallfarm.co.uk; 2D/1D or T, all en suite, 1T private bathroom; ☞; WI-FI; ⓛ). B&B comes in at £47.50-55pp (sgl occ from £85). In the evening, as long as they are not too busy the owner is happy to give walkers a lift to the nearest pub for dinner (though you need to make your own way back).

Continuing along the Cotswold Way, you'll come to *Colgate Farm* (mob ☎ 07549-297996, ☎ 07980-607867, 🖳 colgate farm.co.uk; 1T/1D/1D or Tr, all en suite; WI-FI; ⓛ; 🐾; Mar-Dec), a working farm with both **B&B** (from £50pp, sgl occ £70) and **camping** (£10pp). Guests in the double rooms, which include a self-contained log cabin and a 'Glass House', both of which have their own well-equipped kitchenette, cook their own breakfast from supplies provided; those in the twin room have breakfast in the main house. You can use their washing machine and dryer for a fiver. Campers will find toilets, hot showers, free wi-fi, and firepits with free wood. Dogs are allowed to stay in the B&B for £10, though for camping those 'that wag their tails' are free.

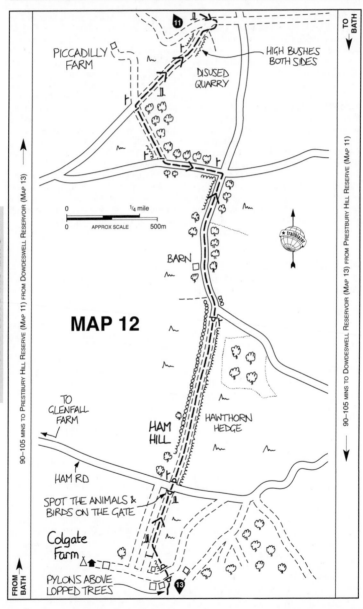

ROUTE GUIDE AND MAPS

PICCADILLY FARM

HIGH BUSHES BOTH SIDES

DISUSED QUARRY

TO BATH

0   ¼ mile
0   APPROX SCALE   500m

★ trailblazer

BARN

MAP 12

90–105 MINS TO PRESTBURY HILL RESERVE (MAP 11) FROM DOWDESWELL RESERVOIR (MAP 13)

90–105 MINS TO DOWDESWELL RESERVOIR (MAP 13) FROM PRESTBURY HILL RESERVE (MAP 11)

TO GLENFALL FARM

HAM HILL

HAWTHORN HEDGE

HAM RD

SPOT THE ANIMALS & BIRDS ON THE GATE

Colgate Farm

PYLONS ABOVE LOPPED TREES

FROM BATH

TO BATH

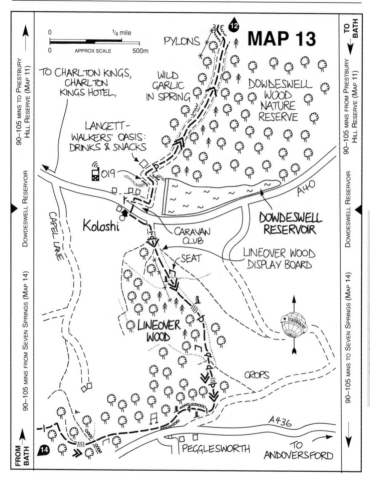

MAP 13

TO BATH

90-105 MINS TO PRESTBURY HILL RESERVE (MAP 11)

90-105 MINS FROM PRESTBURY HILL RESERVE (MAP 11)

TO CHARLTON KINGS, CHARLTON KINGS HOTEL,

PYLONS

WILD GARLIC IN SPRING

DOWDESWELL WOOD NATURE RESERVE

LANGETT- WALKERS' OASIS: DRINKS & SNACKS

019

Koloshi

CAPEL LANE

DOWDESWELL RESERVOIR

DOWDESWELL RESERVOIR

A40

CARAVAN CLUB

DOWDESWELL RESERVOIR

LINEOVER WOOD DISPLAY BOARD

SEAT

LINEOVER WOOD

CROPS

trailblazer

ROUTE GUIDE AND MAPS

90-105 MINS FROM SEVEN SPRINGS (MAP 14)

90-105 MINS TO SEVEN SPRINGS (MAP 14)

A436

FROM BATH

14

PEGGLESWORTH

TO ANDOVERSFORD

CHARLTON KINGS   [off MAP 13]

A couple of places on London Rd offer **B&B** within less than a mile (1.6km) of the trail. Closest is *Charlton Kings Hotel* (☎ 01242-231061, 🖥 charltonkingshotel.co .uk; 2T/9D/1Tr, all en suite; 🍺; WI-FI; 🐾), some three-quarters of a mile (1.2km) to the west. Rates vary, but walkers can expect to pay £27.50-57.50pp (sgl occ from £55) for B&B in comfortable modern rooms,

including a triple room with three single beds. For **food**, the nearest pub, *The Royal* (☎ 01242-228937, 🖥 royalpub.co.uk; food Mon-Thur noon-2.30pm & 6-9pm, Fri to 3pm & 5-9pm, Sat noon-9pm, Sun to 8pm; WI-FI; 🐾 in bar area) is about three-quarters of a mile closer to Cheltenham.

Almost opposite, a narrow lane leads across the River Chelt to *Detmore House*

(☎ 01242-582868, 🖳 detmorehouse.com; 1T/2D/1Tr, all en suite; ☛; WI-FI; (Ⓛ), set amid fields and an orchard. B&B here costs £50-60pp (sgl occ from £85).

Almost next to the hotel is East End Service Station, where there's an **ATM** and small Mace **shop** (daily 7am-9.30pm), though you'll find more variety at East End Stores across the road (Mon-Sat 7am-8pm, Sun 8am-7pm).

Several **bus** services call here (Pulham's No 801, Swanbrook's No 853; Stagecoach's 51 and B services); for details see pp48-50. The NX444 **coach** service (see box p47) also stops here.

NEAR DOWDESWELL RESERVOIR
[MAP 13, p111]

At the foot of the hill leading down towards the reservoir, welcoming hot and cold **drinks and snacks** – with every item £1! – await the weary at Langett.

At the bottom of the hill is *Koloshi* (☎ 01242-516400, 🖳 koloshi.co.uk; 1D/1T, both en suite; WI-FI), an Indian restaurant with rooms. You'll pay £47.50pp for **B&B** (£45 sgl occ). However, do note that the restaurant (**food** Tue-Sun noon-2.30pm & 5.30-10pm) is closed on a Monday.

Pulham's No 801 **bus** (see pp48-50) stops outside Koloshi on request. Since there is no official bus stop here, if you want to be picked up be sure to stand somewhere conspicuous and where it can safely pull over – just outside the restaurant car park is best.

SEVEN SPRINGS   [MAP 14]

There is really little more than a pub and a small roadside diner at this busy junction, but see box p114. Stagecoach's **bus** No 51 (see pp48-50) calls at the bus stop here.

Set in a layby off the A436 is the *Cotswold Diner* (🖳 thecotswolddiner.co .uk; Mon-Fri 7.30am-2pm, Sat 8am-2pm, exc bank hols), a converted but comfortable bus offering warmth and succour to weary walkers. Stop for tea or coffee, breakfast or baguettes, and even ice-cream in the summer months. More permanent is the *Seven Springs* (☎ 01242-870219, 🖳 hungryhorse .co.uk; food daily 11am-9pm; WI-FI; small 🐾 on lead). Part of the Hungry Horse chain, it has a huge menu at bargain prices, with glossy pictures to match; finesse is not the order of the day. Alongside pub favourites from £7.99, there are baguettes, wraps and hot dogs.

LECKHAMPTON HILL TO BIRDLIP   MAPS 15-17

From Leckhampton Hill it's a fairly straightforward **5¾-mile (9.25km)** walk to Birdlip, taking about **2¾ to 3¼ hours**. The route primarily follows the line of the escarpment, with attendant views in good weather. If you're less lucky, warming up at Air Balloon pub (see p117) is an appealing prospect; it's worth lingering at **Crickley Hill** (see p117), both to explore the hill fort and surrounding area.

ULLENWOOD   [MAP 15, p115]

The good people at National Star College in the grounds of Ullenwood Manor have set up a couple of ventures that are perfect for walkers along the Cotswold Way. **Campers** will find relative comfort in the four wooden **camping pods** at *Ullenwood Star Glamping* (☎ 01242-527631, 🖳 national star.org/products-services-facilities/star- glamping; WI-FI; 🐾) and food, in the form of a hamper, is available by prior

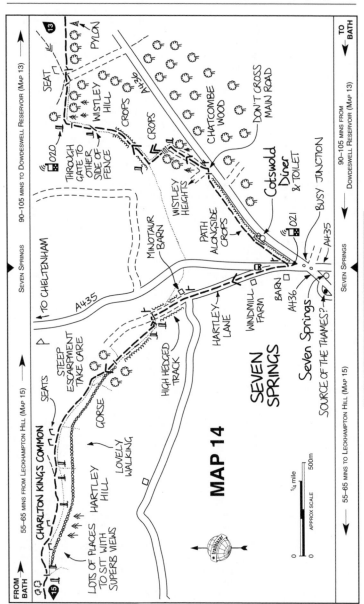

ROUTE GUIDE AND MAPS

arrangement. As well as two pods sleeping up to two (£40 for one or two people), and a third up to four (£45/50 for three/four), there's the oak-timbered Shire House (1D; £50 for one or two) and a **yurt** (Apr-Sep 1D; £60 for one or two). Expect toilets and showers, of course, but you'll need to bring your own sleeping bags, towels etc.

On the same site is *StarBistro* (☎ 01242-535984; Mon-Fri 8.30am-4pm, Sat 9am-3.30pm; WI-FI; 🐕 only on their cov-

ered patio), which serves coffee, lunch and afternoon tea during the week (hot food till 2pm), except on bank holidays. On Saturday they have a brunch menu (till 2pm) and after that only cakes/snacks. The bistro is staffed by youngsters with disabilities from the college, working with a resident chef.

There is also a small **shop** on site selling souvenirs, sandwiches and snacks.

ROUTE GUIDE AND MAPS

❏ Seven Springs – the true source of the Thames?

Mention Seven Springs to those who've done the Cotswolds Way and the chances are, if they remember the place at all, it will be as a rather busy, noisy roundabout; indeed, many will consider it to be a contender for the least attractive part of the entire trail. But the place does – possibly – boast one rather important distinction. For some people consider this place to be the true source of the River Thames.

Most people consider the source of the Thames to be at Trewsbury Mead, south-west of Cirencester. It is here that the Thames Path starts, and Ordnance Survey maps have always labelled as the Thames's true source. Even the local pub, about half a mile away, is called Thames Head Inn.

This site, near Kemble, was first identified as the source of England's most important river way back in 1546 by John Leland, and if you visit the site today you'll find an impressive stone monument stating:

'THE CONSERVATORS OF THE RIVER THAMES
1857-1974
THIS STONE WAS PLACED HERE TO MARK THE
SOURCE OF THE RIVER THAMES'

All of which sounds pretty conclusive. But to those in the know, the claims of Seven Springs are even stronger. On the opposite side of the A436 to the Seven Springs pub, seven small trickles of water drip down a mossy wall into a pool. These, of course, are the Seven Springs after which the area was named. Study the stonework more closely and you'll discover a carving in the stone that reads '*Hic tuus o Tamesine Pater septemceminus fons*', which translates, rather poetically, as 'Here, O Father Thames, is your sevenfold spring'.

But it that true? Well, the water from these springs combines to form a small river called the Churn. This in turn feeds the Thames. And when a river has more than one source, it is usual to declare the one that is the highest as the true source. Seven Springs sits, according to my GPS, at around 207m, whereas the Trewsbury Mead site is over 100m lower at 106m. So there is a strong case to be made for declaring Seven Springs as the true source of the Thames – and relegating the site at Trewsbury Mead to that of a mere tributary.

It's doubtful, of course, that Seven Springs will ever be officially considered the start of the Thames. Which is actually a bit of a pity. For if it *were* ever viewed as the official source it would add about another 15 miles to the river, which would make it longer than the Severn – and thus the longest river in the UK!

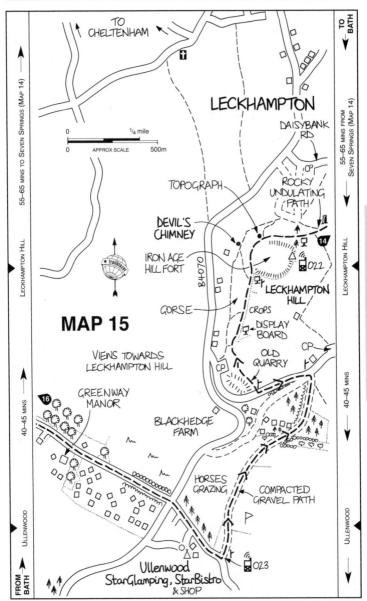

TO CHELTENHAM

LECKHAMPTON

DAISYBANK RD

CP

ROCKY UNDULATING PATH

TOPOGRAPH

DEVIL'S CHIMNEY

IRON AGE HILL FORT

GORSE

B4070

LECKHAMPTON HILL

CROPS

DISPLAY BOARD

OLD QUARRY

CP

CP

022

14

MAP 15

VIEWS TOWARDS LECKHAMPTON HILL

GREENWAY MANOR

16

BLACKHEDGE FARM

HORSES GRAZING

COMPACTED GRAVEL PATH

P

023

Ullenwood
StarGlamping, StarBistro & SHOP

55–65 MINS TO SEVEN SPRINGS (MAP 14)
55–65 MINS FROM SEVEN SPRINGS (MAP 14)

LECKHAMPTON HILL

LECKHAMPTON HILL

40–45 MINS

40–45 MINS

ULLENWOOD

ULLENWOOD

FROM BATH

TO BATH

ROUTE GUIDE AND MAPS

0   1/4 mile
0   APPROX SCALE   500m

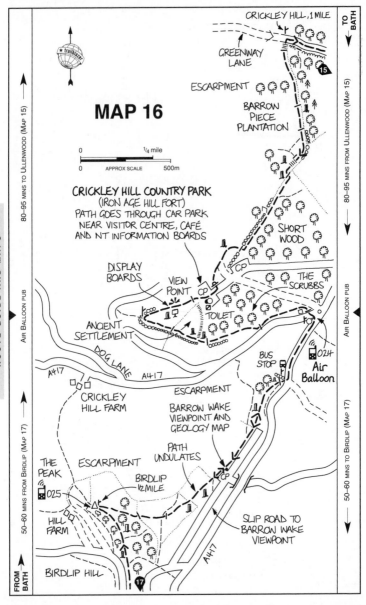

MAP 16

CRICKLEY HILL, 1 MILE

TO BATH

GREENWAY LANE

ESCARPMENT

BARROW PIECE PLANTATION

15

80-95 MINS FROM ULLENWOOD (MAP 15)

80-95 MINS TO ULLENWOOD (MAP 15)

0   1/4 mile
0   500m
APPROX SCALE

CRICKLEY HILL COUNTRY PARK
(IRON AGE HILL FORT)
PATH GOES THROUGH CAR PARK
NEAR VISITOR CENTRE, CAFÉ
AND NT INFORMATION BOARDS

SHORT WOOD

CP

THE SCRUBBS

DISPLAY BOARDS

VIEW POINT

CP

TOILET

AIR BALLOON PUB

ANCIENT SETTLEMENT

024

DOG LANE

A417

BUS STOP

Air Balloon

CRICKLEY HILL FARM

A417

ESCARPMENT

BARROW WAKE VIEWPOINT AND GEOLOGY MAP

50-60 MINS FROM BIRDLIP (MAP 17)

THE PEAK

025

ESCARPMENT

BIRDLIP 1/2 MILE

PATH UNDULATES

CP

50-60 MINS TO BIRDLIP (MAP 17)

HILL FARM

SLIP ROAD TO BARROW WAKE VIEWPOINT

A417

BIRDLIP HILL

17

FROM BATH

AROUND CRICKLEY HILL [MAP 16]

Popular locally with families and dog walkers, **Crickley Hill Country Park** (🖥 natio naltrust.org.uk) covers 143 acres (58 ha) protecting both the site of an ancient hill fort (see box on p122) and a natural environment which attracts a broad diversity of birds, butterflies and wild flowers, including the rare bee orchid (see pp63-4). There's a small *café* (daily Apr-Sep 8am-6pm, Oct-Mar 8am-5pm) here run by Gloucestershire Wildlife Trust and some toilets.

For somewhere to eat, head for *Air Balloon* (☎ 01452-862541, 🖥 chefand brewer.com; **food** Mon-Sat noon-10pm, Sun noon-9pm; WI-FI; 🐾 bar area), a big,

friendly pub with a garden, which is especially popular on Sundays. The menu covers the full works with some excellent-value meals from £7.79 to steaks (£12.29-19.99, though cheaper on their Thursday steak night), not to mention sandwiches and jackets (until 4pm, Mon-Sat), plus coffee, tea and lots of puds.

Community Connexions' No 21 **bus** (see pp48-50) stops near the pub when heading northbound towards Gloucester.

If you're planning to stop in this area, note that Little Witcombe (see p119) is almost as close to Birdlip Hill as it is to Cooper's Hill.

BIRDLIP [MAP 17, p118]

Although the Cotswold Way passes within 200m of Birdlip, it is easy to miss the tiny village entirely. But negotiate the steep and busy road and you'll come to the stone-built *Royal George Hotel* (☎ 01452-862506, 🖥 oldenglishinns.co.uk; 24D/8T/2Tr, all en suite; ✆; WI-FI; Ⓛ; 🐾). B&B rates vary daily and are usually best for

online bookings, but expect to pay £30-60pp (sgl occ room rate); special deals are regularly available. **Meals** (daily noon-10pm) can be taken in the restaurant, or more informally in the bar or garden, or on the terrace.

Community Connexions' No 21 **bus** (see pp48-50) stops here about 100m up the road from the hotel.

BIRDLIP TO PAINSWICK   MAPS 17-20

For much of the next **6¾ miles** (**10.9km, 3¼-3¾hrs**) you'll continue along the Cotswold escarpment through a woodland fringe, which opens out occasionally to reveal hillside areas such as **Cooper's Hill** (Map 18), site of the annual cheese-rolling competition (see box below), and tantalising glimpses north-west to the

---

❑ **Cheese rolling**   [Map 18, p120]

Picture the scene at Cooper's Hill near Brockworth on the Whitsun Bank Holiday Monday at the end of May. At the top, a group of contestants is set on chasing a giant Double Gloucester cheese down the almost sheer hillface for no other reason than to win the cheese – and the glory. Add in the unpredictable English weather and it's a spectacle that will gladden the heart of anyone who thought British eccentricity was dying out. It's a risky affair, with paramedics kept busy throughout the five races, but that hasn't stopped the proceedings – yet.

In 2010, as international popularity threatened to swamp this once strictly village event, the official line was that it was cancelled for safety reasons. While it looked like the end, participants were less easily convinced. Cheese rolling has a long history in this neck of the woods, and local rivalries are not that easily put down. The event went ahead anyway, as it has done every year since, so if you're timing your walk at the end of May, be prepared to share the hill with some 4000 spectators.

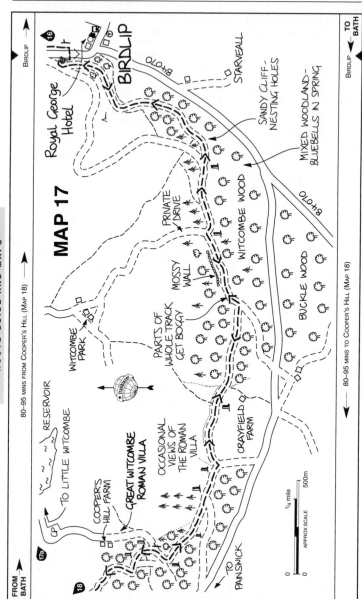

MAP 17

BIRDLIP →

FROM BATH →

80-95 MINS FROM COOPER'S HILL (MAP 18) →

Royal George Hotel

BIRDLIP

B4070

STARVEALL

SANDY CLIFF-
NESTING HOLES

MIXED WOODLAND-
BLUEBELLS IN SPRING

B4070

WITCOMBE WOOD

BUCKLE WOOD

PRIVATE DRIVE

MOSSY WALL

PARTS OF WHOLE TRACK GET BOGGY

WITCOMBE PARK

trailblazer

RESERVOIR

TO LITTLE WITCOMBE

COOPER'S HILL FARM

GREAT WITCOMBE ROMAN VILLA

OCCASIONAL VIEWS OF THE ROMAN VILLA

CRAYFIELD FARM

TO PAINSWICK

¼ mile

APPROX SCALE

500m

0

0

← 80-95 MINS TO COOPER'S HILL (MAP 18)

BIRDLIP → TO BATH

Malvern Hills. Be particularly careful to follow the waymarked path up here, and not to wander off the edge of the escarpment in misty weather; the rough picket fence would do little to break a fall.

Painswick Beacon (Map 19), site of an Iron-Age hill fort (see box on p122) follows, before you reach one of the trail's architectural highlights: **Painswick**. It was east of the town, in the Slad Valley, that the three-year-old Laurie Lee was famously 'set down from the carrier's cart', thus beginning his evocative autobiographical work, *Cider with Rosie*. While the world has moved on, many of the views along this part of the route are probably little changed – at least superficially – since Lee's childhood.

LITTLE WITCOMBE   [MAP 17a]
A steep walk down from the trail brings you to **Great Witcombe Villa** (Map 17), which was constructed during Roman times, but abandoned around the 5th century AD. The foundations are still clearly visible, but almost as interesting is an unmown section of grass which in summer yields numerous wild flowers, including the pyramidal orchid (see p63 and photo opposite p64).

Just a short walk across the main road is *Twelve Bells* (☎ 01452-862521, 💻 beefeater.co.uk; breakfasts Mon-Fri 6.30-10.30am, Sat & Sun 7-11am; Mon-Fri noon-10pm, Sat & Sun to 11pm; WI-FI), part of the Beefeater chain. The adjacent *Premier Inn* (☎ 0871 527 8458, 💻 premierinn.com; 59D, all en suite; 🛏; WI-FI) is a dependable choice, with some of the rooms having space for additional children (though not adults). Pricing varies widely and depends in part on whether you have a Saver rate (where you pay when you book) or a Flex rate (where you can cancel up to 1pm on the day you are booked), but can be as little as £36 for the room (albeit generally only for a Sunday night and for a Saver

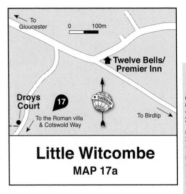

Little Witcombe
MAP 17a

rate). Breakfast – taken at the pub – is all you can eat and costs £7.50 for a continental breakfast, or £9.50 for a full English cooked to order. They also have a 'meal deal' at £24.99, which includes a two-course evening meal and drink and an all-you-can-eat breakfast.

Community Connexions' No 21 **bus** (see pp48-50) stops here.

CRANHAM CORNER [MAP 18, p120]
Not so much a village as a point on the map where the road to Cranham (and the Way) meets the A46, Cranham Corner is nevertheless served by a **bus**, Stagecoach's No 66; see pp48-50. The village itself, almost a mile (1.3km) east of the trail, is where Gustav Holst (see p107) lived for a period and in 1906, while here, he composed the first setting to music of *In the Bleak Midwinter*, a poem by Christina Rosetti.

If a spot of wildlife appeals, or a hot drink, the **Bird and Deer Park** (☎ 01452-812727, 💻 thebirdpark.com; daily Mar-Oct 10am-5pm, Nov-Feb 10am-4.30pm), on Prinknash Estate, might appeal. Tickets are £8.90, though if you're just using Oak Visitor centre to get a drink there's no need to pay the entry fee. It's located west of the trail, off the A46, and is home to both deer and an array of exotic birds.

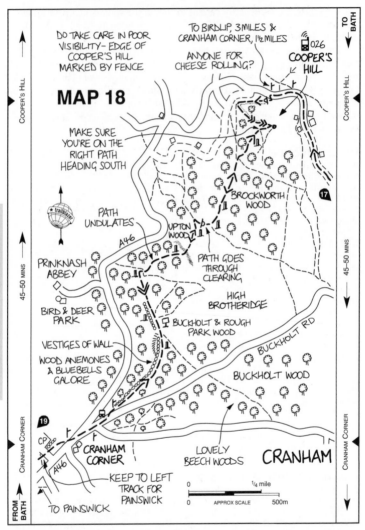

DO TAKE CARE IN POOR VISIBILITY– EDGE OF COOPER'S HILL MARKED BY FENCE

TO BIRDLIP, 3MILES & CRANHAM CORNER, 1½ MILES

ANYONE FOR CHEESE ROLLING?

026

COOPER'S HILL

MAP 18

MAKE SURE YOU'RE ON THE RIGHT PATH HEADING SOUTH

COOPER'S HILL

PATH UNDULATES

BROCKWORTH WOOD

A46

17

UPTON WOOD

PRINKNASH ABBEY

PATH GOES THROUGH CLEARING

HIGH BROTHERIDGE

BIRD & DEER PARK

45-50 MINS

BUCKHOLT RD

BUCKHOLT & ROUGH PARK WOOD

VESTIGES OF WALL

WOOD ANEMONES & BLUEBELLS GALORE

BUCKHOLT WOOD

19

CP

CRANHAM CORNER

LOVELY BEECH WOODS

CRANHAM

A46

KEEP TO LEFT TRACK FOR PAINSWICK

TO PAINSWICK

0   ¼ mile
0   APPROX SCALE   500m

FROM BATH

CRANHAM CORNER

COOPER'S HILL

TO BATH

45-50 MINS

CRANHAM CORNER

❑ **Important note – walking times**
All times in this book refer only to the time spent walking. You will need to add 20-30% to allow for rests, photography, checking the map, drinking water etc.

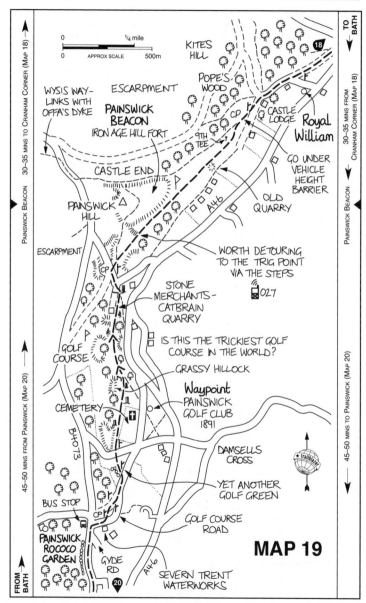

0 ¼ mile
APPROX SCALE
0 500m

KITES HILL

POPE'S WOOD

WYSIS WAY - LINKS WITH OFFA'S DYKE

ESCARPMENT

PAINSWICK BEACON
IRON AGE HILL FORT

9TH TEE

CASTLE LODGE

Royal William

CASTLE END

PAINSWICK HILL

GO UNDER VEHICLE HEIGHT BARRIER

OLD QUARRY

ESCARPMENT

A46

WORTH DETOURING TO THE TRIG POINT VIA THE STEPS

027

STONE MERCHANTS - CATBRAIN QUARRY

IS THIS THE TRICKIEST GOLF COURSE IN THE WORLD?

GOLF COURSE

GRASSY HILLOCK

CEMETERY

Waypoint
PAINSWICK GOLF CLUB 1891

B4073

DAMSELLS CROSS

YET ANOTHER GOLF GREEN

BUS STOP

GOLF COURSE ROAD

PAINSWICK ROCOCO GARDEN

GYDE RD

MAP 19

SEVERN TRENT WATERWORKS

30-35 MINS TO CRANHAM CORNER (MAP 18) →

PAINSWICK BEACON

45-50 MINS FROM PAINSWICK (MAP 20) →

FROM BATH

TO BATH

30-35 MINS FROM CRANHAM CORNER (MAP 18)

PAINSWICK BEACON

45-50 MINS TO PAINSWICK (MAP 20)

ROUTE GUIDE AND MAPS

PAINSWICK HILL   [MAP 19, p121]
A short walk from the trail on the A46 is the independent *Royal William* pub (☎ 01452-813650, 🖥 royalwilliam.co.uk; food daily noon-9pm; WI-FI; 🐾 bar area), where a wide-ranging menu is served. Take your pick from burgers, salads and steaks, and more, washed down with real ale. And isn't it good to see a pub that is independently owned and run – bucking the modern trend.

PAINSWICK   [MAP 20a, p125]
The small town of Painswick, which harks back to the Domesday Book, may come as something of a surprise for those more familiar with the Cotswold villages further north. The off-white stone of the buildings, many built by wool merchants during the 18th century, comes without the golden hue found to the north and the whole style is more elegant.

If you've the energy, count the 99 yew trees in the grounds of **St Mary's Church** (legend has it that the Devil won't let the 100th one grow), seek out the tea-caddy gravestones, or look for the **spectacle stocks** by the churchyard wall. And while you're there, note the clock on the tower, erected to celebrate the millennium.

Pretty well on the trail, some three-quarters of a mile (1.3km) north of Painswick, is the exceptionally friendly *Waypoint* (Map 19; ☎ 01452-812180, 🖥 painswickgolf.com; summer Tue-Sat 9am-6pm, Sun to 4pm, winter Tue-Sun to 4pm; WI-FI; 🐾) at Painswick Golf Club. Open for coffee and cake and a carvery on Sunday, it has a sunny balcony with glorious views over the Slad valley. Note that the carvery has to be booked.

The Arts and Crafts Movement (see box on p76) was influential here in the early 20th century and the tradition continues. Today's artists exhibit at **The Painswick Centre** (🖥 painswickcentre .com; Tue-Sat 10am-5pm; free), on Bisley St, which has regular artists in residence and is the focus of Painswick's art festival, Artburst (see box p16), in August. There are also art exhibitions at Painswick Pooch (see Where to eat), an art café.

If you're here at the weekend, don't miss **Ashton Beer Collection** (mob ☎ 07828-930050, 🖥 ashtonbeercollection .wixsite.com/beer; May-Oct Sat 2-5.30pm or by appointment; £5), housed in the old Christ Church on Gloucester St, whose central window was designed by Sir Edward

---

❏ **Hill forts**
Painswick Beacon (Map 19), also known as Kimsbury Camp, is just one of 35 **Iron-Age hill forts** that have been identified in Gloucestershire, this one dating back to around 400BC. From the layman's perspective, it is arguably the fort that gives greatest vent to the imagination along the Cotswold Way, with steep sides leading up to the fort area from where there are extensive views. Although golf has been played here since 1891, and quarrying has left its mark, the outline of the fort on the ground can still clearly be seen. Today, steps have been cut into the hill to prevent further damage to the ramparts.

Other notable hill forts along the Cotswold Way include those at **Leckhampton Hill** (Map 15, p115), **Crickley Hill** (Map 16, p116), **Haresfield Beacon** (Map 21, p127) and – just off the trail – **Uley Bury** (Map 26, p136). Some of the earlier settlements, including the one at Crickley Hill, are at least 5000 years old, although the hill fort there is far more modern, occupied around 500BC. Although little of these sites is visible on the ground today, there are some excellent interpretive panels along the trail, including an artist's impression at Crickley Hill of how a hill fort might have looked.

The thin soil on these sites, and the fact that they have never been ploughed, means not only that it is relatively easy to make out the lines of the forts on the ground, but also that they are particularly rich environmentally, and several – including Painswick Beacon – have been designated as SSSIs (see p61).

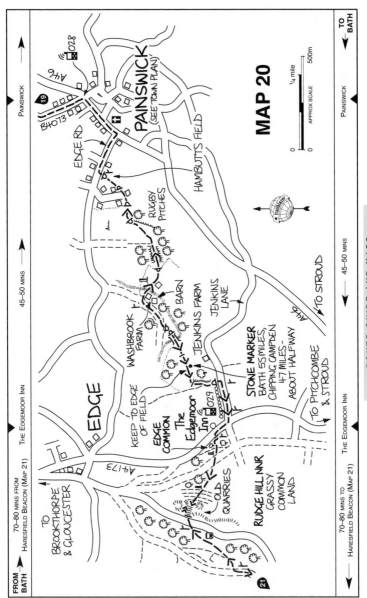

MAP 20

PAINSWICK
(SEE TOWN PLAN)

¼ mile

0   500m

APPROX SCALE

FROM BATH   70-80 MINS FROM   THE EDGEMOOR INN   45-50 MINS   PAINSWICK
HARESFIELD BEACON (Map 21)

PAINSWICK   45-50 MINS   THE EDGEMOOR INN   70-80 MINS TO   TO BATH
HARESFIELD BEACON (Map 21)

A46

B4073

EDGE RD

HAMBUTTS FIELD

RUGBY PITCHES

WASHBROOK FARM

BARN

JENKINS FARM

JENKINS LANE

TO STROUD

STONE MARKER
BATH 55 MILES,
CHIPPING CAMPDEN
47 MILES -
ABOUT HALFWAY

A4173

EDGE

EDGE COMMON

KEEP TO EDGE OF FIELD

The Edgemoor Inn

TO PITCHCOMBE & STROUD

TO BROOKTHORPE & GLOUCESTER

RUDGE HILL NNR
GRASSY COMMON LAND

OLD QUARRIES

PAINSWICK

Burne-Jones and made by William Morris's company. Here, John Ashton Beer has displayed around 600 items from his Arts and Crafts collection, lovingly assembled over four decades.

Transport

Stagecoach's No 66 **bus** (see pp48-50) stops outside St Mary's church.

For a **taxi**, try RM Goddard (☎ 01452-812240), or Painswick Taxis (☎ 07833-444607, or ☎ 07810-212837).

Services

Painswick's **tourist information centre** (☎ 01452-812278, 🖥 painswicktouristinfo.co .uk; Apr-Oct Mon-Fri 10am-4pm, Sat 10am-1pm) is in the Gravedigger's Hut on the southern side of St Mary's churchyard and is run by volunteers.

There is no bank in the town, but there's an **ATM** at the small best-one **supermarket** (Mon-Sat 7am-8pm, Sun 8am-5pm) on St Mary's St. Sadly, the **post office** (Wed & Fri 9.30-11.30am) has been moved into the Town Hall from its beautiful half-timbered building on New St, dating back to the 15th century.

There's a doctor's **surgery** (☎ 01452-812545, 🖥 painswicksurgery.nhs.uk; Mon-Fri 8.30am-6pm) to the north of the town at Hoyland House on Gyde Rd, off Gloucester St, and the handy Painswick **Pharmacy** (Mon-Fri 9am-1pm & 2-6pm, Sat 9am-noon) on New St.

Where to stay

Most of Painswick's places to stay are near the town centre. Two **B&Bs** are close to each other on Gloucester St, along the trail. At *Troy House* (☎ 01452-812339, 🖥 troy guesthouse.co.uk; 1D/3D or T/1Tr/1Qd, all en suite; ☕; WI-FI; Ⓛ; 🐾; Feb-Dec), where there is a variety of rooms in either the house, a self-contained cottage, or an annex across the courtyard from the main house. You'll pay from £42.50pp; for sgl occ it's £75 on Mon-Thur, though you'll have to pay the full room rate at weekends.

Opposite is *St Anne's* (☎ 01452-812879, 🖥 st-annes-painswick.co.uk; 1T/2D, all en suite; WI-FI; Ⓛ; 🐾), a cottagey place with flowers in the rooms. They also have drying facilities and a utility room with a large sink for washing off kit and filling water bottles. Rates are from £40pp (sgl occ £60). They offer a pick up and drop off at Leckhampton if you stay two nights.

Also on the trail is *Falcon* (☎ 01452-814222, 🖥 falconpainswick.co.uk; 2T/2D/7D or T, all en suite; ☕; WI-FI; Ⓛ; 🐾), New St, a 16th-century coaching inn with a 21st-century twist. Rooms can be booked online and prices fluctuate, with the highest at weekends, but expect to pay £40-60pp (sgl occ room rate). On the corner at The Cross, there's an air of grandeur about *Cardynham House* (☎ 01452-814006, 🖥 cardynham.co.uk; 6D/2Tr/1Qd, all en suite; ☕; WI-FI), too. Here there are four grades of room, costing £45-110pp (sgl occ £70-220), depending on the day and time of

---

❏ **Painswick Rococo Garden**   **[Map 19, p121]**
Not far from the trail, this garden (☎ 01452-813204, 🖥 www.rococogarden.org.uk; daily mid Jan to end Oct 10.30am-5pm, Nov to 4pm; £7.50) is claimed to be the only complete English Rococo garden still in existence. It was planted in the 1740s, but so quickly did the fashion change that the original was soon replanted and the garden was later abandoned. Over 240 years later, in 1984, restoration was put in hand thanks to a painting made in 1748 showing the original design. Flights of fancy characterise a fairly structured and geometric layout, with fruit and vegetables forming a part of the whole rather than hidden away. A maze created to commemorate the garden's 250th anniversary is an added attraction; the gardens are renowned for their display of snowdrops in early spring and for the bluebell walk.

Coffee, tea, cakes and light lunches are served in the old *Coach House* (food to 4.30pm, lunch noon-2pm; WI-FI; 🐾).

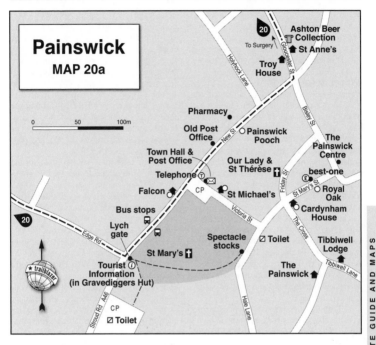

Painswick MAP 20a

ROUTE GUIDE AND MAPS

year; for true indulgence, how about the pool room – 'great fun, if expensive' according to one reader – with its own covered, heated swimming pool at £220 for two sharing? Note that wi-fi here is only reliably available in the lounge because of the thick stone walls.

At *Tibbiwell Lodge* (☎ 01452-812748 or mob ☎ 07872-310393, 🖥 tibbiwelllodge painswick.webs.com; 1T private facilities, 1D/ 1Tr, both en suite; 🛏; WI-FI; Ⓛ; 🐾; Mar-late Nov), a short way down Tibbiwell Lane, there's an interesting choice of rooms (£35-49.50pp, sgl occ from £50 but room rate at the weekend). The room that can sleep up to three people has a balcony and the double has a terrace; both of these rooms look over the valley. Useful facilities include a drying room and boot wash area.

Top of the range in accommodation terms, *The Painswick* (☎ 01452-813688, 🖥 thepainswick.co.uk; 7D/9D or T, all en

suite; 🛏; WI-FI; 🐾) is an imposing three-storey stone building on a quiet lane – and pretty much as good as it gets when it comes to B&Bs on the trail. Luxurious and stylish, the rooms are so popular that it can be difficult to book despite the high room-only rates that start at about £65pp but can easily rise to £130pp or more (sgl occ from £149). B&B costs £85.50-198pp (sgl occ from £178).

Closed for the last edition of this guide, *St Michael's* (☎ 01452-812712, 🖥 stmichaelsbistro.co.uk; 5D, all en suite; 🛏; WI-FI; Ⓛ; 🐾 restaurant only) has reopened as a rather upmarket B&B and restaurant. The décor in the rooms is striking to say the least – the suite, for example, features retro '70s furnishings including a hanging perspex bubble chair, portable record player and 'vintage' board games – but there's no denying the quality and comfort of this place. B&B rates start at £65pp (sgl occ full room rate). Though solo trekkers are officially obliged to pay the room rate, it's worth checking on 💻 booking.com where significant discounts may be available for single occupancy depending on the season.

Where to eat and drink
Painswick is something of a mecca for foodies, so it could be worth timing your walk for a stop here at some stage of the day. At the time of research there was something of a revolution, however, with the local deli, Olivas, up for sale and the trekkers' favourite café, The Patchwork Mouse, undergoing a transformation that that has seen it become the dog-friendly *Painswick Pooch* (☎ 01452-8125600, 💻 thepainswickpooch.wixsite.com/thepains wickpooch; Mon & Wed-Sat 9.30am-5pm, Sun 10am-4pm; WI-FI; 🐾) to advertise its canine credentials. At the moment the renovations are still ongoing but they plan to have a dog chaise longue and to introduce dog ice-cream. For humans they have daily wraps and bagels, cakes and 'walker packs' (packed lunches).

Thankfully, Painswick's two venerable inns are still going strong and remain highlights. The *Royal Oak* (☎ 01452-813129; food Mon-Sat noon-2.30pm & 6.30-9pm, Sun noon-2.30pm; WI-FI; 🐾), on St Mary's St, remains a proper real-ale pub (with beers from Stroud or Butcombe breweries, see box p23), cosy and stone built. Standard pub fare is augmented by the likes of whole mackerel with crushed new

potatoes (£17.95), or pork belly with sweet potato fondant and veg (£16.50). More stylish is *Falcon* (see Where to stay; daily noon-2.30pm, Mon-Sat 6.30-9.30pm, Sun to 8.30pm), where you'll dine in relaxed but contemporary surroundings with excellent service. Locals and visitors flock here for the diverse menu (so you may need to book), but many walkers will appreciate their range of pies at £13.95; the special board contains such notable dishes as pigeon breast for starters (£7.95), and pork belly for mains (£16.50).

Pretty tablecloths set the scene for the **bistro** at *Cardynham House* (see Where to stay; Tue-Sun noon-3pm, Tue-Sat 6.30-9.30pm), which serves everything from baguettes and jacket potatoes at lunchtime, to a regularly changing menu in the evening with mains starting at around £14.50.

The award for the finest eatery in town, however, probably goes to *St Michael's Bistro* (see Where to stay; food Wed-Thur 10am-2.30pm, Fri & Sat 10am-2pm & 7-8.15pm, Sun noon-2.30pm), with locally sourced ingredients and a great range of imaginative dishes, with lunches starting at £6.50 for the Italian bean soup, while in the evenings it's two courses for £26.50, three for £34, with dishes such as plaice with an anchoiade & walnut crust and rib-eye steak on the menu. Do note the limited opening hours, however.

For a more rural repast, consider Rococo Gardens (see box p124).

PAINSWICK TO STONEHOUSE   MAPS 20-23

This **8½-mile (13.4km, 4¼-4¾hr)** section marks the halfway point along the Cotswold Way; indeed, you'll pass a stonemarker (Map 20) stating 'Bath 55' on one side – and 'Chipping Campden 47' on the other – which clearly *isn't* halfway, but it's close. After the open countryside of the first few miles the trail enters a narrow strip of woodland, following the edge of the escarpment as it twists and turns around **Haresfield Beacon** (Map 21). With unimpeded (not to mention spectacular) views in almost every direction, and sheer slopes on two sides, it's no surprise that it was chosen as the site of an Iron-Age hill fort (see box on p122).

The descent through woods and fields to **Stroudwater (Ebley) Canal** (Map 23) gives little indication of the urban sprawl to the east that is the town of Stroud. No wonder, then, that the appearance of first the railway, then two busy

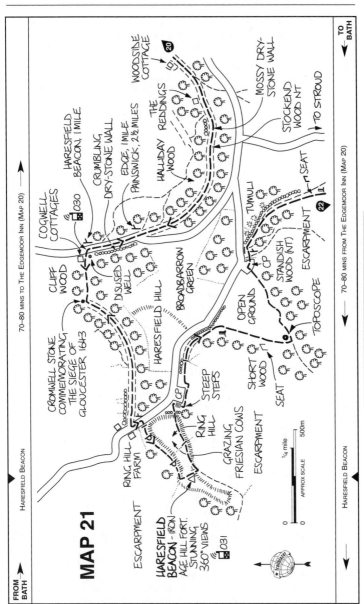

MAP 21

HARESFIELD BEACON

HARESFIELD BEACON - IRON AGE HILL FORT. STUNNING, 360° VIEWS 📷 031

ESCARPMENT

RING HILL FARM

GRAZING FRIESIAN COWS

RING HILL

STEEP STEPS

ESCARPMENT

HARESFIELD BEACON

SHORT WOOD

SEAT

OPEN GROUND

TOPOSCOPE

STANDISH WOOD (NT)

ESCARPMENT

SEAT

TUMULI

CP

BROADBARROW GREEN

HARESFIELD HILL

DISUSED WELL

CLIFF WOOD

CROMWELL STONE COMMEMORATING THE SIEGE OF GLOUCESTER 1643

COGWELL COTTAGES 📷 030

HARESFIELD BEACON, 1 MILE

CRUMBLING DRY-STONE WALL

EDGE, 1 MILE PAINSWICK, 2½ MILES

HALLIDAY WOOD

THE REDDINGS

WOODSIDE COTTAGE 20

MOSSY DRY-STONE WALL

STOCKEND WOOD NT

TO STROUD

22

TO BATH

¼ mile
500m
0
0
APPROX SCALE

N

parallel roads, jars the senses. Yet the canal between these, just a few metres above sea level and the lowest point along the route, is one of the few areas of water along the Cotswold Way and introduces a very different environment.

EDGE   [MAP 20, p123]

Right on the Cotswold Way on the busy A4173, opposite the entrance to Edge Common (part of Rudge Hill National Nature Reserve), *The Edgemoor Inn* (☎ 01452-813576, 🖳 edgemoorinn.uk; food Mon-Sat noon-2pm & 6.30-8.45pm, Sun sittings at 12.15pm & 2.15pm; WI-FI) could be a good staging post. Expect daily specials on the menu and a range of real ales such as Wickwar's BOB (see box p23). Dogs are only allowed on the patio.

RANDWICK   [MAP 22]

On the western outskirts of Stroud are the villages of Randwick and Westrip (see below), a short but steep walk down from the trail.

The local **pub** up the hill in **Randwick** does a good job of satisfying walkers' hunger pangs – except on Sunday evenings and Monday. *Vine Tree Inn* (☎ 01453-763748, 🖳 thevinetreerandwick.co.uk; food served Tue 6-9pm, Wed-Fri noon-2pm & 6-9pm, Sat noon-9pm, Sun noon-3.30pm; WI-FI; 🐾), where lunchtime ciabattas at £7.25 vie with Hungarian sausage & bread (£8.50), or glazed ham, egg & chips (£8.95). Note that the pub is closed all day on Monday and till Tuesday evening.

Cotswold Green's No 230 **bus** (see pp48-50) from Stroud stops here.

WESTRIP   [MAP 22]

Further south, Westrip boasts *The Carpenters Arms* (☎ 01453-762693, 🖳 the-carpenters-arms-westrip.co.uk; food Tue-Sat 6-8pm, Sun noon-2pm; no WI-FI; 🐾), a real-ale pub where mains (mainly pub classics) are never more than £8.95. Note that it's open only in the evenings and all-day Sunday.

STONEHOUSE   [MAP 23, p131]

As the Cotswold Way emerges into the valley that links Stonehouse to the west and Ebley to the east, there's little to delay the walker.

Stonehouse **railway** station, a little over half a mile (1km) from the trail, off the B4008, is served by GWR (see p84) and offers straightforward access to the Cotswold Way at this point.

Stagecoach's **bus** Nos 61, 66 and 66S (see pp48-50) stop on the B4008.

See box p16 for details of Frocester Beer Festival which is held near here in August.

STONEHOUSE TO PENN WOOD   MAPS 23-24

At this point, the Cotswold Way offers two alternatives. The **shorter route**, which runs close to King's Stanley, is only **1½ miles (2.5km)** long, taking about **40-50 minutes** to walk. Predominantly urban with an agricultural fringe, its attractions are of a practical nature, with a couple of B&Bs, a pub and a useful shop in King's Stanley itself.

The more **scenic route**, which follows in part the restored **Stroudwater (Ebley) Canal** then goes on to cross Selsley Common, is just over **3 miles (5km, 1½-1¾hrs)**, so about twice the distance. Unless time is of the essence, opt for the longer walk; the rewards are infinitely greater, with the common

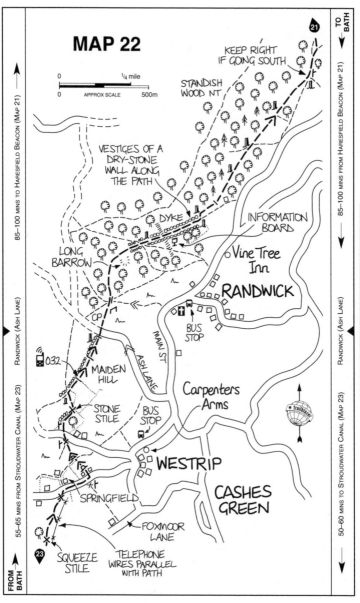

MAP 22

0 · ¼ mile · APPROX SCALE · 0 · 500m

TO BATH

85–100 MINS FROM HARESFIELD BEACON (MAP 21)

RANDWICK (ASH LANE)

50–60 MINS TO STROUDWATER CANAL (MAP 23)

KEEP RIGHT IF GOING SOUTH

STANDISH WOOD NT

VESTIGES OF A DRY-STONE WALL ALONG THE PATH

DYKE

INFORMATION BOARD

Vine Tree Inn

RANDWICK

LONG BARROW

BUS STOP

CP

MAIN ST

Carpenters Arms

032

MAIDEN HILL

ASH LANE

STONE STILE

BUS STOP

WESTRIP

CASHES GREEN

SPRINGFIELD

FOXMOOR LANE

SQUEEZE STILE

TELEPHONE WIRES PARALLEL WITH PATH

85–100 MINS TO HARESFIELD BEACON (MAP 21)

55–65 MINS FROM STROUDWATER CANAL (MAP 23)

FROM BATH

RANDWICK (ASH LANE)

TO BATH

ROUTE GUIDE AND MAPS

itself one of the trail's highlights. Open and windswept, it offers glorious walking at any time of the year, but is at its best in summer when the grass is thick with orchids and other wild flowers.

Both routes converge in **Penn Wood**, just a quarter of a mile (0.45km) or so above (almost literally) Middleyard.

EBLEY [on SCENIC ROUTE, MAP 23]

Less than quarter of a mile (0.4km) east of the oak tree where the re-routed Cotswold Way turns away from Ebley Canal is **Ebley Wharf**, a development across the bridge from Ebley Mill. There's no longer a shop at the wharf – you'll need to head a further half-mile along the main road to the **Cainscross** branch of the Co-op (Mon-Sat 7am-10pm, Sun 10am-4pm) for that – but

there is *Kitsch Coffee and Wine Bar* (☎ 01453-350930; Mon-Thur & Sat 9am-6pm, Fri to 10pm, Sun 10am-3pm) which can provide sanctuary if it's raining. Also here is *Boho Bakery* (🖳 thebohobak ery.co.uk).

Cotswold Green's No 230 **bus** service calls at Ebley as do Stagecoach's Nos 61 & 66 (see pp48-50).

SELSLEY [off MAP 23; MAP 24, p133]
[on SCENIC ROUTE]

The village of Selsley is notable for the Victorian **All Saints' Church** (Map 24), clearly visible on the hill from the canal and a little way from the heart of the community. The church was influential in the development of the Arts and Crafts Movement (see box on p76), its stained-glass windows being one of the first commissions for William Morris's design company. Work was contributed by Dante Gabriel Rossetti and Edward Burne-Jones, as well as by Morris himself. The church lies alongside **Selsley Common**, itself a haven for any number of wild flowers, including the pyramidal orchid (see p63).

Both lodging and sustenance are on hand in the centre of the village at *The Bell*

Inn (off Map 23; ☎ 01453-753801, 🖳 the bellinnselsley.com; 1D/1Tr, both en suite; WI-FI; Ⓛ; 🐾), a couple of hundred yards (200m) from the trail. There are two classy bedrooms with king-size beds, contemporary bathrooms and plenty of mod cons. **B&B** costs £37.50-47.50pp in the smaller room, or £50-62.50pp in the larger, which has a separate living room with sofa bed. For single occupancy in either room you'll pay the room rate. In the **restaurant** (Mon-Sat noon-2.30pm & 6-9pm, Sun noon-3.30pm), mains in the evening are £14-17, or – perhaps more manageable at lunchtime – sandwiches with fries & salad are £8.

Stagecoach's Nos 65 & 66S **bus** services (see pp48-50) stop by All Saints' Church.

KING'S STANLEY   [MAP 24, p133]
[on SHORTER ROUTE]

Only a short walk west of the trail across playing fields, King's Stanley offers most of the services essential to walkers.

The **Co-op** (Mon-Sat 7am-10pm, Sun 8am-10pm) has all the necessities, including a **post office** counter (open the same hours) and a useful **ATM**. Opposite is a small **newsagent**, Yew Tree Stores.

For **B&B**, try *Orchardene* (☎ 01453-822684, 🖳 orchardene.co.uk; 1T en suite/1D with private bathroom; 🛏; WI-FI; Ⓛ; 🐾), reached by heading away from the

shops along Castle St. A 19th-century stone house down a narrow drive, it's a friendly place, offering local organic food, including their own honey. B&B comes in at £42.50pp (sgl occ room rate).

For **food**, pub grub is available at the *King's Head* (☎ 01453-828293, 🖳 thekings headstonehouse.co.uk; food Wed-Sat noon-2.30pm & 5.30-9pm, Sun noon-3pm), by the war memorial, with evening main dishes for £9.95-16.95. The pub is open on Monday and Tuesday (generally 9am-9pm) but food is not served.

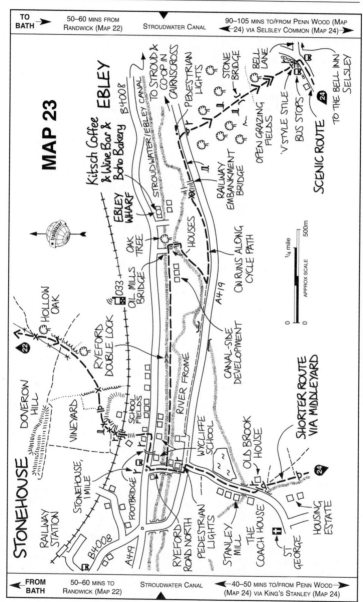

MAP 23

EBLEY

Kitsch Coffee & Wine Bar & Boho Bakery

B4008

STROUDWATER/EBLEY CANAL

TO STROUD & CO-OP IN CAINSCROSS

PEDESTRIAN LIGHTS

STONE BRIDGE

BELL LANE

EBLEY WHARF

OAK TREE

OIL MILLS BRIDGE

Q033

RYEFORD DOUBLE LOCK

22

HOLLOW OAK

DOVERON HILL

VINEYARD

STONEHOUSE, 1 MILE

HOUSES

A419

CN RUNS ALONG CYCLE PATH

RAILWAY EMBANKMENT BRIDGE

OPEN GRAZING FIELDS

'V STILE

BUS STOPS

24

TO THE BELL INN SELSLEY

SCENIC ROUTE

CANAL-SIDE DEVELOPMENT

RIVER FROME

SCHOOL FIELDS

STONEHOUSE

RAILWAY STATION

B4008

A419

FOOTBRIDGE

WYCLIFFE SCHOOL

OLD BROOK HOUSE

SHORTER ROUTE VIA MIDDLEYARD

24

RYEFORD ROAD NORTH

PEDESTRIAN LIGHTS

STANLEY MILL

THE COACH HOUSE

ST GEORGE

HOUSING ESTATE

¼ mile

500m

APPROX SCALE

0

0

ROUTE GUIDE AND MAPS

There's also a Chinese takeaway, *Ben's* (☎ 01453-828855, 🖥 benstakeaway.co.uk; Tue-Sun 4.30-11pm), almost hidden down a narrow street that runs between Shute St and the playing fields. Note that on a Monday evening both the pub and Ben's are closed, so you may have to take a taxi somewhere for supper.

Stagecoach **bus** No 66S (see pp48-50) stops by the war memorial.

MIDDLEYARD   [MAP 24]
[on SHORTER ROUTE]

The Cotswold Way runs through Middleyard, a small ribbon of old and new stone houses up the hill from King's Stanley, yet within easy walking distance of the larger village's facilities.

Backing on to farmland, with direct access clearly signposted from the trail, the aptly named *Valley Views* (☎ 01453-827458, 🖥 valley-views.com; 1T/1D both en suite, 1D private bathroom; 🛏; WI-FI; ①; Mar-end Oct), 12 Orchard Cl, is a modern, very comfortable house where guests have their own sitting room and sunroom. B&B costs £40-45pp (sgl occ from £70), the higher rate is for the large double with a balcony.

Stagecoach **bus** No 66S (see pp48-50) stops in the village.

PENN WOOD TO DURSLEY   MAPS 24-27

Further ribbons of steeply banked beech woods characterise this **6½-mile (10.25km, 3¼-4hrs)** stretch, broken up by two significant highlights as well as a couple of interesting long barrows.

The views from **Coaley Peak** (Map 25) look not just west to the Severn, but onward to Cam Long Down and the Tyndale Monument – a taste of things to come. **Cam Long Down** (Map 27) itself is all too short, the steep climb up being richly rewarded with 360° views: a place to be savoured before the descent into **Dursley**. Be careful up here if the weather is poor, though; there are some sheer drops.

The area is also home to two of the trail's most interesting long barrows (see box below), at **Nympsfield** (Map 25) and **Uley** (Map 26), and two very different mansions: **Woodchester Mansion** (see box p134) and **Owlpen Manor** (off Map 26; see box p138), although the latter is no longer open to the public.

❑ **What is a long barrow?**
Essentially another name for a communal burial ground, the long barrow is known locally as a '*tump*'. These were the graveyards of the Neolithic people, early settlers who were the first to farm the land over 5000 years ago. In addition to human remains, archaeologists have identified the remains of fires that indicate some form of ritual or religious activity.

Of almost 100 long barrows in the Cotswolds, several are along the Cotswold Way including **Nympsfield Long Barrow** (Map 25) near Coaley Peak, dating from 2500BC, and others at Leckhampton Hill and in Standish Wood. Notable among them are **Belas Knap** (Map 9; see box on p100) and – just off this stretch of the route – **Uley Long Barrow** (Map 26), more evocatively known as **Hetty Pegler's Tump**. Best approached along the road rather than by scrambling up the steep hill through the woods, Hetty Pegler is worth the detour, since here you can crawl inside the chamber itself. You'll need a torch – but don't spend too long, for folklore has it that, if you do, the fairies will start to work their magic on the passing of time.

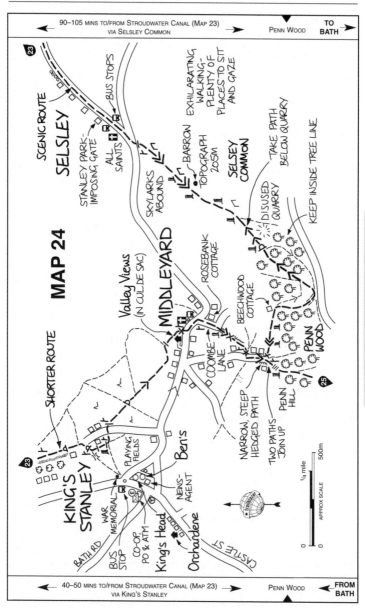

PENN WOOD   TO BATH →

MAP 24

SCENIC ROUTE

SELSLEY

STANLEY PARK IMPOSING GATE

BUS STOPS

ALL SAINTS

SKYLARKS ABOUND

BARROW TOPOGRAPH 205M

SELSEY COMMON

EXHILARATING WALKING – PLENTY OF PLACES TO SIT AND GAZE

TAKE PATH BELOW QUARRY

DISUSED QUARRY

KEEP INSIDE TREE LINE

Valley Views (IN CUL DE SAC)

MIDDLEYARD

ROSEBANK COTTAGE

BEECHWOOD COTTAGE

PENN WOOD

SHORTER ROUTE

COOMBE LANE

NARROW, STEEP HEDGED PATH

PENN HILL

TWO PATHS JOIN UP

KING'S STANLEY

Ben's

PLAYING FIELDS

WAR MEMORIAL

BATH RD

BUS STOP

CO-OP PO & ATM

King's Head

NEWS-AGENT

Orchardene

CASTLE ST

trailblazer
APPROX SCALE
¼ mile
500m

PENN WOOD   ← FROM BATH

ROUTE GUIDE AND MAPS

NYMPSFIELD   [off MAP 25]

About half a mile off the trail from Coaley Peak, in the heart of the village of Nympsfield, *The Rose and Crown Inn* (☎ 01453-860612, 🖳 therosecrownnympsfields.com; **food** Tue-Fri noon-3pm & 6-9pm, Sat noon-9pm, Sun noon-6pm; WI-FI) offers a solid menu heavy with top-quality

steaks (from £16.95) and burgers (from £12.50) as well as a few pub favourites. Note that the pub is closed every Monday other than on bank holiday Mondays.

Stagecoach's No 65 **bus** service (see pp48-50) calls here.

ULEY   [MAP 26, p136]

Although it's over half a mile (1km) from the Cotswold Way, Uley does at least justify the diversion. Probably many people's idea of a proper village, it boasts a pub, a decidedly imposing church, St Giles, and a **post office cum shop** (☎ 01453-861592, 🖳 uleycommunitystores.co.uk; Mon-Fri 8am-6pm, Sat 8am-4pm, Sun 8am-noon; post office Mon, Tue, Thur & Fri 9am-1pm & 2-.5.30pm, Wed 9am-1pm & 2-4pm, Sat 9am-12.30pm); it even has its own brewery (see box p23) and a posh manor house – Owlpen Manor – a short distance away. The village is also notable for the hill fort of Uley Bury (see box on p132), which is much closer to the trail.

The highlight of the village for many, however, is *The Vestry Café* (☎ 01453-861177, 🖳 prema.org.uk/cafe; Tue-Sat

9am-4pm; WI-FI; 🐾) in Prema Arts Centre; it has an inventive menu including the delicious Vestry hash (hash brown potato topped with a poached egg; £8). Note, however, that the café closes for 2-3 weeks during the summer school holidays.

The whitewashed *Old Crown* (☎ 01453-860502, 🖳 theoldcrownuley.co.uk; 2T/2D, all en suite; WI-FI; (L); 🐾), with a terrace garden at the rear, does **B&B** at £40-60pp (sgl occ from £50). There is a standard **pub menu** (food Mon-Fri noon-2pm & 6-9pm, Sat & Sun noon-9pm) and plenty of real-ale choices to accompany your meal. They always have at least one if not two Uley Brewery (see box p23) beers on tap.

Stagecoach's No 65 and Cotswold Green's No 65A **bus** services (see pp48-50) stop near the post office.

❏ **Woodchester Mansion and Park**   [Map 25]

Despite its imposing architecture, the three-storey Victorian **Woodchester Mansion** (🖳 woodchestermansion.org.uk; £8, NT & English Heritage members £7), near Nympsfield, was never finished, its rooms being inhabited by five species of bat, but never by humans. It is usually open to the public from Easter to October (Fri-Sun & bank hols 11am-5pm), but do check their website first. Visitors may explore the house, including the drawing room, which was the only room to be completed, and upstairs along boarded corridors. Lunches, tea and coffee in their *tea room* should help to restore a sense of normality.

The mansion is set in the grounds of **Woodchester Park**, a peaceful wooded valley with a chain of lakes that is owned by the National Trust (☎ 01452-814213, 🖳 nationaltrust.org.uk; daily dawn-dusk; parking £3, NT members free). Designated as an SSSI (see p61), the estate is notable not just for the bats, but for a broad diversity of birds and wild flowers. Waymarked trails through the grounds are accessible to the public all year.

Visitors arriving on foot can access the mansion along the main drive; otherwise entry is via the National Trust car park to the south, from where it's a 10- to 15-minute walk to the house.

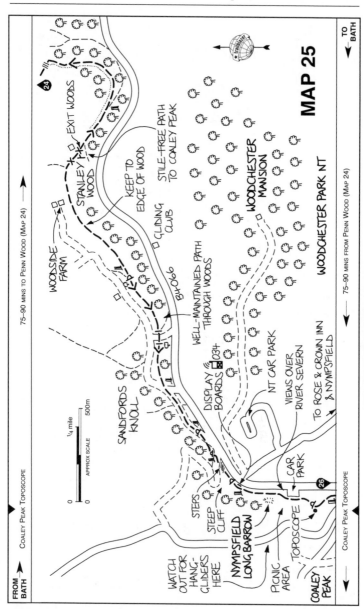

MAP 25

FROM BATH

TO BATH

COALEY PEAK TOPOSCOPE

75–90 MINS TO PENN WOOD (MAP 24)

75–90 MINS FROM PENN WOOD (MAP 24)

COALEY PEAK TOPOSCOPE

WATCH OUT FOR HANG-GLIDERS HERE

NYMPSFIELD LONG BARROW

PICNIC AREA

TOPOSCOPE

COALEY PEAK

STEPS

STEEP CLIFF

SANDFORDS KNOLL

WOODSIDE FARM

EXIT WOODS

STANLEY WOOD

KEEP TO EDGE OF WOOD

GLIDING CLUB

STILE-FREE PATH TO COALEY PEAK

B4066

WELL-MAINTAINED PATH THROUGH WOODS

WOODCHESTER MANSION

WOODCHESTER PARK NT

DISPLAY BOARDS 034

NT CAR PARK

VIEWS OVER RIVER SEVERN

TO ROSE & CROWN INN & NYMPSFIELD

CAR PARK

26

24

¼ mile

0   500m

APPROX SCALE

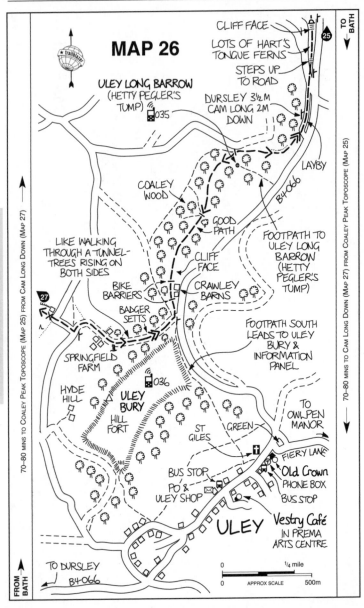

70–80 MINS TO COALEY PEAK TOPOSCOPE (MAP 27) FROM CAM LONG DOWN (MAP 27)

70–80 MINS TO COALEY PEAK TOPOSCOPE (MAP 27) FROM CAM LONG DOWN (MAP 25)

MAP 26

ULEY LONG BARROW
(HETTY PEGLER'S
TUMP) 035

CLIFF FACE

LOTS OF HART'S
TONGUE FERNS

STEPS UP
TO ROAD

25

TO
BATH

DURSLEY 3½ M
CAM LONG 2 M
DOWN

LAYBY

B4066

FOOTPATH TO
ULEY LONG
BARROW (HETTY
PEGLER'S
TUMP)

COALEY
WOOD

GOOD
PATH

CLIFF
FACE

CRAWLEY
BARNS

LIKE WALKING
THROUGH A TUNNEL—
TREES RISING ON
BOTH SIDES

BIKE
BARRIERS

27

BADGER
SETTS

FOOTPATH SOUTH
LEADS TO ULEY
BURY &
INFORMATION
PANEL

SPRINGFIELD
FARM

036

HYDE
HILL

ULEY
BURY

HILL
FORT

TO
OWLPEN
MANOR

ST
GILES

GREEN

FIERY LANE

Old Crown
PHONE BOX

BUS STOP

PO &
ULEY SHOP

BUS STOP

ULEY

Vestry Café
IN PREMA
ARTS CENTRE

TO DURSLEY
B4066

0   ¼ mile

0   500m
APPROX SCALE

TO BATH

FROM BATH

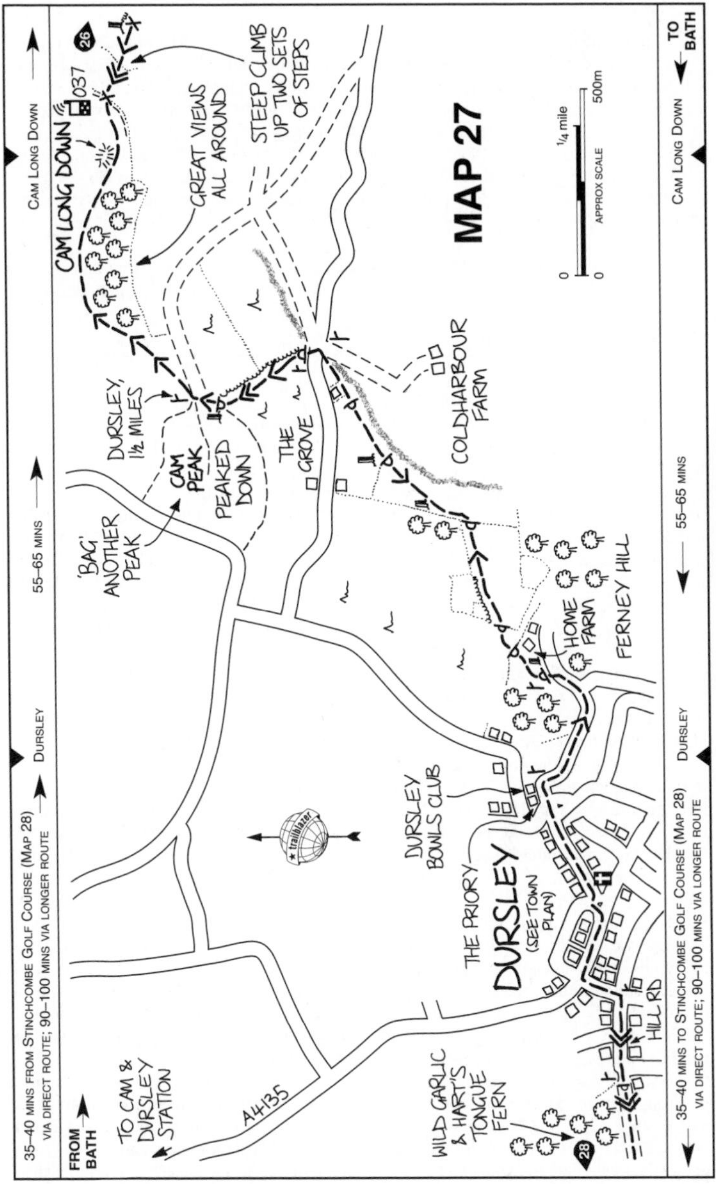
35–40 mins from Stinchcombe Golf Course (Map 28) via direct route; 90–100 mins via longer route
Dursley
55–65 mins
Cam Long Down
From Bath
To Cam & Dursley Station
A4135
Wild Garlic & Hart's Tongue Fern
28
Hill Rd
The Priory
Dursley (see town plan)
Dursley Bowls Club
Home Farm
Ferney Hill
'Bag' another peak
Cam Peak
Peaked Down
The Grove
Dursley, 1½ miles
Coldharbour Farm
Cam Long Down
037
Great views all around
Steep climb up two sets of steps
26
MAP 27
0
¼ mile
0
Approx scale
500m
35–40 mins to Stinchcombe Golf Course (Map 28) via direct route; 90–100 mins via longer route
Dursley
55–65 mins
Cam Long Down
To Bath

❏ **Owlpen Manor**   **[off Map 26, p136]**

Almost hidden from view in a valley along a short avenue of trees, Owlpen Manor (🖥 owlpen.com) is an enchanting Tudor manor house, complete with great hall, dating in part back to 1450. It was abandoned early in the 19th century, but was rescued in 1926 in line with the principles of the Society for the Protection of Ancient Buildings (🖥 spab.org.uk), a body formed by William Morris. While most of the furniture and decoration date to an earlier era, the Arts and Crafts Movement founded by Morris is also represented. Outside, the formal gardens with their neatly clipped yews lead to beech woods with a series of walks, while above looms an elaborate Victorian church.

Sadly, the manor, which remains in private hands, is no longer open to the public except for private functions and group tours, though you can visit the gardens in summer (Apr-Sep Mon-Fri noon-5pm; £5).

DURSLEY   **[MAP 27a]**

Only a few years ago, it was difficult not to echo the sentiments of one local resident, that Dursley had been 'very successfully ruined' by the planning authorities. Now, as houses and shops have materialised on the building sites that marred the centre, so the town has settled into a new phase, marked by a strong sense of community.

At one end of the pedestrianised Parsonage St, which boasts a decent range of traditional shops and facilities, stand the pillared Georgian **Market House** and the parish church of **St James the Great**. Cars follow the newer road that runs almost parallel, lined with a supermarket which seems to have given the town a boost, and a leisure complex undergoing a facelift at the time of research. For the walker, Dursley has one further card up its sleeve: the CAMRA award-winning Old Spot pub (see p140), which is one of the best along the trail.

Like many other Cotswold towns, Dursley was founded on the wool trade; today its weaving skills have turned towards billiard-table baizes and the covers for tennis balls. It was also home to the Lister family, of engineering fame, who still have a presence here. To get an idea of the town's history, including its industrial past, pop into the **Heritage Centre** (Tue-Sat 10.30am-12.30pm).

See box on p16 for details of the walking festival held here in October.

Transport

GWR **trains** (see p84) run to Cam & Dursley station, nearly three miles (4.8km) north of the town.

The town's **bus station** is on May Lane, squeezed between the modern, tinted-glass library and the Old Spot – the old and the new. Stagecoach's No 60 bus runs between the station and Dursley, while their No 61, 62, 65 & Cotswold Green's 65A services call at the bus station but *not* the railway station. See pp48-50.

For **taxi** services, try A 2 B Taxis (☎ 01453-548483), or Cam & Dursley Taxis (mob ☎ 07525-142295).

Services

While the town has no **tourist information** centre as such, staff at the **library** (Mon & Thur 9.30am-5pm, Tue & Fri to 6.30pm, Wed to 2pm, Sat to 4pm) are extremely helpful and they have a good selection of leaflets for visitors. Lloyds **bank** has a branch with an ATM; there's an ATM at Sainsbury's (see below), too. The **post office** (Mon-Sat 9am-5.30pm), with a bureau de change and ATM, is now housed in Dursley Local Store by Market House, at the end of Parsonage St.

A large Sainsbury's **supermarket** (Mon-Sat 8am-10pm, Sun 10am-4pm) & ATM may have brought a new dimension to Dursley, but its traditional shops along the pedestrianised Parsonage St are more than hanging on. This is where you'll find an independent **bakery**, a **butcher** with good cheese and pies, and a florist that doubles as a **greengrocer**. Crisps, sandwiches and drinks can also be bought at Hewitt's, the **newsagent**. A **farmers' market** is held at Market House on the second Saturday of each month (9am to 1pm).

If you've any problems with your **boots**, Dursley Cobblers (☎ 01453-542918; Mon, Tue, Thur & Fri 9am-5pm, Wed & Sat to 4pm), on Parsonage St, may be able to repair them. If the situation has got really bad, salvation may come in the form of **Simply Foot Care** (☎ 07920-018416, 🖥 simplyfootcare.uk; Mon-Tue, Thur & Fri

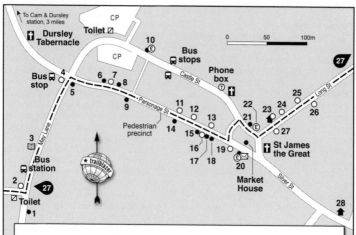

Dursley MAP 27a

Where to stay and eat
2 The Old Spot
4 Della Casa
7 Time Out
11 Hummingbird Café
12 Mezze Restaurant in
   King's Head
13 Dursley & Cam's Kebab &
   Pizza House
16 Belle's Kitchen
19 Bank Café
23 Ye Olde Dursley Hotel
24 Bengal Lounge
25 Dil Raj
26 Golden Wall
27 La Toscana
28 Ormond House
   (The Garden Flat)

Other
1 May Lane Surgery &
   Lloyds Pharmacy
3 Library
5 Co-operative Pharmacy
6 Dursley Cobblers
8 Bakery
9 Butcher
10 Sainsbury's & ATM
14 Simply Foot Care
15 Greengrocer
17 Boots
18 Hewitt's (newsagent)
20 Dursley Local Store, PO & ATM
21 Heritage Centre
22 Lloyds Bank & ATM

9am-4pm, Sat to 1pm), which can deal with corns, calluses, toenail trimming – or simply sell you a pair of orthopaedic slippers.

Although there's a branch of Lloyds **pharmacy** attached to May Lane surgery almost right on the trail, more central are two other chemists – Boots (Mon-Sat 9am-5.30pm) and the Co-op (Mon-Fri 9am-5.30pm, Sat to 5pm) – along Parsonage St.

Where to stay

There's a shortage of **B&B** accommodation in Dursley.

Well recommended is *The Garden Flat* (☎ 01453-545312; 1T; ✆; WI-FI; Marend Oct), a self-contained annexe of **Ormond House**, at 13 Silver St. Large, light and airy, with its own kitchen and bathroom, it looks over a pretty garden and costs from £40pp (sgl occ £42.50) for B&B; the fridge is stocked with basic ingredients so that guests can cook their own breakfast.

Back in town, *Ye Olde Dursley Hotel* (☎ 01453-542821, ☐ yeoldedursley@out look.com; 2S/1D/4T/1Tr, five en suite rest shared facilities; ✆; WI-FI; ⚓ bar only), on Long St, is a friendly place. The public areas are rather shabby but the rooms are fine and it's cheap, particularly for single occupancy: you'll pay £30pp for B&B, regardless of room size and number of people sharing (£25pp if you forego breakfast). The downside is that the rooms are above a busy bar, with a nightclub operating in the latter half of the week.

Where to eat and drink

Arguably one of the best reasons for stopping in Dursley is to pay a visit to *The Old Spot* (☎ 01453-542870, ☐ oldspotinn.co .uk; food Mon-Sat noon-3pm, Sun noon-4pm). Regularly featured among the top CAMRA awards, it is a stronghold among ale drinkers (see box on p23), such that food is normally served only during the day – albeit with the occasional gourmet evening. That's a shame, but don't let it put you off; they can rustle up some good platters or cheeseboards for sharing (both £12), and their Sunday roast is so popular that it runs to two sittings (noon and 2.15pm).

At *Ye Olde Dursley Hotel* (see Where to stay; food Mon-Sat 10am-9pm, Sun 11am-5pm but hours do vary depending on demand) you're looking at standard pub fare; there's also a beer garden and a games room here.

Mezze Restaurant (☎ 01453-519170, ☐ mezzerestaurants.com/dursley; food Tue-Sat 10am-10pm, Sun to 4pm) is housed in the old King's Head pub. The food offers a fantastic range of mezze (£5.50 each). There's also a few standard pub mains (from £10.95 for a cheese burger) and, up to 5pm, they offer a range of delicious and excellent-value stews (£7.95) with fries, mash or rice. A little further down, *Belle's Kitchen* (☎ 01453-549962, ☐ belleskitchendursley .co.uk/WP; Mon-Wed 9am-5pm, Thur-Sat 9am-9pm; WI-FI) is a friendly place serving food throughout the day, including a great fish-finger sandwich at lunch (£6.95).

Heading to the Mediterranean, *Della Casa* (☎ 01453-549679, ☐ dellacasa.co.uk; Mon-Fri noon-3pm & 5-10pm, Sat noon-10.30pm, Sun noon-9.30pm), on Parsonage St, is cool and classy. It focuses on Italian cuisine, from pizzas and risotto to an Italian version of steak & chips (£16.75).

For breakfast, lunch or a cup of tea during the day, the choice has burgeoned in recent years. Near Market House, try *Bank Café* (☎ 01453-543920, ☐ bankcafe.uk; ⚓; Mon-Sat 9am-5pm, Sun 10am-4pm), where squashy sofas meet functional chairs and tables in a big old banking hall. Despite being the smartest place in town, it's also one of the few that allows dogs.

The pedestrianised section of Parsonage St also boasts *Hummingbird* (☎ 01453-299276, ☐ hummingbird-cafe.co .uk; Mon, Tue & Thur 8.30am-3.30pm, Wed 9am-3.30pm, Fri & Sat 8.30am-4.30pm; WI-FI), their breakfast, tea and scones offset by Caribbean specialities such as curried goat, rice & peas for £7.65.

Next to the bakery is *Time Out* (mob ☎ 07986-505424; Mon-Sat 8.30am-3pm; WI-FI), where the emphasis is not surprisingly on fresh bread, cakes and pies, as well as light meals.

Indian cuisine is represented by two restaurants on Long St: *Bengal Lounge*

ROUTE GUIDE AND MAPS

(☎ 01453-519711/2, 🖥 bengalloungedurs ley.co.uk; Sun-Thur 5.30-11pm, Fri, Sat & bank hols to 11.30pm) and *Dil Raj* (☎ 01453-543472, 🖥 dilraj.co; daily noon-2pm, Sun-Thur 5.30-11.30pm, Fri & Sat to midnight). On the same street is *La Toscana* (☎ 01453-543999; Mon-Thur 5-11pm, Fri & Sat noon-2pm & 5-11pm, Sun noon-9pm), an Italian with a fine line in

risottos (£11.95-14.95). Otherwise you'll be looking at a takeaway, perhaps from the Chinese *Golden Wall* (🖥 goldenwalldurs ley.co.uk, Sun, Tue-Thur & bank hol Mon 5-10.30pm, Fri & Sat to 10.45pm), also on Long St, or *Dursley & Cam's Kebab and Pizza House* (daily 3pm-midnight) at 57 Parsonage St.

DURSLEY TO WOTTON-UNDER-EDGE   MAPS 27-30

The Cotswold Way offers another choice at this stage. The **longer (scenic) route**, a 6¾-mile (11km, 3¼-3¾hrs) stretch, climbs steeply from Dursley and circumnavigates Stinchcombe Hill – and the golf course – before coming almost full circle. The **more direct route** (just 4½ miles/7.2km, 2¼-2¾hrs) cuts straight across what looks on the map like the stem of a leaf. Which you choose should depend on time and the weather.

On a clear day, the views from **Stinchcombe Hill** (Map 28) more than justify the detour, but if you're lumbered with English weather at its worst, going straight across may be the better option. Either way, you'll have the opportunity to climb the **Tyndale Monument** (Map 29), perhaps to see those views from on high.

NORTH NIBLEY   [MAP 29, p143]

The demise of the shop-cum-post office has rather ripped the heart of North Nibley, at least as far as trekkers are concerned. That said, the village does still boast a couple of facilities of interest to trekkers, including a campsite. It's one of the few where campers don't have to trudge far for the night, as there's a campsite at *Nibley House* (☎ 01453-543108, 🖥 nibleyhouse.co.uk), just a few yards off the trail. It's a working farm, where **campers** (WI-FI; ℄; 🐾) pay £10pp, with an outside toilet and shower, and plenty of space to explore. For £9 a head, they'll even make your breakfast. Those with delusions of grandeur might prefer to lord it over the campers in the Georgian manor house itself, a family home set in extensive flower gardens: the rooms (1T private facilities, 1D or T/1Qd, both en suite; WI-FI; ℄; 🐾) are large and cost £45–55pp (sgl occ £75-85) for **B&B**.

The village pub, *Black Horse Inn* (☎ 01453-543777, 🖥 blackhorse-northnibley .co.uk; 2D/1T/1Qd, all en suite; WI-FI; ℄;

🐾), Barrs Lane, is right on the Cotswold Way and offers room-only rates for £27.50-37.50pp (sgl occ room rate). Breakfast is extra and costs £7.50pp for a full English but there are other options. There is also a restaurant and bar; the menu (**food** Mon-Fri noon-2.30pm & 6-9pm, Sat noon-3.30pm & 6-9pm, Sun noon-4pm) includes standard pub fare (dinner mains from £11.95) with some vegetarian options.

After the steep climb through the woods from North Nibley, the additional ascent of the stone **Tyndale Monument** (entry £1) on Nibley Knoll may seem 121 steps too far. It's worth it, though, for some splendid views in every direction. The monument was erected in 1866 to the memory of Sir William Tyndale, who in defiance of the authorities translated the New Testament into English. He was burnt at the stake for heresy in 1536.

Stagecoach's No 60 **bus** service (see pp48-50) stops near the pub.

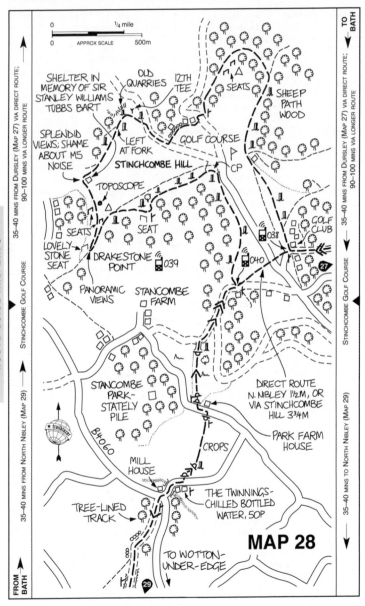

0   ¼ mile
APPROX SCALE   500m

SHELTER IN MEMORY OF SIR STANLEY WILLIAMS TUBBS BART

OLD QUARRIES

12TH TEE

SEATS

SHEEP PATH WOOD

SPLENDID VIEWS; SHAME ABOUT M5 NOISE

LEFT AT FORK

GOLF COURSE

STINCHCOMBE HILL

CP

TOPOSCOPE

SEATS

SEAT

GOLF CLUB

LOVELY STONE SEAT

DRAKESTONE POINT 📱 039

📱 038

📱 040

27

PANORAMIC VIEWS

STANCOMBE FARM

STANCOMBE PARK-STATELY PILE

B4060

DIRECT ROUTE N. NIBLEY 1½M, OR VIA STINCHCOMBE HILL 3¾M

PARK FARM HOUSE

CROPS

MILL HOUSE

THE TWINNINGS-CHILLED BOTTLED WATER, 50P

TREE-LINED TRACK

★ trailblazer

MAP 28

TO WOTTON-UNDER-EDGE

29

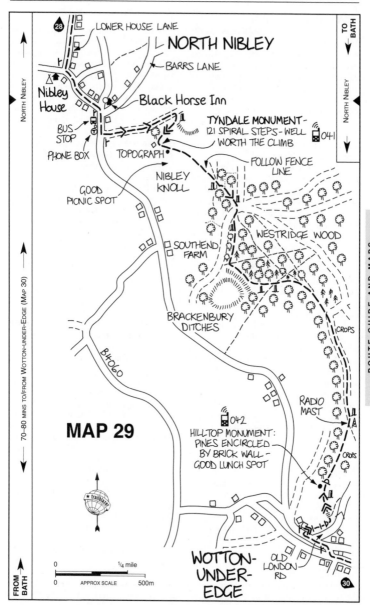

28

LOWER HOUSE LANE

NORTH NIBLEY

BARRS LANE

TO BATH

NORTH NIBLEY

NORTH NIBLEY

Nibley House

Black Horse Inn

BUS STOP

PHONE BOX

TYNDALE MONUMENT—
121 SPIRAL STEPS—WELL
WORTH THE CLIMB

041

TOPOGRAPH

FOLLOW FENCE LINE

NIBLEY KNOLL

GOOD PICNIC SPOT

WESTRIDGE WOOD

SOUTHEND FARM

BRACKENBURY DITCHES

CROPS

B4060

MAP 29

042

HILLTOP MONUMENT:
PINES ENCIRCLED
BY BRICK WALL—
GOOD LUNCH SPOT

RADIO MAST

CROPS

70–80 MINS TO/FROM WOTTON-UNDER-EDGE (MAP 30)

FROM BATH

★ trailblaze

0   ¼ mile

0   APPROX SCALE   500m

WOTTON-
UNDER-
EDGE

OLD LONDON RD

30

ROUTE GUIDE AND MAPS

WOTTON-UNDER-EDGE
[MAP 30a, p147]

It's a friendly place, Wotton-under-Edge, and very community spirited. Almost everything happens on the appropriately named Long St, which morphs from the High St, extending downhill the length of the town. The Cotswold Way runs along this street, passing most of the shops and many pubs and cafés. The trail also takes you past some **almshouses** on Church St and near some on Culverhay; there are also almshouses on Tabernacle Pitch.

The trail continues past the 13th-century parish church of **St Mary the Virgin** before rejoining open countryside. More visible than any of these from above the town is the former **Tabernacle Church**, now an auction room.

East of the town, the Cotswold Way passes through the grounds of **Newark Park** (Map 30; ☎ 01453-842644, 🖳 national trust.org.uk; Mar-Oct Wed-Mon 11am-5pm; Feb Wed-Mon 11am-4pm, Mar-Oct to 5pm, Nov & Dec Sat & Sun only 11am-4pm; £8.60; garden only £6.20), with almost direct footpath access from the trail. Built as a Tudor hunting lodge, it has commanding views to the south-west from its ridge-top location. Following a chequered history, during which it was converted to a fashionable house, it was finally abandoned during the war years and was given to the National Trust in 1949. Since then, both house and garden have been restored and the place is once again inhabited, with an eclectic collection of art on view to the public.

See box on p15 for details of Wotton's Arts Festival.

Transport
Stagecoach's No 60, 84 & No 85 **bus** services call here as do Cotswold Green's No 40 and the No 626 operated by Euro Taxis; see pp48-50.

For **taxis**, try AK Taxis (☎ 01453-842673, or Coombe Valley Taxis (☎ 01453-845071).

Services
For **tourist information**, find your way to the **Heritage Centre** (☎ 01453-521541, 🖳

wottonheritage.com; Apr-end Oct Sun-Tue, Thur & Fri 10.30am-4pm, Sat 10am-3pm, Nov-end Mar Mon-Tue & Thur-Fri 10.30am-3pm, Sat 10am-2pm), on the corner of Market St and The Chipping. Run entirely by volunteers, it has good displays relating to the town's history as well as offering all the normal information services. A range of leaflets and tourist information is also available from the council's **One Stop Shop** (🖳 wotton-under-edge .com/one-stop-shop; Mon-Fri 9am-12.30pm) on the corner of Bradley and Bear streets.

The only bank in town these days is Lloyds, on Long St, which has an **ATM**, as does the Co-op **supermarket** (Mon-Sat 7am-10pm, Sun 10am-4pm), which also now houses the local **post office** (Mon-Fri 8am-6pm, Sat 8am-2pm). A few steps further down the road is a second supermarket, Tesco Express (daily 7am-10pm). More personal than either of these are the excellent Relish **Deli** (with paninis, salads, pizza and pies for lunch on the way – and space to eat in) and Parson's **bakery**, with a second bakery – Walkers – further down the road. A **farmers' market** (Feb-Dec first Sat of month 9am-1pm) in the Town Hall on Market St. Teas (summer Sun 2-5pm) are also served in the town hall; each week they are run by a different charity.

For **waterproofs** and other outdoor clothing, make your way to WH Thomas & Son (closed Wed & Sun), at the bottom of Long St; 'gentleman's outfitters' since 1896, they also have women's sizes. The **pharmacy**, a branch of Lloyds (Mon-Fri 8.30am-6.30pm, Sat 9am-5pm), is here, too, with two **medical surgeries** relatively close by: Chipping Surgery (☎ 01453-842214, 🖳 thechippingsurgery.co.uk; Mon-Fri 8am-6.30pm), on Symn Lane, and Culverhay (☎ 01453-843893, 🖳 culverhay surgery.com; Mon 8am-8pm, Tue-Fri 8am-6pm), on Culverhay.

The town scores on the entertainment stakes, run at least in part by volunteers. Electric Picture House **cinema** (☎ 01453-844601, 🖳 wottoncinema.com), on Market St, has several screenings a week. Close to

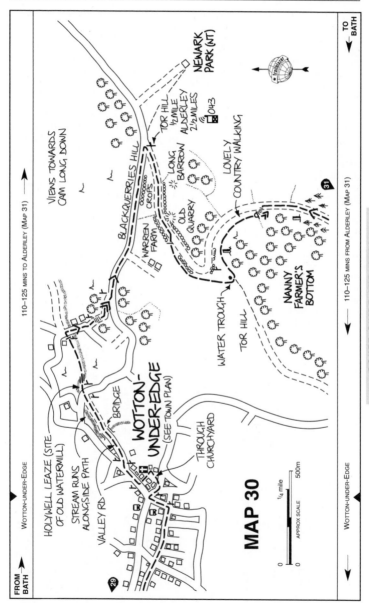

MAP 30

FROM BATH ▶ WOTTON-UNDER-EDGE

110–125 MINS TO ALDERLEY (MAP 31) ➞

VIEWS TOWARDS CAM LONG DOWN

TO BATH

NEWARK PARK (NT)

TOR HILL ALDERLEY 2½ MILES

LONG BARROW

LOVELY COUNTRY WALKING

BLACKQUERRIES HILL

WARREN FARM CROFTS

OLD QUARRY

WATER TROUGH

TOR HILL

NANNY FARMER'S BOTTOM

HOLYWELL LEAZE (SITE OF OLD WATERMILL)

STREAM RUNS ALONGSIDE PATH

VALLEY RD

BRIDGE

WOTTON-UNDER-EDGE (SEE TOWN PLAN)

THROUGH CHURCHYARD

¼ mile

500m

APPROX SCALE

WOTTON-UNDER-EDGE

110–125 MINS FROM ALDERLEY (MAP 31)

WOTTON-UNDER-EDGE

ROUTE GUIDE AND MAPS

the car park, **Under the Edge Arts** (🖥 utea
.org.uk), a community venture in Chipping
Hall, hosts regular displays and a pro-
gramme of events throughout the year.
There's even a week-long Arts Festival (see
box p15) at the end of April/early May.

For a reviving dip at the end of a day's
walking, check out the open-air **swimming
pool** (☎ 01453-842086, 🖥 wottonpool.co
.uk; end Apr-mid Sep, Mon-Fri 3.30-5pm &
6.30-8pm, Sat/Sun 2-4pm; times slightly different in school holidays), on Symn Lane.

Where to stay

Accommodation options in Wotton have
diminished in recent years, but there's still
a good hotel and two B&Bs.

Both B&Bs are on Merlin Haven,
reached along a footpath to the west of the
swimming pool, or by following Westfields
into Dryleaze, then turning left and left
again into Merlin Haven.

Number Eleven (☎ 01453-843576, or
☎ 07966 729741, 🖥 g.ellis.bankside
@gmail.com; 1S/1T both with private facilities; WI-FI; mid Mar to end Oct), at No 11,
charges from £40pp (sgl occ £55) for B&B;
they use the eggs from the hens at the bot-

tom of the garden and smoked salmon and
avocado can be served as an alternative if
requested. *Hawks View* (☎ 01453-521441,
🖥 maggiecodde@gmail.com; 1D en suite;
WI-FI; (L); Mar-Nov), is also on the left as
you're coming from the town. Here B&B
costs from £32.50pp (sgl occ room rate)
and, subject to prior arrangement, there's an
evening meal option around £10pp.

Back in town, the helpful and welcoming *Swan Hotel* (☎ 01453-843004, 🖥 swan
hotelwotton.com; 4D/5D or T/3Tr/1Qd, all
en suite; 🛏; WI-FI; (L); 🐾), on Market St,
has attractive rooms. B&B rates are £47.50-
62.50pp (sgl occ £85-115).

Another option, on Chase Lane in
Wickwar, is *Mounteney's Farmhouse* (☎
07534 701683 or ☎ 01454-294700, 🖥
mounteneysfarmhouse.co.uk; 1D en suite,
1D shared bathroom; WI-FI; (L)). B&B
costs £42.50-47.50pp (sgl occ rates on
request). Since they are out of town and
about eight minutes by car from the
Cotswold Way, if arranged in advance they
are happy to provide a pick up/drop off
service for walkers. Evening meals are
available at the pub in the village.

WOTTON-UNDER-EDGE

Where to stay
1 Hawks View
2 Number Eleven
11 Swan Hotel

Where to eat and drink
4 Royal Oak Inn
6 Bunter's Café
7 Wotton British
  Takeaway
8 Pizza Planet
9 The Star Inn
10 Reg's Kebab,
  Chicken
  & Pizza
11 Swan Hotel
15 Singing Teapot
16 The Ark Coffee
  Shop
19 The Wotton Coffee
  Shop
22 The Edge Coffee
  Shop
28 The Falcon
  Steakhouse
29 Hong Kong Kitchen
30 India Palace

Other
3 Chipping Surgery
5 One Stop Shop
12 Cinema (Electric
  Picture
  House)
13 Heritage Centre &
  Tourist Information
14 Under the Edge Arts
17 Lloyds Pharmacy
18 Parson's Bakery
20 Lloyds & ATM
21 Walkers Bakery
23 Co-op, post office &
  ATM
24 Relish Deli
25 Tesco Express
26 Cotswold Book Room
27 WH Thomas & Son
31 Culverhay Surgery

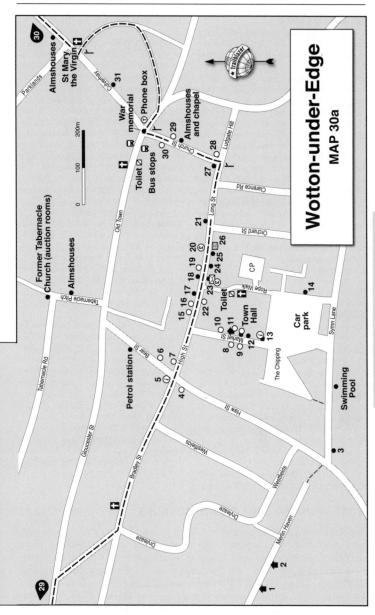

Wotton-under-Edge
MAP 30a

St Mary, the Virgin
Almshouses
Parklands
Culverhay
31
War memorial
Phone box
Almshouses and chapel
29
30
Church St
28
Ludgate Hill
27
Clarence Rd
Toilet
Bus stops
Old Town
Former Tabernacle Church (auction rooms)
Almshouses
Tabernacle Pitch
21
Long St
Orchard St
Tabernacle Rd
Gloucester St
18 19 20
15 16 17
22 23 24 25 26
CP
Rope Walk
14
10
11
Market St
Town Hall
12 13
8 9
6
7
Bear St
High St
5
4
The Chipping
Car park
Symn Lane
Swimming Pool
3
Haw St
Westfields
Bradley St
Westfields
Dyrleaze
Merlin Haven
Dyrleaze
2
1
29
30

0 100 200m

Where to eat and drink

Cafés and takeaways dominate the foody outlets in Wotton-under-Edge, but there are some good **pubs** too. Of these, *The Star Inn* (☎ 01453-844651, 🖥 starinnwotton.co .uk; food daily noon-2pm; WI-FI; 🐾) offers a daily homemade special alongside the normal (and very cheap) pub basics, with mains no more than £5.95 and baguettes £3.50).
Walkers (mud and all) are very welcome here and, outside of their food-serving hours, you can bring in food from outside.

At *Royal Oak Inn* (☎ 01453-844366, 🖥 www.theroyaloakwotton.com; food Mon-Sat noon-2.30pm & 6-9pm, Sun noon-3pm; WI-FI; 🐾 bar area only), on Haw St, you can eat inside or in their large garden. Their 'lunchtime ' menu (Mon-Sat), includes sandwiches and other pub standards, while a second, 'main' menu boasts dishes such as pan-fried calves liver with crispy pancetta and a blackcurrant & rosemary jus (£11.95).

Rather smarter is *Swan Hotel* (see Where to stay; food Mon-Fri noon-3pm, Mon-Thur 5-9pm, Fri 5-9.30pm, Sat noon-9.30pm, Sun noon-8pm) – 'no muddy boots', please – whose extensive menus include a range of British tapas (3 dishes for £12), 'gourmet' burgers from £10, as well as more formal dining.

Right at the bottom of Long St, on the corner of Church St, *The Falcon Steakhouse* (☎ 01453-521894, 🖥 falcon steakhouse.com; daily noon-9pm) is a very popular venture, run by a local farm, so it is worth booking. Their menu is heavy with meat from their own farm, such as an 7oz sirloin steak (£23) all the way up to a 50oz version for £60.95 (Wed only)!

Away from the pubs, Long St will serve you well, with breakfast, light lunches

and tea served in various styles. Relatively modern is *The Edge Coffee Shop* (☎ 01453-844108; Mon-Sat 9am-5pm; WI-FI; 🐾), whose offerings include a range of sandwiches (£4.75 up to £6.75 for the fish-finger sandwich), pancakes (£4.50) and a decent take on the Full English (£8).

On the other side of the road, several smaller places vie for your custom. The tiny *Singing Teapot* (☎ 07769-267455; Tue-Sat 9.30am-4pm; no WI-FI; 🐾) offers tea, cakes and light lunches in a genuinely welcoming environment. Close by is *The Ark Coffee Shop* (☎ 01453-521838; Mon-Fri 9am-noon & 2-4.30pm, Sat 9.30am-12.30pm; no WI-FI), where a team of Christian volunteers serves up coffee and cakes.

And a few doors further down is *The Wotton Coffee Shop* (☎ 01453-520448; Mon-Sat 9am-5pm; WI-FI) with plenty of choice on the menu and there's a lovely 16th-century garden in which to eat.

If you're tempted by a cooked breakfast, try *Bunter's Café* (Mon-Fri 7.30am-2pm, Sat 9am-noon), just off Long St, where the full English will set you back just £5.95.

Ethnic cuisine comes from *India Palace* (🖥 theindiapalace.co.uk; Sun-Thur 5.30-11.30pm, Fri & Sat to midnight), Church St, which has a restaurant as well as a takeaway service, and the nearby *Hong Kong Kitchen* (Tue-Sun 5-10pm), which also serves fish & chips, but is takeaway only. There's also *Wotton British Takeaway* (Mon-Sat 11.30am-2pm & 5-10pm), on High St, for fish, chicken and pies, or perhaps *Pizza Planet* (Mon-Sat 4.30-11pm, Sun to 10.30pm), on Market St. *Reg's Kebab, Chicken & Pizza* (Sun-Thur 3-11pm, Fri-Sat 3pm-midnight) is also here.

WOTTON-UNDER-EDGE TO OLD SODBURY   MAPS 30-35

This **12¼-mile (19.7km)** section will take about **6-6¾ hours**, passing through open, rolling fields, interspersed with the occasional tract of woodland, and a number of small villages with attractive stone churches. Of these, one of the most intriguing, primarily for its cubed yews, is St Mary the Virgin at Hawkesbury (Map 33), but it's a long downhill detour off the Cotswold Way. Similarly, tantalising glimpses through the trees of **Horton Court** (Map 34)

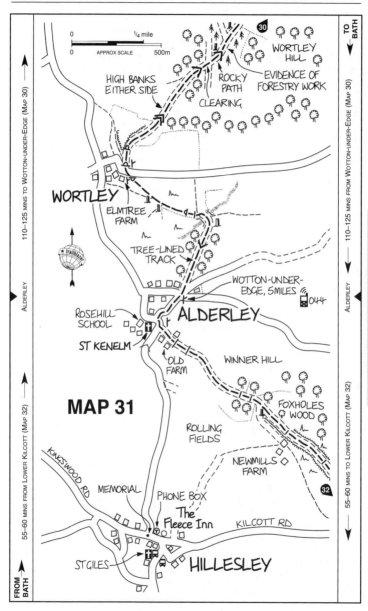

TO BATH

FROM BATH

110–125 MINS TO WOTTON-UNDER-EDGE (MAP 30)

ALDERLEY

55–60 MINS FROM LOWER KILCOTT (MAP 32)

110–125 MINS FROM WOTTON-UNDER-EDGE (MAP 30)

ALDERLEY

55–60 MINS TO LOWER KILCOTT (MAP 32)

¼ mile

0

0   500m

APPROX SCALE

30

WORTLEY HILL

EVIDENCE OF FORESTRY WORK

ROCKY PATH

CLEARING

HIGH BANKS EITHER SIDE

trailblazer

WORTLEY

ELMTREE FARM

TREE-LINED TRACK

WOTTON-UNDER-EDGE, 5 MILES

044

ALDERLEY

ROSEHILL SCHOOL

ST KENELM

OLD FARM

WINNER HILL

FOXHOLES WOOD

MAP 31

ROLLING FIELDS

NEWMILLS FARM

32

KINGSWOOD RD

MEMORIAL

PHONE BOX

The Fleece Inn

KILCOTT RD

ST GILES

HILLESLEY

might tempt the walker to tackle the very steep path down for closer inspection but see p152 before contemplating this; most will be happy to stick to the trail and the lovely drovers' road south of Hawkesbury. If the walk lacks drama, it certainly makes up for it in nomenclature: who could resist the appeal of a dip that glories in the name of **Nanny Farmer's Bottom** (Map 30)? And if you find yourself tiring, there's always the prospect of a sandwich or dinner at the Dog Inn in Old Sodbury to act as a spur.

ALDERLEY [MAP 31, p149]

There's an air of exclusivity about Alderley, from the timeless solidity of the **Church of St Kenelm** to the old stone houses which are surrounded by well-maintained gardens. Stagecoach's No 84 and 85 **buses** (see pp48-50) stop by the church.

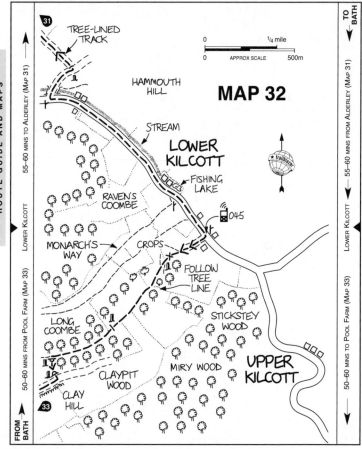

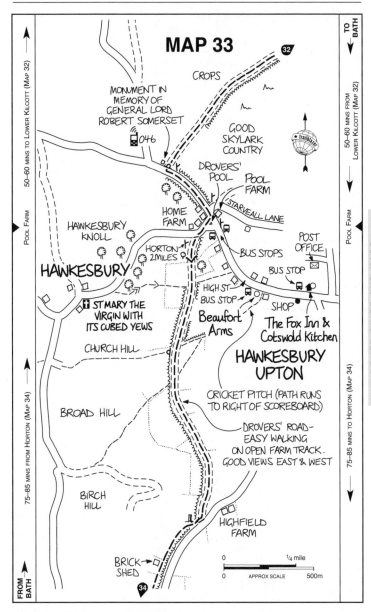

MAP 33

32

TO BATH

CROPS

MONUMENT IN MEMORY OF GENERAL LORD ROBERT SOMERSET

046

GOOD SKYLARK COUNTRY

trailblazer

DROVERS' POOL

POOL FARM

STARVEALL LANE

HOME FARM

HAWKESBURY KNOLL

POST OFFICE

BUS STOPS

HORTON 2 MILES

BUS STOP

HAWKESBURY

HIGH ST BUS STOP

SHOP

ST MARY THE VIRGIN WITH ITS CUBED YEWS

Beaufort Arms

The Fox Inn & Cotswold Kitchen

HAWKESBURY UPTON

CHURCH HILL

CRICKET PITCH (PATH RUNS TO RIGHT OF SCOREBOARD)

BROAD HILL

DROVERS' ROAD - EASY WALKING ON OPEN FARM TRACK. GOOD VIEWS EAST & WEST

BIRCH HILL

HIGHFIELD FARM

BRICK SHED

34

0   1/4 mile
0   APPROX SCALE   500m

50–60 MINS TO LOWER KILCOTT (MAP 32)

POOL FARM

75–85 MINS FROM HORTON (MAP 34)

FROM BATH

TO BATH

50–60 MINS FROM LOWER KILCOTT (MAP 32)

POOL FARM

75–85 MINS TO HORTON (MAP 34)

ROUTE GUIDE AND MAPS

HILLESLEY [MAP 31, p149]

Little more than a cluster of individual stone cottages with a church and a pub, Hillesley is another attractive village around half a mile (1km) from the trail.

The local watering hole, *The Fleece Inn* (☎ 01453-520003, 🖳 thefleeceinn hillesley.com; **food** Wed-Sat noon-2.30pm & 6-9pm, Sun noon-4pm; WI-FI; 🐾 bar only), is a haven for those who love their real ales (it was CAMRA's regional pub of the year for 2018). Saturday night is steak night here, with a rump steak just £10 and even a rib-eye just £14.95. The pub is open Monday and Tuesday but only from 4.30pm.

Stagecoach's No 84 and 85 **buses** (see pp48-50) stop by the Church of St Giles.

HAWKESBURY UPTON [MAP 33, p151]

Is there no end to the attractive villages in this area? The heart of this one lies about quarter of a mile (0.4km) off the Cotswold Way, but with a pleasant B&B pretty close and a range of other facilities, it has plenty to offer the walker.

Beaufort Arms (☎ 01454-238217, 🖳 beaufortarms.com; food daily noon-2.30pm & 6.30-9.30pm; WI-FI; 🐾 bar only) is very much a village hub, with plenty of real ales and scarcely a nod to the 21st century. Their 'five-fifty favourites' menu includes eight pub classics such as chilli con carne and faggots, peas & chips all wonderfully priced at, you've guessed it, £5.50; though even on their regular menu there's only one item, the lamb shank (£12.75), that breaks the £10 barrier.

At the far end of the village, about half a mile (0.8km) from the trail, *The Fox Inn* (☎ 01454-238558, 🖳 thefoxinnhawkesbury .co.uk; 2D/2Tr, all en suite; ●; WI-FI; ⓛ; 🐾 bar area only) has attractive rooms from £40pp (sgl occ £60) but the rate does not include breakfast which must be ordered separately (£8pp for the full English). Part of the same establishment is *Cotswold Kitchen* (food Tue-Sat noon-3pm & 5-9pm, Sun noon-4pm), which specialises in pizzas as well as delicious mains – from £12.95 for the halloumi kebab up to £19.95 for the surf & turf option. Guests staying at the Fox Inn can have an evening meal even though the kitchen is officially closed.

Also up this way is the excellent village **shop** (Mon-Sat 8am-6pm, Sun 8am-12.30pm), with all the basics, filled rolls made to order, and a good range of pastries. The **post office** (Mon, Tue & Thur-Sat 9am-1pm, Wed to noon) is located a short way beyond the pub.

Stagecoach's No 84 and 85 **buses** (see pp48-50) stop in the village.

HORTON [MAP 34]

While the village of Horton is on the Cotswold Way, most walkers will bypass its main attraction, the National Trust property of **Horton Court** (🖳 nationaltrust.org.uk; £5), which lies at the bottom of a steep footpath off the Cotswold Way (or you could walk back along the road from the village school). It's a rather grand name for the seemingly modest but picturesque property that sits in a cottage-style garden close to the **church of St James the Elder**. At its heart is a 12th-century Norman hall, all that remains of what may be the oldest rectory in England. Other parts of the building date to Tudor times, with significant expansion and the addition of an Italianate loggia during the 16th century, and further changes in the 1920s. Though the main house is closed to visitors, the hall, Tudor Ambulatory and parts of the garden are open to the public; however, due to limited parking space you'll need to book in advance if you wish to visit and the opening times are rather limited (late July to end Sep Wed & Sat 2-5pm only).

Stagecoach's No 84 and 85 **buses** (see pp48-50) stop in the village.

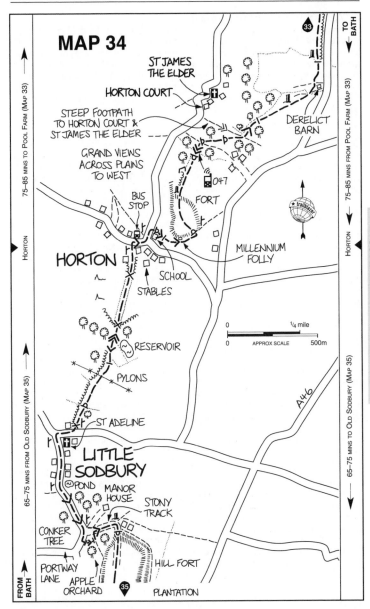

LITTLE SODBURY   [MAP 34, p153]

This pretty village is set apart by the hill-top **church of St Adeline**, offering a perfect vantage point from which to survey the landscape unrolling ahead. The churchyard is a fine place to rest your feet for a few minutes.

There are no facilities right in the village but three-quarters of a mile (1.25km)

west along Portway Lane (Map 34, p153) is *Cotswold Meadow Camping* (☎ 07789 081899, 🖳 cotswoldmeadowcamping.co.uk; 🐾 on leads) which opened recently. They charge £10 for one adult and a tent and also have ready-erected Lotus Belle tents for glampers: £50/85 for 2/4-berth. There are fire pits, toilets and showers.

OLD SODBURY   [MAP 35]

The trail passes through the grounds of the beautiful **St John the Baptist Church**, up on the hill, before dropping down to the village itself. In the shadow of its larger neighbour to the west, Chipping Sodbury, the village nevertheless has a lot to recommend it to the walker. Badminton Horse Trials (see box p15) in early May is likely to make accommodation hard to find.

Coachstyle's No 41 and Stagecoach Nos 84, 85 & 620 **buses** (see pp48-50 for details) stop opposite the Dog Inn. For a **taxi** try Grab-a-Cab (☎ 01454-313883, 🖳 grab-a-cab-online.co.uk) which is based in Chipping Sodbury.

In the centre of the village, and right on the trail, the popular *Dog Inn* (☎ 01454-312006, 🖳 the-dog-inn.co.uk; 3D or T/1Tr, all en suite; 🛏; WI-FI; Ⓛ; 🐾) offers a welcome respite. **B&B** costs from £42.50pp (sgl occ £60). In the bar, real ales (including Sharp's Doom Bar; see box on p23) and an extensive menu (**food** Mon-Fri noon-2.30pm & 6-9pm, Sat noon-9pm, Sun to 8pm) are the order of the day. No one will go hungry with a good choice of curries as well as steaks, plenty of fresh fish, pasta and jacket potatoes, and there are varied vegetarian, vegan and gluten-free options as well.

Right across the road, so convenient for both pub and path, *Rock Cottage* (☎ 01454-314688, 🖳 rock-cottage-old-sodbury-bed-and-breakfast .co.uk; 2D/1Tr, all en suite; 🛏; WI-FI; Ⓛ; 🐾) has some lovely rooms, a guests' sitting room as well as a pleasant garden that you can enjoy on a sunny day. Rates (from £35pp, sgl occ £55) are fair.

Some 300m from the trail is the upmarket *Sodbury House* (☎ 01454-312847, 🖳 sodburyhouse.co.uk; 3S/1D/3D or T, all en suite; 🛏; WI-FI; Ⓛ), which offers B&B from £48pp (sgl £64, sgl occ £68). In the evening, most guests gravitate towards The Dog Inn for dinner or – in the other direction – The Bell.

Another option is *Courtlands Farm* (☎ 01454-316366, 🖳 me.thebarn@yahoo .com; 2D/1T shared bathroom; 🛏; WI-FI; Ⓛ; 🐾) about a mile off the trail. Run by the former owners of a B&B in Little Sodbury, which you will have walked past on your way into the village, this B&B may not be the most convenient for the trail but it's flat, easy walking to the property and they do offer lifts to the pub in the evening (though you will have to make your own back again afterwards). Dogs aren't allowed in the rooms but can sleep in the stables. Rates are from £45pp (£55 sgl occ) for B&B.

Rather over half a mile (1km) in the other direction, on the main A46, the 14th-century *Cross Hands Hotel* (☎ 01454-313000, 🖳 oldenglishinns.co.uk; 6S/2T/12D/1Qd, all en suite; 🛏; WI-FI; 🐾) is just by the bus stop. Rates for B&B vary daily and are usually best for online bookings but expect to pay £41.25-56.25pp (sgl £62.50-82.50, sgl occ room rate). They also have a **restaurant** (daily noon-10pm).

Cotswold Service Station (Mon-Fri 6.30am-8pm, Sat 8am-6pm), on the other side of the crossroads, is handy for stocking up on drinks and snacks for your walk.

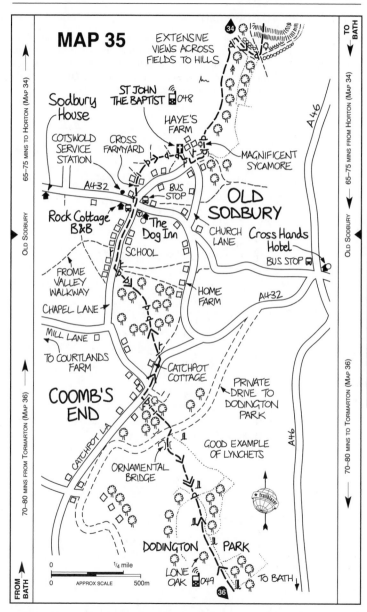

OLD SODBURY TO COLD ASHTON   MAPS 35-39

Despite being divided by the M4, this **8½-mile (13.7km, 4¼-4¾hrs)** part of the walk has much to recommend it. In place of many (but not all!) of the ups and downs further north are broad expanses of farmland, an unexpectedly rewarding walk across **Dodington Park**, and the glimpsed glory of **Dyrham Park** (Map 37; see p158), which most certainly merits a visit.

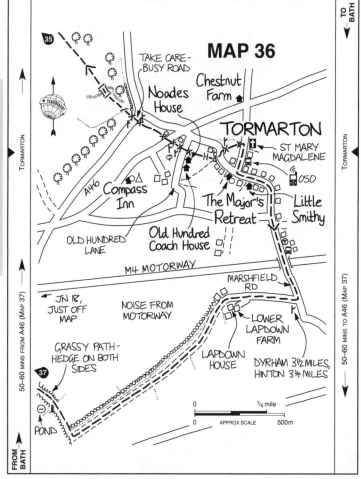

TORMARTON [MAP 36]

In spite of its proximity to the busy M4, the village of Tormarton remains relatively unscathed by noise, or even by the 21st century, so it's an unexpectedly good place to stop for the night. With a welcoming hotel, a pub with rooms, a choice of B&Bs and even a place to camp, there are plenty of options, too.

The village is served by the No 41 **bus**, run by Coachstyle; see pp48-50.

Rather unexpectedly, **campers** (🐾) can pitch a tent at *Compass Inn* (☎ 01454-218242, 🖥 compass-inn.co.uk) in return for a donation to their charity box. There are no outdoor facilities, but they do provide a keycard so you can use the public toilets inside (available 24hrs). The hotel itself is something of a rabbit warren, independently owned but marketed under the Best Western umbrella, and with extensive gardens. It's about 500m from the village, quite close to the motorway and within sight of the A46, so noise is a factor, but it's not too bad. **Rooms** (7T/13D/4Tr/2Qd, all en suite; ☞; WI-FI; (Ⓛ); 🐾) have all the accoutrements of a business hotel, costing £39.75-50pp (sgl occ room rate) though the rates can vary. **Breakfast** (£3.95-12.50) and packed lunches are available for all. Service is friendly and the **food** (Mon-Sat 7am-9pm, Sun 8am-8.30pm), served in the bar, restaurant or garden, is a pleasant surprise; good sandwiches at lunchtime, from £5.95, come with a proper salad.

With the Cotswold Way at the bottom of the garden, *Noades House* (☎ 01454-218278, 🖥 noadesstudio.co.uk; 1T/1D

both en suite, 1T private bathroom; ☞; WI-FI; (Ⓛ); Mar-end Oct), on the quiet Old Hundred Lane, is exceptionally well placed. Rates for B&B are £42.50pp, or £65 for single occupancy.

Right next door, *Old Hundred Coach House* (☎ 01454-218420, 🖥 oldhundred coachhouse.co.uk; 1T, private bathroom; ☞; WI-FI; (Ⓛ); 🐾) charges from £30pp (sgl occ £30) for B&B.

At a stone's throw from the pub is *Little Smithy* (☎ 01454-218412, 🖥 little smithy.com; 1T/1D, both en suite; ☞; WI-FI; (Ⓛ)), where you'll pay from £45pp, or from £65 for single occupancy. Breakfast is eaten in the main house, but the rooms, both self-contained, are in an adjoining cottage, where there's also a lounge that guests can share. They require a minimum two-night stay between November and March.

In the village centre, *The Major's Retreat* (☎ 01454-218263, 🖥 majorsretreat .co.uk; 3T, all en suite) offers B&B in rooms above the pub; they charge from £27.50pp (sgl occ £45). No-nonsense **pub grub** (daily noon-2.30pm & 7-9.30pm) is excellent value, with a wide range of satisfying pub favourites, most of which are less than a tenner. Real ales may include Pig's Ear from the Uley Brewery and Mole Best from Moles Brewery.

Up the road and over the crossroads, the rooms at *Chestnut Farm* (☎ 01454-218563, 🖥 cfbb.co.uk; 1T/3D, all en suite; WI-FI; (Ⓛ); 🐾) are grouped together in a converted barn. You'll pay from £32.50pp (£40 sgl occ).

TOLLDOWN (South of the M4) [MAP 37, p158]

South of Tormarton, on the main A46 about 500 yards from the trail, **B&B** is available at *The Crown* (☎ 01225-891166, 🖥 the-crowntolldown.co.uk; 3D/6D or T, all en suite; ☞; WI-FI; (Ⓛ); 🐾), where rooms are in a separate building behind the pub. B&B generally costs £42.50-60pp, but rates do vary – especially during Badminton Horse Trials.

Their **food** (Mon-Sat noon-3pm & 6-9pm, Sun noon-8pm) is highly regarded and

includes a very good Sunday roast (around £14.95).

On the opposite corner, at **Marshfield Bakery** (☎ 01225-891709; Mon-Fri 9am-5pm), biscuits and cakes are sold alongside sandwiches and pasties to present the perfect packed lunch. Next door, **Fine Cheese Company** (☎ 01225-448748, 🖥 finecheese shops.co.uk) also has a *café* (Mon-Fri 10am-4pm) – the perfect place to pile on all the cholesterol and calories that you've lost along the way.

ROUTE GUIDE AND MAPS

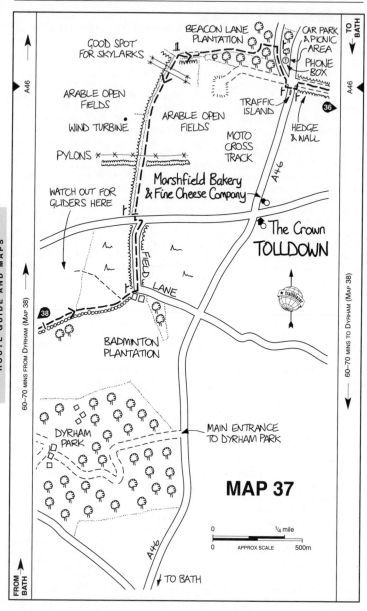

TO BATH

A46

BEACON LANE PLANTATION

CAR PARK & PICNIC AREA

PHONE BOX

GOOD SPOT FOR SKYLARKS

ARABLE OPEN FIELDS

WIND TURBINE

ARABLE OPEN FIELDS

TRAFFIC ISLAND

36

HEDGE & WALL

MOTO CROSS TRACK

PYLONS

WATCH OUT FOR GLIDERS HERE

Morshfield Bakery & Fine Cheese Company

A46

The Crown TOLLDOWN

FIELD LANE

38

trailblazer

BADMINTON PLANTATION

60–70 MINS FROM DYRHAM (MAP 38)

60–70 MINS TO DYRHAM (MAP 38)

DYRHAM PARK

MAIN ENTRANCE TO DYRHAM PARK

MAP 37

0   ¼ mile
0   APPROX SCALE   500m

A46

TO BATH

FROM BATH

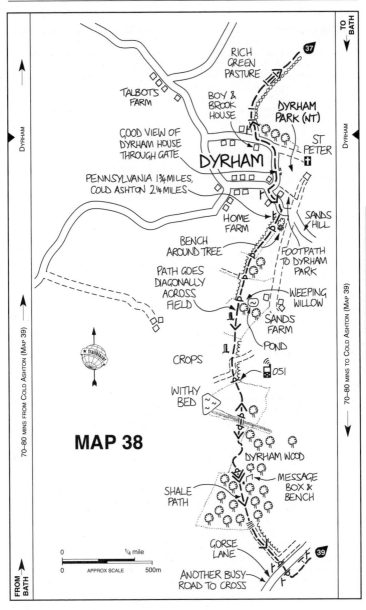

TO BATH

DYRHAM

DYRHAM

ROUTE GUIDE AND MAPS

RICH GREEN PASTURE

37

TALBOT'S FARM

BOY & BROOK HOUSE

DYRHAM PARK (NT)

GOOD VIEW OF DYRHAM HOUSE THROUGH GATE

ST PETER

DYRHAM

PENNSYLVANIA 1¾ MILES, COLD ASHTON 2¼ MILES

SANDS HILL

HOME FARM

BENCH AROUND TREE

FOOTPATH TO DYRHAM PARK

PATH GOES DIAGONALLY ACROSS FIELD

WEEPING WILLOW

SANDS FARM

POND

CROPS

051

70–80 MINS FROM COLD ASHTON (MAP 39)

70–80 MINS TO COLD ASHTON (MAP 39)

★ trailblazer

WITHY BED

MAP 38

DYRHAM WOOD

MESSAGE BOX & BENCH

SHALE PATH

GORSE LANE

0   ¼ mile

0   APPROX SCALE   500m

ANOTHER BUSY ROAD TO CROSS

39

FROM BATH

❏ **Dyrham Park**   **[Map 37, p158 & Map 38, p159]**
As the Cotswold Way wends through the tiny village of Dyrham, it passes the ornamental gates of Dyrham Park (☎ 0117-937 2501, 🖳 nationaltrust.org.uk; park daily
10am-5pm or dusk; garden mid Feb-Dec daily 10am-5pm, Jan-early Feb 10am-4pm;
house Mar-Oct daily 11am-5pm, Nov-Dec 10am-4pm; house, garden & park £12.50,
NT members free), affording a splendid vista up the long drive to the house and
church. If you're not pushed for time it's well worth getting sidetracked.

Familiar to many film buffs as the set location for *Remains of the Day*, the
Baroque-style house nestling at the bottom of a steep valley was built at the end of
the 17th century. A strong Dutch influence pervades the original décor and furnishings, and the Victorian kitchens give an indication of how life must have been for
those below stairs. The church alongside, however, is medieval and the estate itself
dates back to Saxon times. Visitors can explore both the house and the formal gardens as well as 274 acres (110 hectares) of rolling parkland.

PENNSYLVANIA   [MAP 39]
Just off the main A46 at Pennsylvania, yet
still relatively peaceful is *Cornflake
Cottage* (☎ 01225-892592, 🖳 cornflake
cottagebandb.co.uk; 1D/1T; ☞; WI-FI; ⓛ).
Its two rooms share a bathroom, but these
are not normally rented out separately
unless to family or friends travelling
together. The cost for B&B is from £45pp,
or £65-75 for single occupancy.

Virtually next door is *Swan Cottage*
(mobile ☎ 07831-422994, ☎ 01225-891419,
🖳 swancottagebandb.co.uk; 1D/2T, all en

suite; WI-FI; ⓛ) which offers B&B (from
£40pp, sgl occ £60) and also boasts an en
suite **shepherd's hut** (1D or T; ⓛ; 🐾;
from £42.50pp, sgl occ from £60, or £30pp
self-catering) with great views overlooking
the farmland. If requested in advance they
will serve an evening meal (2 courses for
£17).

On the main road itself there's a **petrol
station** (daily 6am-10pm) with a branch of
Londis that sells drinks, sandwiches and
other snacks.

COLD ASHTON
                [MAP 39; MAP 40, p162]
With its location between the busy A420
and the even busier A46, Cold Ashton
might seem to be blighted, but the reality is
entirely different. Most of the village lies
along a quiet lane to the south, beyond the
church, and its cluster of small stone houses stands peacefully against a backdrop of
rolling fields.

When the village pub closed, the
neighbouring *Cold Ashton Café* (Map 39;
mobile ☎ 07939-076324, or ☎ 01225-
891849, 🖳 thecoldashtoncafe@gmail.com;
Tue-Fri 8.30am-2.30pm, Sat & Sun 9am-
2.30pm; 🐾), at **Folly End Farm,** came to
the rescue, offering breakfast, lunch, tea
and home-made cakes. Their opening hours

can vary so check their Facebook page
before going. If booked in advance they
also provide homely evening meals for
those staying at local B&Bs. The café is
licensed and, as an added bonus, they may
drive walkers back to their accommodation after dinner. **Campers** (🐾 only if
very well trained) don't miss out, either;
you can pitch a tent in the field alongside
the sheep, donkeys and emus (!) for free
with access to hot and cold water and an
outside toilet.

About half a mile (1km) south of the
trail to the right of the busy A46,
Whiteways (off Map 39; ☎ 01225-891333,
🖳 whiteways@live.co.uk; 2Qd, both en
suite; WI-FI but may be weak; ⓛ; 🐾) is

surprisingly well insulated from the traffic that thunders past. You'll find two very big and well-equipped rooms in a purpose-built annexe. B&B costs from £45pp (sgl occ £80). Packed lunches must be booked well in advance and guests can benefit from the evening meal option at Folly End Farm (see opposite) if booked in advance.

Sheltered at the bottom of the steep Greenway Lane, *Hill Farm* (Map 40; ☎ 01225-891952, mob ☎ 07870-358627, 🖳 hillfarmbath.com; WI-FI; Ⓛ; Apr-Sep) is a real find. Up to four guests stay either in the **Shepherd's Hut** (1D or T; from £50pp, sgl occ £70), a self-contained traditional wagon on wheels with en suite facilities and a kitchen area, or – rather more con-

ventional – in the **Trough** (1D or T; from £50pp, sgl occ £70), a converted barn with en suite facilities and a private kitchen/dining area. Either way, everything is set up for near-effortless self-catering with the makings for breakfast and – with advance notice – dinner (£15pp for two courses and a glass of wine or beer). Best of all is the stunning view from the terrace, where guests are free to enjoy a drink or dinner.

If you fancy a cup of tea but don't want to leave the trail to get it, the *Special Plant Nursery* (daily 10am-5pm), about 20 minutes after Cold Ashton, serves hot beverages and flapjacks.

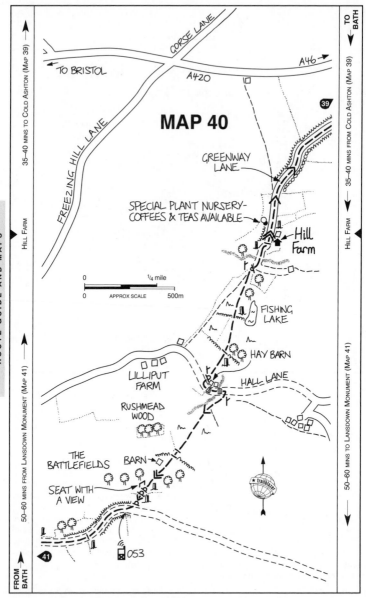

CORSE LANE

TO BRISTOL

A420

A46

MAP 40

39

FREEZING HILL LANE

GREENWAY LANE

SPECIAL PLANT NURSERY-
COFFEES & TEAS AVAILABLE

Hill
Farm

0   ¼ mile

0   APPROX SCALE   500m

FISHING
LAKE

HAY BARN

HALL LANE

LILLIPUT
FARM

RUSHMEAD
WOOD

THE
BATTLEFIELDS

BARN

SEAT WITH
A VIEW

053

trailblazer

35-40 MINS TO COLD ASHTON (MAP 39)

HILL FARM

ROUTE GUIDE AND MAPS

50-60 MINS FROM LANSDOWN MONUMENT (MAP 41)

FROM
BATH

41

35-40 MINS FROM COLD ASHTON (MAP 39)

HILL FARM

50-60 MINS TO LANSDOWN MONUMENT (MAP 41)

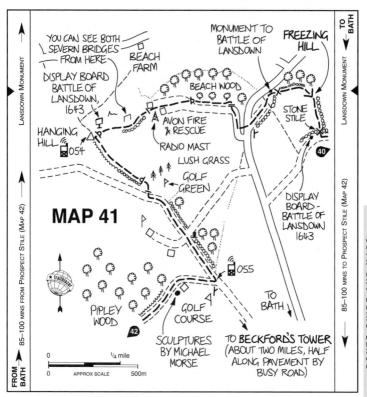

MAP 41

YOU CAN SEE BOTH SEVERN BRIDGES FROM HERE

BEACH FARM

DISPLAY BOARD BATTLE OF LANSDOWN, 1643

MONUMENT TO BATTLE OF LANSDOWN

FREEZING HILL

BEACH WOOD

STONE STILE

HANGING HILL 054

AVON FIRE & RESCUE

RADIO MAST

LUSH GRASS

GOLF GREEN

40

DISPLAY BOARD - BATTLE OF LANSDOWN 1643

055

TO BATH

TRAILBLAZER

PIPLEY WOOD

42

GOLF COURSE

SCULPTURES BY MICHAEL MORSE

TO BECKFORD'S TOWER (ABOUT TWO MILES, HALF ALONG PAVEMENT BY BUSY ROAD)

0   ¼ mile

0   APPROX SCALE   500m

LANSDOWN MONUMENT

85-100 MINS FROM PROSPECT STILE (MAP 42)

FROM BATH

TO BATH

LANSDOWN MONUMENT

85-100 MINS TO PROSPECT STILE (MAP 42)

ROUTE GUIDE AND MAPS

❑ **Battle of Lansdown**   **[Map 40 & Map 41]**
If it were not for the signboards and the monument to Sir Bevil Grenville, the walker on the Cotswold Way might cross the field at the top of **Freezing Hill** (Map 41)
without a second glance. Yet little has changed since the night of 5 July 1643 when
the final stages of the Battle of Lansdown were played out between two almost equally matched armies of the Royalists and the Parliamentarians.

In command of the opposing forces were two friends of long standing: Sir
William Waller in charge of the Parliamentarian defence of Bath against Sir Ralph
Hopton leading a Royalist attack. It was a bloody affair, with 'legs and arms flying
all over the place', during which the Royalist Grenville was mortally wounded, having led the Cornish infantry in the charge up Lansdown Hill. While the battle itself
was indecisive, casualties were severe. The Parliamentarians withdrew under cover
of darkness, and the Royalists were thwarted in their pursuit of capturing Bath and
moving on to the richer prize of Bristol.

❑ **Beckford's Tower**   **[off Map 41, p163]**
Although the Cotswold Way passes a couple of miles to the west of Beckford's Tower
(weekdays ☎ 01225-460705, weekends during opening season ☎ 01225-422212, 🖥
beckfordstower.org.uk; Mar-end Oct Sat, Sun & bank hol Mon 10.30am-5pm; £4.50),
you can't miss its distinctive outline and no trip to Bath would be complete without
a brief nod towards William Beckford (1760-1844). Beckford's grandfather was a
17th-century plantation owner and his father three times Lord Mayor of London;
Beckford himself inherited a cool £2 million, no mean fortune in the 18th century.
Having built Fonthill Abbey near Salisbury, he retired to Lansdown Crescent in Bath,
where he set about building the tower as a personal retreat. The land around it was
consecrated as a cemetery in 1848 and is where Beckford was laid to rest.
   The tower is now owned by Bath Preservation Trust. For walkers it's more
important to know that, when it's open, the views from the top are worth the climb if
the weather's on your side. There's also an interesting museum focusing on
Beckford's colourful life. If you fancy the detour – it's nearly two miles (3km) from
the Cotswold Way – you could walk from the golf course to the main road, then
downhill along the pavement to the tower.

COLD ASHTON TO BATH   MAPS 39-43

After Cold Ashton comes the final **10-mile (16km, 5-5¾hrs)** stretch to Bath.
Leaving the busy A46, the Cotswold Way returns to rolling hills dotted with cattle and sheep, the noise of traffic replaced with birdsong. It's a gradual climb to
the top of the slope near Lansdown Hill, where the trail crosses the very field
where the **Battle of Lansdown** (see box on p163) took place in 1643. The area
is clearly demarcated with orange 'flags' and informative signboards, as well as
a memorial; it doesn't take much to conjure up the chaos that must have ensued
that summer evening.
   As you pass **Bath racecourse** (Map 42), do make time to stop at **Prospect
Stile** (now a kissing gate!), which at 230m (755ft) affords superb views across
Bath (albeit marred by the gasworks) and over the Severn estuary.
   The last couple of miles of the trail beyond **Weston** (Map 43) see some
unexpected ups and downs as the route twists to make the most of open terrain,
before the final descent past Lansdown Crescent to the grandeur of Bath Abbey.
   If you'd rather stay on the downward slope, you could cut across the golf
course (Map 41) to Lansdown Rd and follow this straight into Bath, taking in
Beckford's Tower (see box above) as you go and ending up with Lansdown
Crescent on your right.

WESTON   [MAP 43, p167]
Heading south, the walk down to Weston
culminates in a return to a more urban world,
but there are bonuses in practical terms.
Well-placed for walkers is *Western Bistro*
(☎ 01225-443017, 🖥 thewesternbistro.com;
Mon-Sat 9am-4pm). There's a branch of
Boots **pharmacy** (Mon-Sat 9am-6pm, Sat

to 1pm) next door; a little further in the
other direction is a small **supermarket**,
Tesco Express (Mon-Sat 7am-11pm, Sun
11am-5pm).
   First's No 9 **bus** (see pp48-50) operates between here and Bath, so if you can't
face the steep climbs there is an alternative.

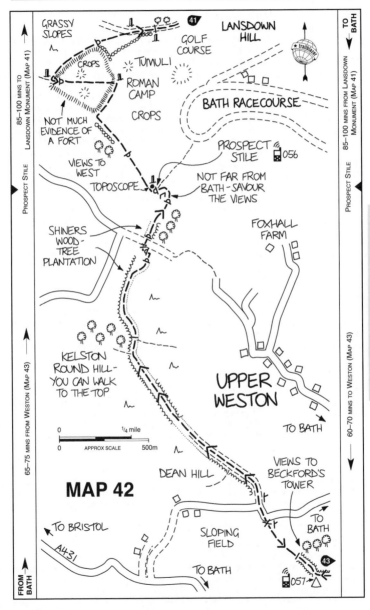

MAP 42

BATH   **[MAP 43a, pp172-3]**

'Oh, who can ever be tired of Bath?'
    Catherine Morland in **Jane Austen**'s
    Northanger Abbey, published in 1817

Not so long ago, as the train drew into the station at Bath, the announcer would intone in measured voice, 'Bath Spa'. It's that word 'spa' that has brought fortune to this western town, attracting 18th-century royalty to take the waters and serving as the catalyst for the construction of what we know today as Georgian Bath.

The city predates Roman times, when it was known as Aquae Sulis, but it is the Georgian buildings that are today revered and which have been protected as a World Heritage Site since 1987. Although George III (1738-1820) moved his allegiance to Cheltenham, sparking another building frenzy, Bath has never really fallen out of favour.

Today's visitors come not just to bathe in the waters at the smart Thermae Spa, but to explore the city's history at the Roman Baths, and to marvel at the soaring roof of Bath Abbey. They come, too, to investigate its museums, and – rather more prosaically – to try out any number of restaurants, hotels and bars that are around every corner. All that against a background of architecture that cannot fail to attract even the least-interested observer.

For the walker, the focal point of the city is the culmination of the trail, Bath Abbey, where you'll be greeted by an engraved limestone circle, sibling to the one in Chipping Campden (see p80).

See box p16 for details of festivals in Bath.

What to see and do

For most walkers on the Cotswold Way, the first sense of the city comes from the glimpse of Lansdown Crescent as you descend Lansdown Hill. Royal Crescent follows, leading to the smart gates of **Royal Victoria Park**, which in themselves represent a symbolic entrance to the city.

Although it is primarily Georgian Bath that draws the crowds, there are hints of medieval times in the ruins of the **city walls** along Upper Borough Walls and Barton St, north of the abbey, while no trip to Bath would be complete without visiting the **Roman Baths** (see p169).

To get a real feel for the city, join one of the two-hour **walking tours** that are run by volunteers from outside the Pump Room [65], right next to the Roman Baths. Tours depart at 10.30am and 2pm Sunday to Friday, and just at 10.30am on Saturday; between May and September, there's an additional evening walk at 7pm on Tuesday and Thursday. There is no charge – and tips are not accepted. Is this one of Bath's best-kept secrets?

A city with this sort of heritage must have the odd ghost hovering in the shadows. If you fancy being scared out of your wits, join a guided **ghost walk** (🖳 ghost walksofbath.co.uk; Thur-Sat 8pm; £8pp), lasting just short of two hours. To take part, just turn up at the allotted time outside the Garrick's Head pub [56] (see p181), though groups of 10 or more need to pre-book.

For those who prefer to guide themselves, there's a **city trail** beneath your feet – quite literally: it's marked out with plaques on the pavements. There's no accompanying map but for an upbeat interpretation see 🖳 bath.co.uk/city-trail. Broadly, the trail starts near the abbey, taking in the Roman Baths and the Pump Room, before moving on to Queen Square, The Circus and the Assembly Rooms, then back towards Pulteney Bridge and Parade Gardens, finishing at Abbey Green.

❏ **Cotswold Way signs in Bath**
Those unfamiliar with the city will need to keep a sharp eye out for the Cotswold Way signs, which have been reduced to discreet roundels featuring the National Trail acorn in a stylish metallic paint on black. Look out for these on lamp posts and bollards; nothing so rustic as a wooden fingerpost here!

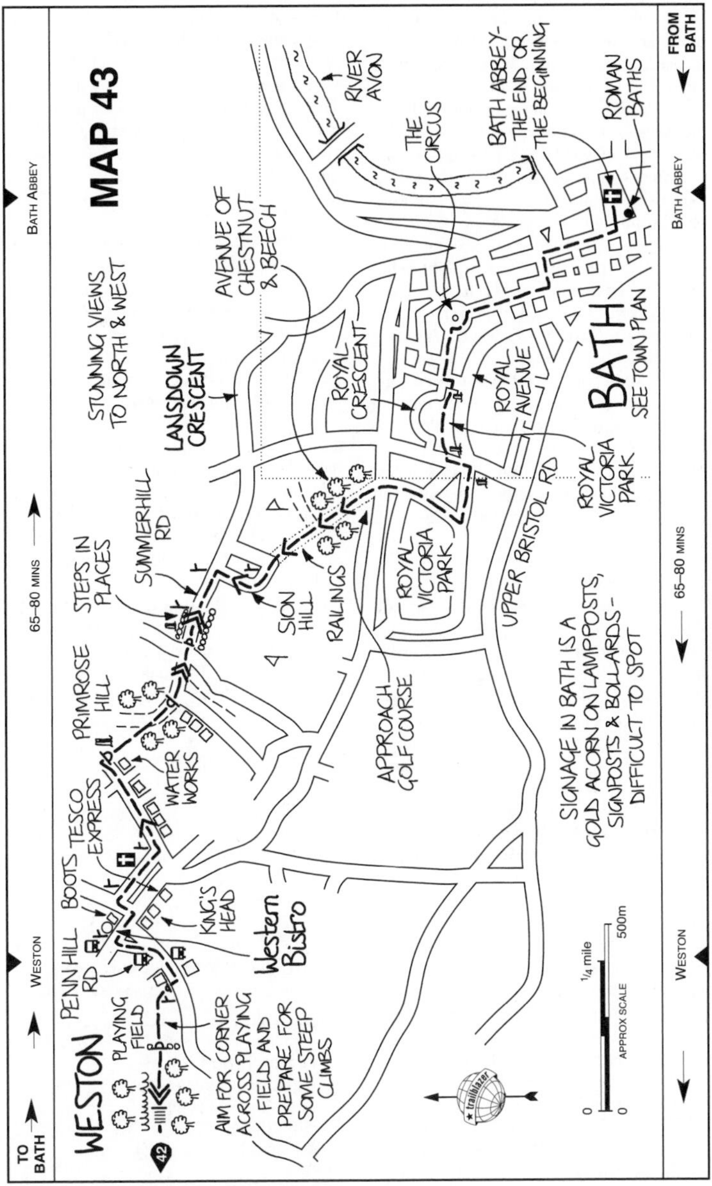

MAP 43

BATH ABBEY ▶

◀ BATH ABBEY

◀ 65–80 MINS ▶

65–80 MINS

STUNNING VIEWS TO NORTH & WEST

AVENUE OF CHESTNUT & BEECH

RIVER AVON

THE CIRCUS

BATH ABBEY – THE END OR THE BEGINNING

ROMAN BATHS

FROM BATH

LANSDOWN CRESCENT

ROYAL CRESCENT

ROYAL AVENUE

BATH
SEE TOWN PLAN

◀ BATH ABBEY

SUMMERHILL RD

STEPS IN PLACES

SION HILL

RAILINGS

ROYAL VICTORIA PARK

UPPER BRISTOL RD

ROYAL VICTORIA PARK

PRIMROSE HILL

WATER WORKS

APPROACH GOLF COURSE

SIGNAGE IN BATH IS A GOLD ACORN ON LAMPPOSTS, SIGNPOSTS & BOLLARDS – DIFFICULT TO SPOT

BOOTS TESCO EXPRESS

KING'S HEAD

Western Bistro

◀ 65–80 MINS ▶

◀ WESTON

WESTON

PENN HILL RD

PLAYING FIELD

AIM FOR CORNER ACROSS PLAYING FIELD AND PREPARE FOR SOME STEEP CLIMBS

42

TO BATH ▶

◀ WESTON

¼ mile

0   500m

APPROX SCALE

0

trailblazer

ROUTE GUIDE AND MAPS

Further afield, the National Trust (🖳 nationaltrust.org.uk/bath-skyline) have devised a 6-mile (10km) **Bath Skyline walk** and a shorter version, **Walk to the View!**; the routes for both can be downloaded from the website. Those who would like to complete the **Cotswold Way in stages** should consider signing up for the walks led by Cotswold Voluntary Wardens, some of them based from Bath; for details, see p29.

If you've had enough of walking, there are always the double-decker **sightseeing buses** (🖳 city-sightseeing.com/en/84/bath) which operate hop-on, hop-off tours with a commentary for £15.50 a head; tickets are valid for 24 hours.

Or you could try a **horse-drawn tour** (🖳 courtyardcarriages.com) which takes in the architectural highlights of Pulteney Bridge, Royal Crescent and The Circus. Trips (Feb-Dec Wed-Sun 11am-4.30pm; 25-30 mins; £12pp) can be prebooked and they start from the eastern end of Cheap St, opposite Parade Gardens.

● **Bath Abbey** One of England's most glorious churches, Bath Abbey (🖳 bath abbey.org; Mon 9.30am-5.30pm, Tue-Fri 9am-5.30pm, Sat 9am-6pm, Sun 1-2.30pm & 4.30-6pm; £4 donation suggested) is the third church to occupy this site. Visitors are welcome to tour the building, with its magnificent flying buttresses and fan-vaulted rafters, but it is during a service, or a concert, that you can best appreciate the architecture as the sound of choral music soars skywards. Tower tours (10am-4pm; Mon-Fri 1/hr, Sat 2/hr; £8) are offered, except in bad weather and on certain days.

Over the years, three separate buildings have occupied the site of the abbey. The first, an Anglo-Saxon church, was replaced by the Normans at the end of the 11th century. When this fell into ruin at the end of the 15th century, the present abbey church was founded, but was abandoned in 1539 at the time of Henry VIII's order for the dissolution of the monasteries. The Gothic church here now was rebuilt during the reign of Elizabeth I and completed in 1616.

Take a look at the abbey doors and you'll see the sacred heart and crown of thorns that proclaim its earlier foundation as a Catholic church. To each side of the doors are statues of St Peter and St Paul, to whom the Norman church was dedicated. The statue to the left was decapitated by Roundheads during the reign of Charles I, with the face recarved at a later date to restore the balance – at least in part. The abbey church itself is dedicated to St Peter.

● **Bath Assembly Rooms** Built in 1771, the lavishly designed Assembly Rooms (🖳 nationaltrust.org.uk/bath-assem bly-rooms; daily Mar-Oct 10.30am-6pm, Nov-Feb 10.30am-5pm; free, except for Fashion Museum), on Bennett St, were the creation of John Wood the Younger, and *the* place to be seen in fashionable Georgian society. Significant damage was caused by a bomb in 1942, but the Assembly Rooms have since been fully restored. Note that the building is sometimes closed for private functions. On the lower-ground floor is the **Fashion Museum** (🖳 fashionmuseum.co .uk; daily Mar-Oct 10.30am-5pm, Nov-Feb to 4pm; £9, see also box below). If you neither know nor care how Georgian formality compares with 20th-century designer chic, perhaps you'd be better off in the chain shops on Stall St. If you do, stay put; you'll even get the chance to try on corsets and crinolines.

● **Herschel Museum of Astronomy** Dedicated to five generations of the Herschel family, this museum (🖳 herschel museum.org.uk; Jan-Jun & Sep-Dec Mon-Fri 1-5pm, Sat-Sun & bank hols 10am-5pm, Jul & Aug daily 11am-5pm; £6.50), 19 New King St, is as much about the interior of an 18th-century townhouse as about astronomy. Already established as a musician, William Herschel moved here in 1777 with his sister, the astronomer Caroline

> ❏ **Combined ticket**
> If planning to visit the Fashion Museum, Roman Baths & Victoria Art Gallery it would be worth getting the combined ticket (£22.50).

Herschel. As a form of relaxation, he took up astronomy himself, building his own telescope and going on to discover the planet Uranus from this garden in 1781. Among the exhibits relating to everyday life is a 7ft (210cm) scale model of his 40ft (12m) telescope. Herschel went on to be appointed Astronomer Royal, forcing a move to Datchet in 1782. He died in 1823 and is buried in Berkshire, in the churchyard of St Lawrence, Upton.

● **The Holburne Museum** Established in 1893 to showcase the collection of Sir William Holburne, this museum (☎ 01225-388569, 💻 holburne.org; Mon-Sat 10am-5pm, Sun/bank hols 11am-5pm; £11, Art Fund members £5; free Wed 3-5pm and 5-9pm on last Fri of month) lies at the end of Great Pulteney St. It is a major provincial gallery with a particularly strong emphasis on Georgian portraiture. To miss the rest of the collection would be a shame, however. Do take a look at the smaller exhibits tucked away in drawers – and allow time for a breather in the contemporary *café* (food till 4.30pm).

● **Museum of Bath Architecture** The setting for this fascinating museum (💻 museumofbatharchitecture.org.uk; The Vineyards, The Paragon; mid Feb-Jun & Sep-Nov Mon-Fri 1-5pm, Sat-Sun & bank hols 10am-5pm, Jul & Aug daily 11am-5pm; £6.50) is the **Countess of Huntingdon's Chapel**, built in 1765 and in use as a place of worship until 1981. The building is interesting in itself, but the real reason for visiting is to find out why – and how – Georgian Bath was built. Work your way through the grand designs of the architects, including the city's principal visionary John Wood, who designed Queen Square, and his son, also John, who was the inspiration behind both The Circus and Royal Crescent. Discover the challenges faced by the stonemasons, carpenters and roofers, then learn about the interior décor, such as applying gold leaf to the ceiling mouldings. Intricate scale models show how the interiors of the houses were constructed – and depict what went on in each of the rooms. Other muse-

> ❑ **Opening hours**
> When planning your trip, note that several establishments, including the Roman Baths, stop selling tickets up to an hour before closing time, so do be sure to give yourself plenty of time.

ums might shout louder, but this is the one to put at the top of your list.

● **Museum of East Asian Art** This museum (💻 meaa.org.uk; Tue-Sat 10am-5pm, Sun noon-5pm; £5), 12 Bennett St, based on the personal collection of a Hong Kong lawyer, offers more of an introduction to Asian art than any great insight. Among the exhibits are ceramics, bamboo carvings and an extensive collection of Chinese jade. Find it off The Circus, just a stone's throw from the Cotswold Way as it enters Bath.

● **Parade Gardens** Right in the centre of Bath, Parade Gardens (Easter-end Sep; £1.50) is a peaceful place to enjoy the colour of an English formal garden. Bands play here regularly in summer.

● **Roman Baths and Pump Room** Probably the single greatest attraction for visitors are the **Roman Baths** (💻 roman baths.co.uk; daily Jan-Feb & Nov-Feb 9.30am-5pm, Mar-mid Jun & Sep-Oct 9am-5pm, mid Jun-Aug 9am-9pm; £16.50, or £17.50 in Jul-Aug; see also box opposite), on Stall St. Dating to between the 1st and 5th centuries AD, and constructed of stone, the colonnaded great bath was built to take advantage of a natural spring from which waters rise at a constant temperature of around 46°C. If the changing rooms, saunas and plunge pools are reminiscent of a modern-day spa, the temple dedicated to the goddess Sulis Minerva puts the whole thing firmly back into context. Included in the admission price is entry to the Georgian **Pump Room**, where the spring water may be sampled. For details of afternoon tea at the Pump Room, see p181.

● **Royal Crescent and Lansdown Crescent** At the far right of **Royal Crescent**, No 1 (🖵 no1royalcrescent.org .uk; Feb-mid Dec daily 10am-5pm; £10.30) was the first house to be constructed and it was built in the Palladian style following designs by John Wood the Younger. The attraction now encompasses the servants' quarters in the neighbouring No 1A. Today's visitor will gain an insight into life both upstairs and downstairs in fashionable Georgian society; don't miss the kitchens or the cabinet of curiosities.

Royal Crescent may get all the accolades, but it is **Lansdown Crescent** (see Map 43, p167) that is first seen by those heading south on the Cotswold Way. With sheep grazing on the grassy hill in front, and fine views over the city, it arguably runs its more famous neighbour very close.

● **Victoria Art Gallery** Facing Pulteney Bridge (designed by Robert Adam and one of only three river bridges in Europe with shops that are integral to the bridge) is Victoria Art Gallery (🖵 victoriagal.org.uk; daily 10.30am-5pm; Upper Gallery is free but special exhibitions in the Victoria Gallery cost £4.50; see also box p168), built at a time of civic pride to show off the city's attributes. While the name suggests it focuses on Victorian art, the reality is a far broader mix, from the 17th century to the contemporary, and including a couple of Gainsborough paintings and Rex Whistler's glorious incarnation of British insularity, *The Foreign Bloke*. Some are linked to the city, but most were donated by wealthy Bath residents, or formed part of their collections. Displays also include sculpture, ceramics, glass, porcelain and pottery. The room downstairs plays host to a series of changing exhibitions. On a practical note, there's a self-service machine dispensing hot drinks into china cups (yes, really!). And if you're nursing sore feet there is plenty of comfortable seating down the centre of the gallery.

Entertainment

Bath does culture very well, but there's light relief on the agenda too. A great place to ease all those post-walk aches and pains,

or to get yourself in a relaxed frame of mind before setting off, is **Thermae Bath Spa** (🖵 thermaebathspa.com; daily 9am-9.30pm; pools closed 9pm; no children under 16) on the gloriously named Hot Bath St. At £36 a head (£40 at weekends) for just a couple of hours, it's expensive – some would say extortionate – but at least the price includes a towel, robe and flipflop slippers (you get to keep the latter), though you need to take a swimming costume/ trunks. If you don't fancy shelling out for the 2hr Thermae Welcome package (which includes access to the open-air bath, the Minerva Bath and the Wellness Suite) at the New Royal Bath, or indeed for one of their 50 treatments and therapies, there's the satellite **Cross Bath** (daily 10am-8pm), just across the road, which is open air but without the view; a 1½-hour session here costs £18, or £20 at weekends.

Bath's **Theatre Royal** (🖵 theatreroyal .org.uk), on Sawclose, stages a wide range of high-quality productions, and – for theatre buffs – shouldn't be missed. If you've a preference for the silver screen, try the multi-screen Odeon **cinema** (🖵 odeon.co .uk) on James St, or – for more offbeat offerings – **Little Theatre Cinema** (🖵 pic turehouses.com/cinema/The_Little), on St Michael's Place.

Boat trips can be organised with *Pulteney Princess* (🖵 pulteneyprincess.co .uk; Apr-Oct up to 6/day), which plies the Avon between Pulteney Weir and Bathampton Mill; a round trip of about an hour costs £9; one-way trips are also possible. If you'd rather set off under your own steam, rowing boats, canoes and punts can be hired from Bath Boating Station (off Map 43a; 🖵 bathboating.co.uk; early Apr-late Sep Wed-Sun & bank hol Mon 10am-5.30pm), whose base is at the end of Forester Rd, north-east of Great Pulteney St. Boats cost £7pp for the first hour, and £4 for every hour after that (£18 for full day).

Spectators rather than participants can check out what's on at **The Rec** (🖵 bath rugby.com), home to Bath Rugby Club – though it's a small ground by today's standards, and tickets can be hard to come by. The Rec is also used for concerts.

Arrival and departure

Whether Bath is the grand finale of your walk, or an historic starting point, there is no shortage of ways to get to and from the city.
● **By train** Bath Spa railway station is at the end of Manvers St, near the river. Services operated by GWR, South Western Railway and Cross Country stop here; for details see box p46.
● **By coach** The coach/bus station is located on Dorchester St, close to both the railway station and SouthGate shopping centre which dominates the southern part of the city. National Express's No 403 service (see box p47) calls here.
● **By bus** Stagecoach's No 620 from Old Sodbury and First's No 9 services (see pp48-50) call at the bus station.
● **By car** Bath is about half-an-hour's drive from junction 18 of the M4.
● **By air** The nearest airport with both domestic and international flights is Bristol; see box p45. The Airdecker bus (🖳 air decker.com; daily 1-2/hr) operates between the airport and Bath.

If you want to abandon your luggage so you can explore the city, you can either leave it with Bath Backpackers (£4 a bag per day, free for guests), or at the YMCA; see p174 for both.

Getting around Bath

The centre of Bath is sufficiently compact that most visitors are happy to wander the streets on foot. Cyclists, however, can pick up a **bike** from any of the 14 nextbike docking stations around the city, and drop it back later. For the visitor, most useful are the five stations close to the city centre: at the railway station [97]; Green Park [62]; Holburne Museum [22]; Orange Grove [50]; and Charlotte St car park [30]. You'll need to download the app or obtain an access card for £2 from 🖳 nextbike.co.uk/ en/bath, or to call ☎ 020-8166 9851. Rentals cost £1 per half hour, up to a maximum of £10 per 24 hours, with a £10 credit deposit required at the time of registration.

At the other end of the energy spectrum, open-top **buses** encircle the tourist areas of the city, anathema to some but a great relief from blistered feet for others.

For details of both these and horse-drawn carriages, see p168.

Registered **taxis**, easily spotted by the light on the roof, can be hailed on the streets. Others, such as ***Abbey Taxis*** [90] (☎ 01225-444444, 🖳 abbeytaxis.co.uk), which is on South Parade, and many of those run by ***V-Cars*** (☎ 01225-464646, 🖳 v-cars .com) must be prebooked. There's also a **taxi rank** in front of the railway station.

Services

Tourist information   The **Visitor Information Centre** [70] (☎ 01225-614420, 🖳 visitbath.co.uk; Mon-Sat 9.30am-5.30pm, mid Feb-end Oct Sun 10am-4pm), Bridgwater House, 2 Terrace Walk, has a prime central spot near where the tour buses pull in.

● **Money matters** All the main high street **banks** have branches with **ATMs** across the city. The most central are on Milsom St, where there are branches of Lloyds [38] and HSBC [39], or south on Southgate, where you'll find branches of Metro Bank [82], Barclays [84] and HSBC [83]. The main **post office** (Mon & Wed-Sat 9am-5.30pm, Tue from 9.30am) is on the corner of Broad and Green streets [42].

● **Shopping** Arguably the most central of the **supermarkets** for those seeking supplies is Waitrose [46] (Mon-Fri 7.30am-9pm, Sat to 8pm, Sun 11am-5pm), which is in The Podium on Northgate St. There's a large branch of Sainsbury's [61] (Mon-Sat 7am-10pm, Sun 11am-5pm) behind the old Green Park Station, and smaller Sainsbury's Locals (daily 7am-11pm) on Monmouth St [58] and opposite the bus station [87].

More interesting by far are some of the smaller, **independent shops**, where you can taste the cheese to go in your lunch before buying. Two to tempt your palate are The Fine Cheese Co [41] (☎ 01225-483407, 🖳 finecheeseshops.co.uk/bath; Mon-Sat 9am-5pm, café from 8am), on Walcot St opposite the Podium, and Chandos Deli [11] (🖳 chandosdeli.com; Mon-Fri 8am-7pm, Sat 9am-7pm, Sun 9am-5pm), on George St. *(cont'd on p174)*

(cont'd on p174)

ROUTE GUIDE AND MAPS

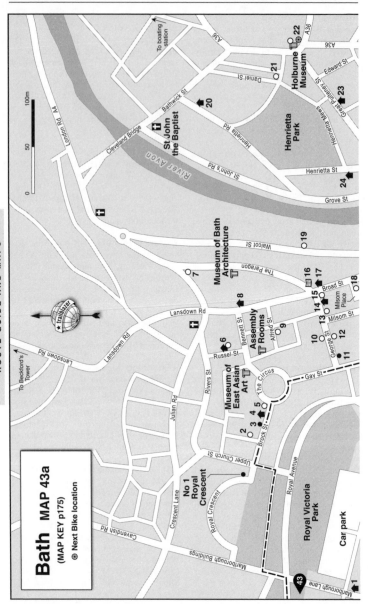

ROUTE GUIDE AND MAPS

Bath MAP 43a
(MAP KEY p175)

⊕ Next Bike location

To Beckford's Tower

Lansdown Rd

Julian Rd

Crescent Lane

Cavendish Rd

Royal Crescent

Marlborough Buildings

No 1
Royal Crescent

Upper Church St

Rivers St

Bennett St

Russel St

6
Museum of East Asian Art

The Circus

Gay St

Royal Victoria Park

Car park

Royal Avenue

Marlborough Lane

43

1

Brock St

2 3 4 5

George St

10 13

11 12

Assembly Rooms

9
Alfred St

Milsom St

8

Lansdown Rd

14 15 16 17

Broad St

18

Milsom Place

Museum of Bath Architecture

The Paragon

7

Walcot St

19

St John's Rd

Henrietta Rd

Bathwick St

Cleveland Bridge

London Rd A4

St John the Baptist

River Avon

20

Daniel St

21

Holburne Museum

22

A36

Edward St

Great Pulteney St

23

Henrietta Mews

Henrietta Park

Henrietta St

Grove St

24

0   50   100m

To boating station

A36

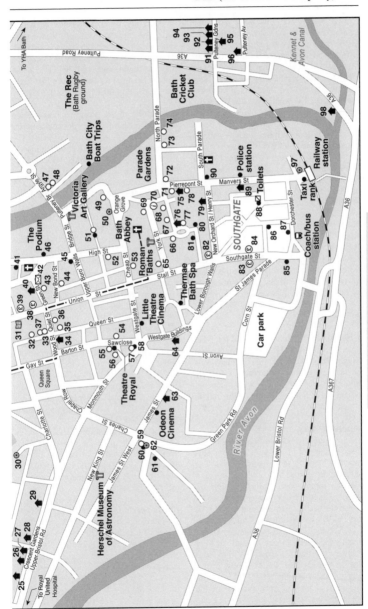

(cont'd from p171) Both have their own licensed *cafés* serving sandwiches prepared to order and lots of other goodies. There are also several food outlets in the **Guildhall Market** [51] (🖥 bathguildhallmarket.co .uk; Mon-Sat 8am-5.30pm but stalls have their own hours) and an excellent **farmers' market** [60] (🖥 bathfarmersmarket.co.uk; Sat 9am-1.30pm) in the old Green Park Station in front of Sainsbury's.

For **outdoor supplies**, such as walking boots, poles and clothing, there are several outlets: BCH Camping & Leisure [85] on Southgate St; Blacks [80] and Cotswold Outdoor [81] on Abbey Gate; Millets [45] on High St; and The North Face [88] in SouthGate shopping centre.

Bath is an easy place to lose a bibliophile, with an excellent independent **bookshop**, Topping & Company [16] (The Paragon; 🖥 toppingbooks.co.uk; daily 8.30am-7pm), at the top of Broad St, where tea and coffee are always on the go. They have a good range of maps and guides, too, as does the large branch of Waterstones [31] (Mon-Sat 9am-6pm, Sun 11am-5pm) on Milsom St.

● **Health** Royal United **Hospital** (off Map 43a; ☎ 01225-428331, 🖥 ruh.nhs.uk) is at Combe Park, about 1½ miles (2.4km) west of the city centre. **Pharmacies** include Boots [86] in SouthGate and the independent Luther & Jhoots [3] right on the trail on Brock St near The Circus.

Where to stay

While there's plenty of accommodation close to the end of the trail, by the abbey, much of it is on the expensive side. The suggestions given here and on pp176-8 include some more reasonable options, many of them grouped together in one or two areas to the south-east and west of the city, and all within easy reach of the trail.

Although seemingly limitless, Bath's accommodation can get booked up very early during Bath Festival (end May-June) and in the summer. Prices almost everywhere vary considerably, taking into account the time of year, the day of the week, the length of stay, and what is going on in the city; those given below are necessarily for guidance, primarily based on a single night midweek during the summer. At weekends, usually defined as Friday and Saturday night, and bank holidays, many places also insist on a **minimum two-night stay**, especially for advance bookings.

● **Hostels** Basic hostel accommodation that is also central comes in various guises (though campers will be out of luck). The largest option, sleeping over 200 people, is the *YMCA* [17] (☎ 01225-325900, 🖥 ymca bathgroup.org.uk), on Broad Street Place. Dorm accommodation (1 x 10-, 2 x 12-, 2 x 15- & 1 x 18-bed dorms, shared facilities; WI-FI) is in the original 135-year-old building; two of the dorms are only for women and one of the 12-bed dorms is men only. The newer building has the private rooms (10S/5D/29T/6Tr/7Qd, some en suite, others with shared facilities; WI-FI). Staying at the YMCA costs £23-26pp in a dormitory, private rooms from £32/28pp for a single/two sharing. All rates include a continental breakfast and at the weekend a cooked option (£3.95) is available. There's a laundry for guests' use, a left-luggage facility (small charge), and a gym (at a reduced rate for residents) – though that's unlikely to be of interest at the beginning or end of a 102-mile hike!

For something more personal, head for the privately run *Bath Backpackers* [75] (☎ 01225-446787, 🖥 hostels.co.uk/Bath-Accommodation.html; 72 beds in 4-, 8-, 10-, or 12-bed dormitories, shared facilities; WI-FI; (L)), at 13 Pierrepont St, where there's a self-catering kitchen and a 'party dungeon' room. A dorm bed costs £10-21pp. There is a 10-bed dorm for women, the other dorms are mixed.

A further option is the hostel at *St Christopher's Inn* [40] (☎ 01225-481444, 🖥 st-christophers.co.uk/bath-hostels; 2 x 6- & 3 x 12-bed dorms, 1T bunk bed/2D; WI-FI), at 9 Green St. A dorm bed costs £10-28.80pp (one dorm is female only); their twin and double rooms (one en suite) start from £18.50pp (sgl occ room rate). Booking online and direct is recommended as the rates are generally lower, also the

BATH – MAP KEY (see map pp172-3)

Where to stay
1 Marlborough House
4 Brocks
6 The Queensberry
8 The Belmont
14 Travelodge Bath Central
17 YMCA
20 Chestnuts House
23 Edgar Townhouse
24 Kennard
25 Bay Tree House
26 Waltons
27 Crescent Guesthouse
28 The Albany
29 The Bath House
34 Harington's Hotel
40 St Christopher's Inn
63 Premier Inn Bath City Centre
64 Travelodge Bath City Centre
75 Bath Backpackers
76 Three Abbey Green
79 The Henry Guest House
89 Anabelle's
91 Avon Guesthouse
92 Lynwood
93 Apple Tree
94 Brindley's

Where to stay *(cont'd)*
95 White Guest House
96 Membland Guesthouse
98 Travelodge Bath Waterside

Where to eat and drink
2 Rustico Bistro Italiano
5 The Circus
6 The Olive Tree
7 The Star Inn
9 Woods
10 Clayton's Kitchen
12 Martini
13 Loch Fyne
15 Wagamama
18 Côte Brasserie
19 Schwartz Bros
21 The Pulteney Arms
32 Salamander
33 Olé Tapas
35 The Raven
36 The Eastern Eye
37 Firehouse Rotisserie
43 The Old Green Tree
44 Volunteer Rifleman's Arms
47 B Bakery
48 Ponte Vecchio

Where to eat & drink *(cont'd)*
49 Browns
52 Pâtisserie Valerie
53 The Roman Baths Kitchen
54 Schwartz Bros
55 Amarone
56 Garrick's Head
57 Thai Balcony
59 Green Park Brasserie
65 Pump Room
66 Crystal Palace
67 Acorn Vegetarian Kitchen
68 Sally Lunn's
69 The Real Italian Pizza Co
71 Salathai
72 The Green Rocket Café
73 Sotto Sotto
74 OPA
77 The Bath Bun
78 Yak Yeti Yak

Other
3 Luther & Jhoots (chemist)
11 Chandos Deli
16 Topping & Company
22 nextbike

Other *(cont'd)*
30 nextbike
31 Waterstones
38 Lloyds Bank & ATM
39 HSBC Bank & ATM
41 Fine Cheese Co
42 Post Office
45 Millets
46 Waitrose (in The Podium)
50 nextbike
51 Guildhall Market
58 Sainsbury's Local
60 Farmers' Market
61 Sainsbury's
62 nextbike
70 Visitor Info Centre
80 Blacks
81 Cotswold Outdoor
82 Metro Bank
83 HSBC & ATM
84 Barclays Bank & ATM
85 BCH Camping & Leisure
86 Boots
87 Sainsbury's Local
88 The North Face
90 Abbey Taxis
97 nextbike

ROUTE GUIDE AND MAPS

rate includes a continental breakfast if booked direct. However, note there may be a two-night minimum stay requirement at weekends. On the down side, it's above the noisy Belushi's bar and restaurant. The plus? You get 25% off food at Belushi's.

The city's YHA hostel, **YHA Bath** (off Map 43a; ☎ 0345-371 9303, 🖳 yha.org.uk /bath; 1 x 2-, 5 x 3-, 1 x 4-, 6 x 5- & 6 x 6-bed room with en suite facilities; 2 x 2-, 2 x 4- & 3 x 6-bed rooms, plus an 8-bed male dorm and 10-bed female dorm, all with shared facilities; WI-FI; (Ⓛ), is over a mile (1.6km) east of the centre on Bathwick Hill. If you don't mind the walk, and fancy staying in an Italianate mansion, it could be worth considering. Pricing is dynamic and fluctuates widely, but members can expect to pay in the range of £14-24pp for a dorm bed, or from £59 for two sharing a private en suite twin room. Some rooms have a double bed and 19 are en suite. Laundry facilities and meals are available, and the hostel is licensed. There are limited self-catering facilities (no hobs or oven, just a microwave, toaster and kettle.

● **Guesthouses and B&Bs**
Central Right on the Cotswold Way as you walk into Bath, near The Circus, is **Brocks** [4] (☎ 01225-338374, 🖳 brocksguesthouse .co.uk; 1T or D/3D/1Tr/1Qd, all en suite; 🖤; WI-FI), 32 Brock St, where B&B costs around £50pp (sgl occ around £10 less than the room rate).

Not far from here, at 7 Belmont, a pedestrian walkway that runs parallel to but above Lansdown Rd, you'll find **The Belmont** [8] (☎ 01225-423082, 🖳 belmont bath.co.uk; 1S/2T/3D, most en suite; 🖤; WI-FI), a traditional B&B run by Archie Watson. The single has a separate bathroom and costs from £45, or it's from £45pp (sgl occ £70).

At the other end of town, close to the railway station, **The Henry Guest House** [79] (☎ 01225-424052, 🖳 thehenry.com; 1S private facilities, 3D/2D or T/1Qd all en suite; WI-FI) offers contemporary rooms in a Georgian townhouse. B&B costs from £50pp (sgl £65, sgl occ £80). They are happy to do a wash & dry for £12.

Similarly convenient for the railway station, albeit rather noisy, is **Anabelle's** [89] (☎ 01225-330133, 🖳 anabellesguest house.co.uk; 2D/1T all en suite, 2D/3T shared facilities; 🖤; WI-FI), where you'll pay £35-43pp for B&B (sgl occ rates on request).

The more central **Three Abbey Green** [76] (☎ 01225-428558, 🖳 threeabbeygreen .com; 3D/5D or T/1Tr/1Qd, most en suite, all with private facilities; 🖤; WI-FI) is a family-run guesthouse occupying a listed townhouse just behind the abbey. Charges vary considerably, but expect to pay £45-80pp (sgl occ is 10% off the room rate).

Across Pulteney Bridge on Henrietta Rd is **Chestnuts House** [20] (☎ 01225-334279, 🖳 chestnutshouse.co.uk; 4D/1Tr, all en suite; 🖤; WI-FI) – a stone-built house with rooms for £40-72.50pp (sgl occ £75-115).

East of the city Outside the immediate centre, there are two gluts of predominantly terraced B&Bs in residential areas that are within easy walking distance of the trail. The first, about 10 minutes' walk east of the abbey across the railway and a short stroll from the Kennet and Avon Canal, runs along **Pulteney Rd and up Pulteney Gardens**. Of these, two are right on the main road, so potentially quite noisy. **Membland Guesthouse** [96] (☎ 01225-336712, mob ☎ 07958-599572, 🖳 memb landguesthouse.co.uk; 2D/1Tr, all en suite; WI-FI), where rooms start at £45-47.50pp (sgl occ room rate).

Then on the corner of Pulteney Gardens, **Avon Guesthouse** [91] (☎ 01225-313009, 🖳 avonguesthousebath.co.uk; 1T/4D/1Tr, all en suite; 🖤; WI-FI; Feb-Dec) charges £37.50-52.50pp (sgl occ £70-95).

Pulteney Gardens itself harbours several Victorian homes offering B&B. At No 23, B&B at **White Guest House** [95] (☎ 01225-426075, 🖳 whiteguesthouse.co.uk; 1S/1T/3D, all en suite; WI-FI) will set you back £35-40pp (sgl £50-55, sgl occ from £65).

On the opposite side at No 6 is **Lynwood** [92] (☎ 01225-426410, 🖳 lyn wood.house; 2S with private facilities,

ROUTE GUIDE AND MAPS

2D/1D or T all en suite; WI-FI), with accommodation for £35-40pp (sgl from £45, sgl
occ room rate). Note that the rate does not
include breakfast but there are lots of
options nearby.

Right next door, No 7, at *Apple Tree*
[93] (☎ 01225-337642, ⌨ appletreeguest
house.co.uk; 5D, all en suite; WI-FI) you'll
pay £47.50-80pp (sgl occ from £85).

At the end on the corner, and in another class entirely, is the self-styled 'boutique
B&B' *Brindley's* [94] (☎ 01225-310444, ⌨
brindleysbath.co.uk; 1T or D/5D, all en
suite; WI-FI). With French-inspired décor,
its rooms – some with king-size beds – cost
£57.50-115pp (sgl occ room rate).

West of the city A second clutch of guesthouses and B&Bs is at **Crescent Gardens**,
an elevated section of **Upper Bristol Rd**
that's just a few minutes' walk from the
trail – and the centre of Bath. Closest of
these is *The Bath House* [29] (mob ☎
07711-119847, ☎ 01179-374495, ⌨ the-
bathhouse.org; 1T or D/4D, all en suite; ☛;
WI-FI), at No 40, a self-styled 'boutique
B&B' where rooms with king-size or four-
poster beds are £34.50-69.50pp (sgl occ
£72-129). They also have two self-catering
apartments, about 100 yards away on
James St. One sleeps up to three people (1T
or D plus a sofa bed; £39.50-79.50pp, sgl
occ £82-129); the other up to five (1T or D/
1Tr; £139-249 for up to five people sharing). In both apartments a complimentary
continental breakfast is provided for the
first morning.

Rooms at *The Albany* [28] (☎ 01225-
313339, ⌨ albanybath.co.uk; 1T or D private facilities, 1T/2D/1Tr and one room
sleeping up to five, all en suite; WI-FI), No
24, cost £45-52.50pp (sgl occ £60-95), but
the rate would be higher if there are only
two in the larger rooms.

At *Crescent Guesthouse* [27] (☎
01225-425945, ⌨ crescentbath.co.uk; 1S/
1T/3D, all en suite; WI-FI), No 21, expect to
pay £35-47.50pp (sgl/sgl occ £55-85).
Rates at *Waltons* [26] (☎ 01225-426528, ⌨
waltonsguesthouse.co.uk; 2S/4D/1Tr, all en
suite; WI-FI), No 17, are £40-45pp (£50-55
for a single, sgl occ room rate).

❏ **Two-night minimum stay**
Virtually all B&B-style accommodation options in Bath require a minimum stay of two nights at weekends
and also at peak periods. But if there
is availability at short notice most
would consider a one-night stay.

Last up is *Bay Tree House* [25] (☎
01225-483699, ⌨ baytreehousebath.co.uk;
2D/1Tr, all en suite, 1D/1T shared bathroom; ☛; WI-FI), No 12, with B&B for
£37.50-60.50pp (sgl occ from £75).

Further up, a turning to the right leads
into **Marlborough Lane**, where the elegant
Marlborough House [1] (☎ 01225-318175,
⌨ marlborough-house.net; 3D/1Tr/2Qd, all
en suite; WI-FI; ☂) is in a class of its own.
For £52.50-87.50pp (sgl occ £105-135) you
can have a room with a king-sized bed, but
also possibly a four-poster. The toiletries in
the rooms are organic as are the ingredients
for breakfast. There is air-con in all the
rooms.

● **Hotels** With B&Bs climbing steadily up
the price ladder, it's not unreasonable to
shop around for one of the cheaper hotels,
especially if you're happy to find a café for
breakfast. Relatively new on the scene is
Premier Inn Bath City Centre [63] (☎
0871-527 9454, ⌨ premierinn.com; 23D/
31Tr/44Qd, all en suite; ☛; WI-FI), on
James St. Saver rates (non refundable and
pay at time of booking) start at around
£41.50 for the room, and Flex rates from
£59 (cancel up to 1pm on the day and pay
on arrival).

In a similar mould are three branches
of **Travelodge** (⌨ travelodge.co.uk); all
have a good number of double, twin and
triple rooms and all rooms are en suite with
baths. The older *Bath Central* [14] (☎
0871-984 6219) is indeed central, on
George St, though has now been upstaged
by the even more central *Bath City Centre*
[64] (Bath Spa; ☎ 0871-984 6523), at 6-10
Westgate Buildings, very close to the
Roman baths. There's also *Bath Waterside*
[98] (☎ 0871-984 6407) on Rossiter Rd and

ROUTE GUIDE AND MAPS

in more tranquil surroundings to the south, on the Kennet and Avon Canal. Once again rates can vary hugely from day to day, though the best are online: saver rates (non-refundable and paid at time of booking) can come in as low as £42 per room and flexible rates (can cancel up to noon on arrival date) are more likely to be from £66. Wi-fi (£3 for 24hrs) and a buffet breakfast (£9.50pp) are extra.

To the east of the abbey, over the river, are several small hotels. These include *Edgar Townhouse* [23] (☎ 01225-420619, 🖳 edgar-townhouse.co.uk; 2S/3T/12D/1Qd, all en suite), at 64 Great Pulteney St, which offers B&B for £37.50-87pp (sgl £69-90, sgl occ rates on request).

Round the corner at *Kennard* [24] (☎ 01225-310472, 🖳 kennard.co.uk; 2S share facilities, 1T/8D/1Tr all en suite; WI-FI), 11 Henrietta St, you'll pay from £65pp (sgl/sgl occ £90-115) for B&B.

Equally central but far more personal is *Harington's Hotel* [34] (☎ 01225-461728, 🖳 haringtonshotel.co.uk; 9D/1D or T/3Tr, all en suite; ♥; WI-FI), 10-11 Queen St, just off the square, where B&B costs £40.50-111.50pp (no discount for sgl occ).

At the top end of the scale, one boutique hotel stands out: *The Queensberry* [6] (☎ 01225-447928, 🖳 thequeensberry.co.uk; 29D or T, all en suite; ♥; WI-FI) on Russel St. Stylish and contemporary, its rooms come in at £50-225pp (sgl occ room rate) excluding breakfast (full English is an extra £12.50pp).

Where to eat and drink

Eating out in Bath is easy. The problem lies in choosing where to go from the broad array of pubs, restaurants, cafés and fast-food joints whose menus demand attention at every turn. The following, then, is no more than a selection of options within easy reach of the centre. Others abound, especially around Kingsmead Square, so you'll be spoiled for choice.

● **Traditional and contemporary** As you walk into (or out of) Bath along the Cotswold Way, you'll pass *The Circus* [5] (🖳 thecircusrestaurant.co.uk; lunch Mon-Fri noon-2.30pm Sat to 2pm, dinner from 5pm and snacks served in between), on Brock St, aptly located near The Circus. You can have breakfast, elevenses, lunch or tea here, or dine in style. Whatever your choice, the décor is pleasantly informal and the menus are both seasonal and sound very appetising; try the South Devon scallops with smoked artichoke purée and prosciutto (£9.70) for starters.

In a prime location right in front of the abbey, and hugely popular with tourists, is *The Roman Baths Kitchen* [53] (🖳 romanbathkitchen.co.uk; Sun-Thur 9am-6pm, Fri-Sat 9am-9pm). Separate daytime and dinner menus have a fairly broad range of

---

❏ **Bath specialities**

● **Bath bun** Created in the 17th century by Sally Lunn, the original Bath bun is a light bread roll, akin to a large French brioche and still served at the eponymous Sally Lunn's (see pp181-2) in Bath. Later, though, the term 'Bath bun' became associated with a sweetened roll sprinkled with sugar and this is now the more widely known of the two.

● **Bath Oliver** The plain savoury biscuit served as an accompaniment to cheese was the creation of one Dr Oliver, who practised in Bath during the 18th century. It's widely available in supermarkets and delicatessens.

● **Bath chap** The breadcrumbed boiled cheek of a pig, these normally come in a cone shape. Find them at the Guildhall Market in Bath.

● **Bath soft cheese** An old Bath recipe is said to lie behind the creation of this cheese, which is available at the city's Saturday morning farmers' market.

● **Bath asparagus** Not so much a culinary speciality as a rare summer delicacy, Bath asparagus grows wild in the hills around the city, the locations a closely guarded secret. As you might expect, it is strictly protected.

dishes, from small and large and sharing plates to grills and salads.

Long a local favourite is *Green Park Brasserie* [59] (☎ 01225-338565, 🖥 green parkbrasserie.com; daily noon-2.45pm, Tue-Sat 5.30-10pm), 6 Green Park Station, where there's the added buzz of live jazz in the evening (Wed-Sat). Rather grandly located in the old booking hall of the restored Green Park Station, it spills over on to the old station concourse. Come at lunch for good-value fixed-price menus (£11/15 for two/three courses), or indulge à la carte (mains £10-24) on dishes such as pan-fried duck breast with Madeira jus and poached pear. However, be aware that they are sometimes closed for a private function so it is best to call in advance to check.

Clayton's Kitchen [10] (🖥 theporter .co.uk/claytons-kitchen; Mon-Thur noon-2.30pm & 6-9.30pm, Fri-Sat noon-2.30pm & 6-10pm, Sun noon-3pm & 6-9pm), on George St, offers a varied menu from sandwiches to deli boards and locally sourced mains, though is probably not a place for a rushed lunch.

Just off Queen Square, *Firehouse Rotisserie* [37] (🖥 firehouserotisserie.co .uk; Mon-Sat noon-10.30pm, Sun to 10pm), John St, describes itself as an American restaurant serving food 'with a hint of southern California'. It is a light and convivial spot that presents a range of innovative 'small plates' along with grills, pizzas and a range of rotisserie chicken (£13).

Close to the nextbike rack on Orange Grove, *Browns* [49] (🖥 browns-restau rants.co.uk; Mon-Thur 9am-10pm, Fri & Sat to 11pm, Sun to 10.30pm) is part of an upmarket but good-value chain and could be a good spot to abandon a bike for lunch. The atmosphere in this former police station and magistrate's court is buzzing, the menu broad and prices (mains from £10.50) reasonable.

Racing paraphernalia adorns the walls of the established *Woods* [9] (🖥 woods restaurant.com; Tue-Sat noon-2.30pm & 5-9.30pm, Sun noon-2.30pm), a family-run place on Alfred St, opposite the Assembly Rooms. Come for their bar menu with goodies such as Provençal fish soup

(£8.50); a two-course fixed-price menu at lunch or early dinner (5.30-7pm); or select from dishes that might include seared Gressingham duck breast with blackcurrant & Marsala sauce (£21.50).

If celebration is in order, a classy venue could be appropriate. Round the corner from Woods, on Russel St, *The Olive Tree* [6] (🖥 olivetreebath.co.uk; Tue-Sun noon-2pm, daily 7-10pm) is the exclusive and top-quality restaurant at The Queensberry Hotel (see Where to stay), exuding calm and contemporary style. At the time of research it is also the only place in Bath with a Michelin star. There's a two-course lunch menu at £26, but tasting menus from £60 are strictly for specials; booking is recommended.

● **Mediterranean** There's more than a passing nod to French café culture at *Côte Brasserie* [18] (🖥 cote-restaurants.co.uk; Mon-Fri 8am-11pm, Sat 9am-11pm, Sun 9am-10.30pm) in Milsom Place, too, where *moules frites* at £12.95 jostle for space on the menu with *poulet breton* (£11.95).

For Italian cuisine in many guises, you'll be spoiled for choice. Combine your meal with a touch of history at the stylish Italian *Amarone* [47] (🖥 www.amaroneris torante.co.uk; Mon-Thur noon-2.30pm & 5.30-10pm, Fri same but to 10.30pm, Sat noon-10.30pm), which occupies the house where Beau Nash lived and died, next to the theatre on Barton St.

At the riverside *Ponte Vecchio* [48] (🖥 pontevecchiobath.com; Mon-Fri noon-3pm & 6-10pm, Sat & Sun noon-10pm) in a prime position overlooking the weir, next to The Rec, it's all about the setting. Dine inside or out in their wood and stainless-steel take on a traditional boathouse from an Italian menu with pizzas from £8.95 and pasta from £12.50.

Rather less scenic is the long-standing *Martini* [12] (🖥 www.martinirestaurant.co .uk; Mon-Fri noon-2.30pm & 6-10.30pm, Sat noon-10.30pm, Sun noon-2.30pm & 6-10pm), on George St. The décor may not be up to much, but traditional food and an old-fashioned Italian welcome bring punters back for more.

Italian is on the menu at 2 Margaret's Buildings, too, where *Rustico Bistro Italiano* [2] (☎ 01225-310064, 🖳 rustico bistroitaliano.co.uk; Tue-Sun noon-2.15pm & 6-9.45pm) serves hearty helpings of Italian classics. But if you're just after a pizza, beat a path to the unpretentious but popular *Real Italian Pizza Co* [69] (🖳 real italianpizza.co.uk; daily 11am-11pm), on York St, where busy chefs do wonders with a wood-fired pizza oven. For the latest Italian success story, though, make your way down to the grotto-like setting of *Sotto Sotto* [73] (☎ 01225-330236, 🖳 sottosotto .co.uk; daily noon-2pm & 5-10pm), on North Parade. Come for the (slightly noisy) atmosphere and for dishes such as *Fegato di vitello con polenta croccante e marmellata di cipolle rosse* (sautéed calf liver with a crispy polenta slice & red onion marmalade for £15).

Tapas are on hand at *Olé Tapas* [33] (🖳 oletapas.co.uk; Sun-Thur noon-10pm, Fri-Sat noon-11pm), 1 John St, a buzzing little place with offerings of fish, chorizo, aubergine and more, at £2.50-16 per dish. And then there's Greek cuisine, as defined at *OPA* [74] (🖳 opabath.com; Mon-Sat noon-2am), also on North Parade.

● **World cuisines** A must for the setting alone is *The Eastern Eye* [36] (☎ 01225-422323, 🖳 easterneye.com; Mon-Fri noon-2.30pm & 6-11.30pm, Sat-Sun noon-11.30pm), 8a Quiet St, even if you're not a huge fan of Indian cuisine – though it's good. Occupying the first floor of a 19th-century building adorned with sculptures of 'Commerce' and 'Genius', it sits beneath a magnificent three-domed ceiling.

Rather less smart is the irresistibly named *Yak Yeti Yak* [78] (🖳 yakyetiyak.co .uk; daily noon-2pm, Mon-Thur 6-10.30pm, Fri-Sat 5-10.30pm, Sun 6-10pm), on Pierrepont St, where Nepalese mains are £6.20-7.10 for vegetarian dishes, and from £8.20 for others; they also have a three-course lunch menu for £14.10.

Just a few steps up the road you can be transported to the Far East at *Salathai* [71] (🖳 salathai-bath.co.uk; daily noon-2.30pm & 6-10.30pm), where set menus cost from £16.95, or £14.95 for vegetarian.

There's also the tranquil setting of *Thai Balcony* [57] (☎ 01225-444450, 🖳 thaibalcony.co.uk; daily noon-2.30pm, & 6-10.30pm), at 1 Seven Dials above the Sainsbury's Local on Sawclose. It has been here since 1990 and is usually busy so reserving a table is recommended. The staff are friendly and it is a relaxing place. The menu is extensive and includes Gaeng Ped Yang (duck red curry) for £11.25 and a good selection of vegetarian dishes with Pad Thai Jay for £11.95.

For a reliable source of good, inexpensive food with plenty of noodles, you can't beat the relaxed *Wagamama* [15] (🖳 waga mama.com/restaurants/bath; Mon-Sat 11.30am-11pm, Sun to 10pm) next to the Travelodge on the corner of George and Broad streets; it's great for vegetarians, too.

● **Vegetarian and fish** Vegetarians and vegans beat a path to *Acorn Vegetarian Kitchen* [67] (🖳 acornvegetariankitchen.co .uk; Wed-Sun noon-3pm & 5.30-9.30pm), 2 North Parade Passage, close to the abbey, and go no further. Formerly the popular Demuths, it has gone up a notch, with two courses a rather pricey £29.90. But then, with dishes such as mushroom tart served with celeriac cooked slowly in its own juice, hazelnut butter, braised king oyster mushroom, red cabbage & red chicory, you'll be spoiled for choice.

Simpler is *The Green Rocket Café* [72] (🖳 thegreenrocket.co.uk; Mon & Tue 9am-4.30pm, Wed-Sat 9am-4.30pm & 6-9.30pm, Sun 10am-4.30pm), on the corner of North Parade & Pierrepont St. Freshly squeezed juices (£3.95) complement a well-chosen and regularly changing lunch menu, from sandwiches to noodles and a mushroom, sundried tomato & basil rice burger (£9.50), with dinner mains up to £11.50 for (smoked mushroom, chestnut & sage) sausages and (mustard) mash. They also offer a takeaway service.

For fish lovers, *Loch Fyne* [13] (☎ 01225-750120, 🖳 lochfyneseafoodandgrill .co.uk; Mon-Thur 7.30am-10.30pm, Fri to 11pm, Sat 8am-11pm, Sun to 10.30pm), on Milsom St, needs little introduction having become familiar on many a British high street in recent years. With fresh fish cooked in open kitchens it remains a popular concept and the place can get very busy.

● **Bars, pubs and pub grub** For the most part, opening hours quoted in this section relate to when **food** is served; almost all venues serve drinks outside these hours.

Just behind the theatre, the *Garrick's Head* [56] (🖥 garricksheadpub.com; daily noon-3pm, Sun-Tue 5.30-9pm, Wed-Sat 5.30-10pm) retains the atmosphere of a pub, with a good bar menu and more. They even brew their own eponymous house ale. Somewhat quirkily, the building, the former home of Beau Nash, marks the start of the city's ghost walk (see p166) – so presumably Banquo could be among the guests.

Despite the onslaught of modernisation, plenty of pubs remain unscathed. For a quiet drink and well-prepared food, *Crystal Palace* [66] (🖥 crystalpalacepub .co.uk; Sun-Thur 11am-9pm, Fri & Sat to 9.30pm), on Abbey Green, is absolutely central; the walled garden behind is an added bonus for lunch in the summer months. Rather less peaceful is *The Pulteney Arms* [21] (🖥 thepulteneyarms.co .uk; Mon-Fri noon-2.30pm & 6-9pm, Sat noon-3pm & 6-9pm, Sun noon-3pm), on the corner of Daniel St and Sutton St. This is the 'rugby' pub, frequented by players and spectators, and heaving when Bath are playing just across the river at The Rec.

There's simple, no-nonsense fare at *The Raven* [35] (🖥 theravenofbath.co.uk; Mon-Sat 11am-9pm, Sun 11am-8.30pm), on Queen St, a no-frills, CAMRA award-winning pub which concentrates on pies – pork pies, steak pies, vegetarian pies, even Heidi pies (about £9.80) – all washed down with real ale.

If you're after nothing more complicated than a good pint, you'll be spoiled for choice (hours given here are **pub hours**, not those for food). Claiming to be the smallest pub in Bath, the *Volunteer Rifleman's Arms* [44] (☎ 01225-425210; daily 11am-11pm) is centrally located on New Bond Street Place; they do serve food here, but for many it's all about the beer.

Close by there's *The Old Green Tree* [43] (☎ 01225-448259; Mon-Sat noon-11pm, Sun to 10.30pm), Green St, then you could move on to *Salamander* [32] (🖥 bathales .com/our-pubs/pid/the-salamander; Mon-Thur 11am-11pm, Fri & Sat to 1am), on John St, for a more Victorian atmosphere, and round off the evening at 16th-century *The Star Inn* [7] (☎ 01225-425072; noon-2.30pm & 5.30pm-midnight, Fri & Sat noon-1am, Sun noon-midnight), with its four small bars, where real ale is drawn straight from the barrel. See box on p23 for more details of the beers.

● **Teahouses and cafés** Walking the Cotswold Way throws up its fair share of trials, from steep hills to unpredictable rain and cold, when a cup of tea is rarely more welcome. Bath doesn't disappoint. Perhaps this is the time to dress up and treat yourself to afternoon tea at the *Pump Room* [65] (☎ 01225-444477, 🖥 romanbaths.co.uk/ pump-room-restaurant; daily Mar-Dec 9.30am-5pm, Jan & Feb from 10am but note that they may close an hour or so earlier if there is a festival or special occasion), one of the great institutions of Bath. Built between 1795 and 1797, the Pump Room exudes the elegance of the era, with its grand chandeliers and classical music played by the Pump Room Trio. Although you can take morning coffee or lunch here, it's at teatime that it comes into its own. You don't have to have the full works of sandwiches, scones, cakes and pastries (£26pp) – but it's certainly tempting. Tables may be reserved during the week and for breakfast and lunch (noon-2.30pm) on Sunday, but not at other times; at busy periods expect to queue for 30-40 minutes. Note that they may close an hour or so earlier if there is a festival or special occasion. If you just want to marvel at the building, you can combine it with a visit to the Roman Baths (see p169).

Old-fashioned tea doesn't have to be quite so posh, though. The oldest house in Bath, at 4 North Parade Passage, dates back to around 1482 and houses *Sally Lunn's* [68] (🖥 sallylunns.co.uk; daily 10am-9pm; dinner from 5pm, advance booking advised). This is the home of the Bath bun (see box on p178), which was created by Ms Lunn when she lived here in the 17th century.

Just round the corner (with another entrance on North Parade Passage), the name has been taken up at *The Bath Bun* [77] (🖥 thebathbun.com; Tue-Sat 9.30am-5pm, Sun & Mon 11am-5pm), where there is pretty china and the colourful cup cakes are very popular. Try their cream tea for £6.50, or traditional high tea at £14.50. Or indulge continental style at a branch of *Pâtisserie Valerie* [52] (🖥 patisserie-val erie.co.uk; daily 9am-7pm), 20 High St, where cream cakes, iced cakes, chocolate cakes and sticky gateaux provide plenty of sweet treats.

If it's a bright and sunny morning, one of our favourite places to sit and have croissants and pain au chocolat for breakfast is at *B Bakery* [47] (☎ 01225-962288, 🖥 bath.b-bakery.com; Mon-Tue & Thur-Sun 10am-5pm), perfectly located by Pulteney Bridge overlooking the weir.

● **Cheap eats and fast food** It's not difficult to find some form of fast food among the many outlets around the city, not to mention the occasional 'greasy spoon' joint where you can get a standard fry up, and any number of sandwich bars.

One of the best proponents of the burger is *Schwartz Bros* (🖥 schwartzbro s.co.uk), with a branch on **Walcot St** [19] (Tue 5.30-10pm, Wed & Thur to 11pm, Fri & Sat noon to midnight, Sun to 10pm), and another on **Sawclose** [54] (Sun-Tue noon-11pm, Wed-Fri to midnight, Sat to 3am).

APPENDIX A – GPS WAYPOINTS

Each GPS waypoint was taken on the route at the reference number marked on the map as below. This list is also available in downloadable form from the Trailblazer website – 🖳 trailblazer-guides.com/gps-waypoints.

MAP	REF	GPS WAYPOINT		DESCRIPTION
Map 1	001	N52° 03.018'	W01° 46.913'	start of Cotswold Way, Chipping Campden
Map 1	002	N52° 03.525'	W01° 47.752'	kissing gate on Dover's Hill
Map 2	003	N52° 01.862'	W01° 49.687'	toposcope – Fish Hill
Map 3	004	N52° 01.458'	W01° 50.165'	Broadway Tower
Map 3	005	N52° 02.197'	W01° 51.172'	junction of road, Broadway
Map 3	006	N52° 01.678'	W01° 52.427'	guidepost, Broadway Coppice
Map 4	007	N52° 00.332'	W01° 52.842'	cattle grid – Shenberrow
Map 4	008	N52° 00.003'	W01° 53.040'	Shenberrow Hill
Map 5	009	N52° 00.403'	W01° 54.146'	corner of road by The Vine, Stanton
Map 5	010	N51° 59.377'	W01° 54.748'	gate to Stanway House
Map 6	011	N51° 58.322'	W01° 53.473'	Stumps Cross
Map 6	012	N51° 58.070'	W01° 54.563'	monument – Beckbury Camp
Map 7	013	N51° 58.157'	W01° 55.655'	leave road by Hailes Abbey
Map 8	014	N51° 57.218'	W01° 57.825'	corner of North St, Winchcombe
Map 9	015	N51° 55.690'	W01° 58.255'	kissing gate by Belas Knap
Map 10	016	N51° 56.542'	W02° 01.018'	Cleeve Hill car park
Map 10	017	N51° 56.160'	W02° 01.328'	Cleeve Hill toposcope
Map 11	018	N51° 55.600'	W02° 01.325'	Cleeve Hill fort, marking track by path junction to Southam
Map 13	019	N51° 52.606'	W02° 01.227'	bridge over spill by Dowdeswell Reservoir
Map 14	020	N51° 51.827'	W02° 02.207'	guidepost, Wistley Hill
Map 14	021	N51° 51.193'	W02° 02.865'	junction with Hartley Lane, Seven Springs
Map 15	022	N51° 51.822'	W02° 04.550'	Leckhampton Hill trig point
Map 15	023	N51° 50.987'	W02° 04.925'	track meets road
Map 16	024	N51° 50.598'	W02° 05.783'	Air Balloon pub
Map 16	025	N51° 50.073'	W02° 06.893'	The Peak
Map 18	026	N51° 49.922'	W02° 09.312'	Cooper's Hill
Map 19	027	N51° 48.358'	W02° 11.518'	steps to trig point, Painswick Hill
Map 20	028	N51° 47.205'	W02° 11.592'	junction with A46, Painswick
Map 20	029	N51° 46.808'	W02° 13.120'	The Edgemoor Inn
Map 21	030	N51° 47.008'	W02° 14.685'	Way leaves road by disused well (Cliff Wood)
Map 21	031	N51° 46.697'	W02° 15.745'	Haresfield Beacon
Map 22	032	N51° 45.325'	W02° 15.522'	gate on Maiden Hill
Map 23	033	N51° 44.395'	W02° 15.192'	Oil Mills Bridge
Map 25	034	N51° 42.702'	W02° 18.037'	Nympsfield display boards
Map 26	035	N51° 41.908'	W02° 18.355'	Uley Long Barrow (Hetty Pegler's Tump)
Map 26	036	N51° 41.527'	W02° 18.610'	Uley Bury
Map 27	037	N51° 41.617'	W02° 19.482'	Cam Long Down
Map 28	038	N51° 40.818'	W02° 22.037'	routes divide by Stinchcombe Hill Golf Club
Map 28	039	N51° 40.803'	W02° 22.938'	Drakestone Point (scenic route)
Map 28	040	N51° 40.725'	W02° 22.247'	convergence of paths, Stinchcombe Hill
Map 29	041	N51° 39.528'	W02° 22.353'	Tyndale Monument

Map 29	042	N51° 38.492'	W02° 21.555'	hilltop monument above Wotton-under-Edge
Map 30	043	N51° 38.347'	W02° 19.310'	Tor Hill & Alderley signpost
Map 31	044	N51° 37.033'	W02° 19.995'	Wotton-under-Edge 5-mile sign, Alderley
Map 32	045	N51° 35.975	W02° 18.482	track meets road
Map 33	046	N51° 35.220'	W02° 19.780'	monument to General Lord Somerset
Map 34	047	N51° 33.663'	W02° 20.453'	wood near Horton Court
Map 35	048	N51° 32.070'	W02° 21.275'	St John the Baptist, Old Sodbury
Map 35	049	N51° 30.906'	W02° 21.032'	lone oak, Dodington Park
Map 36	050	N51° 30.427'	W02° 20.087'	Tormarton bus stop
Map 38	051	N51° 28.200'	W02° 22.735'	kissing gate above withy bed
Map 39	052	N51° 27.182'	W02° 21.584'	Cold Ashton church
Map 40	053	N51° 25.875'	W02° 23.392'	kissing gate at top of hill
Map 41	054	N51° 25.787'	W02° 24.892'	Hanging Hill
Map 41	055	N51° 25.405'	W02° 24.317'	turn by Lansdown Golf Course
Map 42	056	N51° 24.782'	W02° 24.832'	Prospect Stile
Map 42	057	N51° 23.720'	W02° 24.062'	Weston trig point
Map 43	058	N51° 22.883'	W02° 21.563'	Bath Abbey (end/start of Cotswold Way)

APPENDIX B – WALKING WITH A DOG

WALKING THE COTSWOLD WAY WITH A DOG

Many are the rewards that await those prepared to make the extra effort required to bring their best friend along the Cotswold Way. You shouldn't underestimate the amount of work involved, though. Indeed, just about every decision you make will be influenced by the fact that you've got a dog: how you plan to travel to the start of the trail, where you're going to stay, how far you're going to walk each day, where you're going to rest and where you're going to eat in the evening etc.

If you're also sure your dog can cope with (and will enjoy) walking, say, 10-14 miles or more a day for several days in a row, you need to start preparing accordingly. Extra thought also needs to go into your itinerary. The best starting point is to study the village and town facilities table on pp34-7 (and the advice below), and plan where to stop and where to buy food.

Looking after your dog

To begin with, you need to make sure that your own dog is fully **inoculated** against the usual doggy illnesses, and also up to date with regard to **worm pills** (eg Drontal) and **flea preventatives** such as Frontline – they are, after all, following in the pawprints of many a dog before them, some of whom may well have left fleas or other parasites on the trail that now lie in wait for their next meal to arrive. **Pet insurance** is also a very good idea; if you've already got insurance, do check that it will cover a trip such as this.

On the subject of looking after your dog's health, perhaps the most important implement you can take with you is a **plastic tick remover**, available from vets for a couple of quid. These removers, while fiddly, help you to remove ticks safely (ie without leaving the head behind buried under the dog's skin).

Being in unfamiliar territory also makes it more likely that you and your dog could become separated. All dogs now have to be microchipped but make sure yours also has a tag with your contact details on it (a mobile phone number would be best if you have one).

When to keep your dog on a lead

● **On the edge of the escarpment** It's a sad fact that, every year, a few dogs lose their lives falling over the edge of steep slopes.

● **When crossing farmland** This is particularly important in the lambing season (around February to May) when your dog can scare the sheep, causing them to lose their young. During this time, most farmers would prefer it if you didn't bring your dog at all. Farmers are allowed by law to shoot at and kill any dogs that they consider are worrying their sheep. Dogs running free in standing crops can also cause damage, so do take care to prevent this. The exception to the 'dogs on leads' rule is if your dog is being attacked by cows. A few years ago there were three deaths in the UK caused by walkers being trampled as they tried to rescue their dogs from the attentions of cattle. The advice in this instance is to let go of the lead, head speedily to a position of safety (usually the other side of the field gate or stile) and call your dog to you.

● **Around ground-nesting birds** It's important to keep your dog under control when crossing an area inhabited by ground-nesting birds, which are usually active between March and June; a dog on the loose at this time could inadvertently destroy the nest, or frighten the adult birds away. Most dogs love foraging around in the woods but make sure you have permission to do so; some woods are used as 'nurseries' for game birds and dogs are only allowed through them if they are on a lead.

● **By roads etc** For obvious reasons.

What to pack

You've probably already got a good idea of what to bring to keep your dog alive and happy, but the following is a checklist:

● **Food/water bowl** Foldable cloth bowls are popular with walkers, being light and taking up little room in a rucksack. You can get also get a water-bottle-and-bowl combination, where the bottle folds into a 'trough' from which the dog can drink.

● **Lead and collar** An extendable one is probably preferable for this sort of trip. Make sure both lead and collar are in good condition – you don't want either to snap on the trail, or you may end up carrying your dog through sheep fields until a replacement can be found.

● **Medication** You'll know if you need to bring any lotions or potions.

● **Bedding** A simple blanket may suffice, or you can opt for something more elaborate if you aren't carrying your own luggage.

● **Poo bags** Essential.

● **Hygiene wipes** For cleaning your dog after it's rolled in, errm, stuff.

● **A favourite toy** Helps prevent your dog from pining for the entire walk.

● **Food/water** Remember to bring treats as well as regular food to keep up the mutt's morale. That said, if your dog is anything like mine the chances are they'll spend most of the walk dining on rabbit droppings and sheep poo anyway.

● **Corkscrew stake** Available from camping or pet shops, this will help you to keep your dog secure in one place while you set up camp/doze.

● **Tick remover** See opposite ● **Raingear** It can rain! ● **Old towels** For drying your dog.

When it comes to packing, I always leave an exterior pocket of my rucksack empty so I can put used poo bags in there (for deposit at the first bin I come to). I always like to keep all the dog's kit together and separate from the other luggage (usually inside a plastic bag inside my rucksack). I have also seen several dogs sporting their own 'doggy rucksack', so they can carry their own food, water, poo etc – which certainly reduces the burden on their owner!

Cleaning up after your dog

It is extremely important that dog owners behave in a responsible way when walking the path. Dog excrement should be cleaned up. In towns, villages and fields where animals graze or which will be cut for silage, hay etc, you need to pick up and bag the excrement.

Staying with your dog

In this guide we have used the symbol 🐕 to denote where a hotel, pub, B&B or campsite allows dogs to stay, although this always needs to be arranged in advance; many places have only one or two rooms that they deem suitable, and in some dogs need to sleep in a separate building. Some places make an additional charge (usually per night but occasionally per stay), while others may require a deposit, which is refundable if the dog doesn't make a mess. Hostels (both YHA and independent) do not permit dogs unless they are an assistance (guide) dog.

When it comes to **eating**, most landlords allow dogs in at least a section of their pubs, though very few restaurants do. Make sure you always ask first, then ensure that your dog doesn't run around the pub but is secured to your table or a radiator.

Henry Stedman

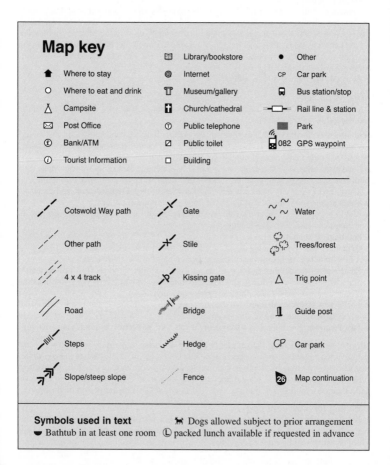

Map key

🏠 Where to stay	📖 Library/bookstore	● Other
O Where to eat and drink	@ Internet	CP Car park
Ⲁ Campsite	🏛 Museum/gallery	🚌 Bus station/stop
⊠ Post Office	✝ Church/cathedral	▬□▬ Rail line & station
ⓔ Bank/ATM	☏ Public telephone	Park
ⓘ Tourist Information	☑ Public toilet	📱082 GPS waypoint
	□ Building	

Cotswold Way path	Gate	~~~ Water
Other path	Stile	Trees/forest
4 x 4 track	Kissing gate	△ Trig point
Road	Bridge	Ⲁ Guide post
Steps	Hedge	CP Car park
Slope/steep slope	Fence	26 Map continuation

Symbols used in text   🐕 Dogs allowed subject to prior arrangement
🛁 Bathtub in at least one room   Ⓛ packed lunch available if requested in advance

INDEX

Page references in **bold** type refer to maps

Tour du Mont Blanc
Jim Manthorpe, 2nd edn, £13.99
ISBN 978-1-905864-92-8, 204pp, 60 maps, 50 colour photos
At 4807m (15,771ft), Mont Blanc is the highest mountain in western Europe. The trail (105 miles, 168km) that circumnavigates the massif, passing through France, Italy and Switzerland, is the most popular long-distance walk in Europe. Includes day walks. Plus – Climbing guide to Mont Blanc

Kilimanjaro – the trekking guide
Henry Stedman, 5th edn, £14.99
ISBN 978-1-905864-95-9, 368pp, 40 maps, 50 colour photos
At 5895m (19,340ft) Kilimanjaro is the world's tallest freestanding mountain and one of the most popular destinations for hikers visiting Africa. Route guides & maps – the 6 major routes. City guides – Nairobi, Dar-es-Salaam, Arusha, Moshi & Marangu.

The Inca Trail, Cusco & Machu Picchu
Alex Stewart & Henry Stedman, 6th edn, £14.99
ISBN 978-1-905864-88-1, 370pp, 70 maps, 30 colour photos
The Inca Trail from Cusco to Machu Picchu is South America's most popular trek. This guide includes hiking options from two days to three weeks. Plus plans of Inca sites, guides to Lima, Cusco and Machu Picchu. Includes the High Inca Trail, Salkantay Trek and the Choquequirao Trail. New 6th edition adds two Sacred Valley treks: Lares Trail and Ausangate Circuit.

Peru's Cordilleras Blanca & Huayhuash
The Hiking & Biking Guide
Neil & Harriet Pike, 1st edn, £15.99
ISBN 978-1-905864-63-8, 242pp, 50 maps, 40 colour photos
This region, in northern Peru, boasts some of the most spectacular scenery in the Andes, and most accessible high mountain trekking and biking in the world. This practical guide contains 60 detailed route maps and descriptions covering 20 hiking trails and more than 30 days of paved and dirt road cycling.

Moroccan Atlas – the trekking guide
Alan Palmer, 2nd edn, £14.99
ISBN 978-1-905864-59-1, 420pp, 86 maps, 40 colour photos
The High Atlas in central Morocco is the most dramatic and beautiful section of the entire Atlas range. Towering peaks, deep gorges and huddled Berber villages enchant all who visit. With 73 detailed maps, 13 town and village guides including Marrakech.

Trekking in the Everest Region
Jamie McGuinness 6th edn, £15.99
ISBN 978-1-905864-81-2, 320pp, 95 maps, 30 colour photos
Sixth edition of this popular guide to the world's most famous trekking region. Covers not only the classic treks but also the wild routes. Written by a Nepal-based trek and mountaineering leader. Includes 27 detailed route maps and 52 village plans. Plus: Kathmandu city guide

TRAILBLAZER'S LONG-DISTANCE PATH (LDP) WALKING GUIDES

We've applied to destinations which are closer to home Trailblazer's proven formula for publishing definitive practical route guides for adventurous travellers. Britain's network of long-distance trails enables the walker to explore some of the finest landscapes in the country's best walking areas. These are guides that are user-friendly, practical, informative and environmentally sensitive.

'The same attention to detail that distinguishes its other guides has been brought to bear here'.
THE SUNDAY TIMES

● **Unique mapping features** In many walking guidebooks the reader has to read a route description then try to relate it to the map. Our guides are much easier to use because walking directions, tricky junctions, places to stay and eat, points of interest and walking times are all written onto the maps themselves in the places to which they apply. With their uncluttered clarity, these are not general-purpose maps but fully edited maps drawn by walkers for walkers.

● **Largest-scale walking maps** At a scale of just under 1:20,000 (8cm or 3¹/₈ inches to one mile) the maps in these guides are bigger than even the most detailed British walking maps currently available in the shops.

● **Not just a trail guide – includes where to stay, where to eat and public transport** Our guidebooks cover the complete walking experience, not just the route. Accommodation options for all budgets are provided (pubs, hotels, B&Bs, campsites, bunkhouses, hostels) as well as places to eat. Detailed public transport information for all access points to each trail means that there are itineraries for all walkers, for hiking the entire route as well as for day or weekend walks.

● **Includes dowloadable GPS waypoints –** Marked on our maps and downloadable from the Trailblazer website.

Cleveland Way *Henry Stedman*, 1st edn, ISBN 978-1-905864-91-1, 208pp, 58 maps
Coast to Coast *Henry Stedman*, 8th edn, ISBN 978-1-905864-96-6, 268pp, 110 maps
Cornwall Coast Path (SW Coast Path Pt 2) *Stedman & Newton*, 6th edn, ISBN 978-1-912716-05-0, 352pp, 142 maps
Cotswold Way *Tricia & Bob Hayne*, 4th edn, ISBN 978-1-912716-04-3, 204pp, 53 maps,
Dales Way *Henry Stedman,* 1st edn, ISBN 978-1-905864-78-2, 192pp, 50 maps
Dorset & South Devon (SW Coast Path Pt 3) *Stedman & Newton*, 2nd edn, ISBN 978-1-905864-94-2, 336pp, 88 maps
Exmoor & North Devon (SW Coast Path Pt I) *Stedman & Newton*, 2nd edn, ISBN 978-1-905864-86-7, 224pp, 68 maps
Great Glen Way *Jim Manthorpe,* 1st edn, ISBN 978-1-905864-80-5, 192pp, 55 maps
Hadrian's Wall Path *Henry Stedman*, 5th edn, ISBN 978-1-905864-85-0, 224pp, 60 maps
Norfolk Coast Path & Peddars Way *Alexander Stewart*, 1st edn, ISBN 978-1-905864-98-0, 224pp, 75 maps,
North Downs Way *Henry Stedman*, 2nd edn, ISBN 978-1-905864-90-4, 240pp, 98 maps
Offa's Dyke Path *Keith Carter*, 5th edn, ISBN 978-1-912716-03-6, 256pp, 98 maps
Pembrokeshire Coast Path *Jim Manthorpe*, 5th edn, ISBN 978-1-905864-84-3, 236pp, 96 maps
Pennine Way *Stuart Greig*, 5th edn, ISBN 978-1-912716-02-9, 272pp, 138 maps
The Ridgeway *Nick Hill*, 4th edn, ISBN 978-1-905864-79-9, 208pp, 53 maps
South Downs Way *Jim Manthorpe*, 6th edn, ISBN 978-1-905864-93-5, 204pp, 60 maps
Thames Path *Joel Newton*, 2nd edn, ISBN 978-1-905864-97-3, 256pp, 99 maps
West Highland Way *Charlie Loram*, 7th edn, ISBN 978-1-912716-01-2, 218pp, 60 maps

'The Trailblazer series stands head, shoulders, waist and ankles above the rest.
They are particularly strong on mapping ...'
THE SUNDAY TIMES

Distance table (upper value in each cell in plain type, lower value in *italic*):

	Chipping Campden	Broadway	Stanton	Wood Stanway	Hailes	Winchcombe	Cleeve Hill	Dowdeswell Reservoir	Seven Springs	Crickley Hill	Birdlip
Broadway	6										
	9.5										
Stanton	10.5	4.5									
	17	*7.5*									
Wood Stanway	12.5	6.5	2								
	20	*10.5*	*3*								
Hailes	16	10	5.5	3.5							
	25.5	*16*	*8.5*	*5.5*							
Winchcombe	18	12	7.5	5.5	2						
	29	*19.5*	*12*	*9*	*3.5*						
Cleeve Hill	24	18	13.5	11.5	8	6					
	38.5	*29*	*21.5*	*18.5*	*13*	*9.5*					
Dowdeswell Res'voir	29	23	18.5	16.5	13	11	5				
	46.5	*37*	*29.5*	*26.5*	*21*	*17.5*	*8*				
Seven Springs	32	26	21.5	19.5	16	14	8	3			
	51	*41.5*	*34*	*31*	*25.5*	*22*	*12.5*	*4.5*			
Crickley Hill	37	31	26.5	24.5	21	19	13	8	5		
	59	*49.5*	*42*	*39*	*33.5*	*30*	*20.5*	*12.5*	*8*		
Birdlip	39.5	33.5	29	27	23.5	21.5	15.5	10.5	7.5	2.5	
	63	*53.5*	*46*	*43*	*37.5*	*34*	*24.5*	*16.5*	*12*	*4*	
Cranham Cnr	43.5	37.5	33	31	27.5	25.5	19.5	14.5	11.5	6.5	4
	69.5	*60*	*52.5*	*49.5*	*44*	*40.5*	*31*	*23*	*18.5*	*10.5*	*6.5*
Painswick	46	40	35.5	33.5	30	28	22	17	14	9	6.5
	73.5	*64*	*56.5*	*53.5*	*48*	*44.5*	*35*	*27*	*22.5*	*14.5*	*10.5*
Stonehouse	54.5	48.5	44	42	38.5	36.5	30.5	25.5	22.5	17.5	15
	87	*77.5*	*70*	*67*	*61.5*	*58*	*48.5*	*40.5*	*36*	*28*	*24*
Selsley Common	56	50	45.5	43.5	40	38	32	27	24	19	16.5
	89.5	*80*	*72.5*	*69.5*	*64*	*60.5*	*51*	*43*	*38.5*	*30.5*	*26.5*
Dursley	63.5	57.5	53	51	47.5	45.5	39.5	34.5	31.5	26.5	24
	101.5	*92*	*84.5*	*81.5*	*76*	*72.5*	*63*	*55*	*50.5*	*42.5*	*38.5*
North Nibley	68.5	62.5	58	56	52.5	50.5	44.5	39.5	36.5	31.5	29
	109.5	*100*	*92.5*	*89.5*	*84*	*80.5*	*71*	*63*	*58.5*	*50.5*	*46.5*
Wotton-u-Edge	70.5	64.5	60	58	54.5	52.5	46.5	41.5	38.5	33.5	31
	113	*103.5*	*96*	*93*	*87.5*	*84*	*74.5*	*66.5*	*62*	*54*	*50*
Hawkesbury Upton	78	72	67.5	65.5	62	60	54	49	46	41	38.5
	125	*115.5*	*108*	*105*	*99.5*	*96*	*86.5*	*78.5*	*74*	*66*	*62*
Little Sodbury	81.5	75.5	71	69	65.5	63.5	57.5	52.5	49.5	44.5	42
	130.5	*121*	*113.5*	*110.5*	*105*	*101.5*	*92*	*84*	*79.5*	*71.5*	*67.5*
Old Sodbury	83.5	77.5	73	71	67.5	65.5	59.5	54.5	51.5	46.5	44
	133.5	*124*	*116.5*	*113.5*	*108*	*104.5*	*95*	*87*	*82.5*	*74.5*	*70.5*
Coomb's End	84	78	73.5	71.5	68	66	60	55	52	47	44.5
	134.5	*125*	*117.5*	*114.5*	*109*	*105.5*	*96*	*88*	*83.5*	*75.5*	*71.5*
Tormarton	85.5	79.5	75	73	69.5	67.5	61.5	56.5	53.5	48.5	46
	137	*127.5*	*120*	*117*	*111.5*	*108*	*98.5*	*90.5*	*86*	*78*	*74*
Pennsylvania	91.5	85.5	81	79	75.5	73.5	67.5	62.5	59.5	54.5	52
	146.5	*137*	*129.5*	*126.5*	*121*	*117.5*	*108*	*100*	*95.5*	*87.5*	*83.5*
Cold Ashton	92	86	81.5	79.5	76	74	68	63	60	55	52.5
	147	*137.5*	*130*	*127*	*121.5*	*118*	*108.5*	*100.5*	*96*	*88*	*84*
Bath	102	96	91.5	89.5	86	84	78	73	70	65	62.5
	163	*153.5*	*146*	*143*	*137.5*	*134*	*124.5*	*116.5*	*112*	*104*	*100*

Cotswold Way
DISTANCE CHART

(route via Selsley Common and Stinchcombe Hill)

miles/*kilometres* (approx)

Distances given as miles (roman) / *kilometres* (italic).

Cranham Corner	Painswick	Stonehouse	Selsley Common	Dursley	North Nibley	Wotton-under-Edge	Hawkesbury Upton	Little Sodbury	Old Sodbury	Coomb's End	Tormarton	Pennsylvania	Cold Ashton	
2.5														Painswick
4														
11	8.5													Stonehouse
17.5	*13.5*													
12.5	10	1.5												Selsley Common
20	*16*	*2.5*												
20	17.5	9	7.5											Dursley
32	*28*	*14.5*	*12*											
25	22.5	14	12.5	5										North Nibley
40	*36*	*22.5*	*20*	*8*										
27	24.5	16	14.5	7	2									Wotton-under-Edge
43.5	*39.5*	*26*	*23.5*	*11.5*	*3.5*									
34.5	32	23.5	22	14.5	9.5	7.5								Hawkesbury Upton
55.5	*51.5*	*38*	*35.5*	*23.5*	*15.5*	*12*								
38	35.5	27	25.5	18	13	11	3.5							Little Sodbury
61	*57*	*43.5*	*41*	*29*	*21*	*17.5*	*5.5*							
40	37.5	29	27.5	20	15	13	5.5	2						Old Sodbury
64	*60*	*46.5*	*44*	*32*	*24*	*20.5*	*8.5*	*3*						
40.5	38	29.5	28	20.5	15.5	13.5	6	2.5	0.5					Coomb's End
65	*61*	*47.5*	*45*	*33*	*25*	*21.5*	*9.5*	*4*	*1*					
42	39.5	31	29.5	22	17	15	7.5	4	2	1.5				Tormarton
67.5	*63.5*	*50*	*47.5*	*35.5*	*27.5*	*24*	*12*	*6.5*	*3.5*	*2.5*				
48	45.5	37	35.5	28	23	21	13.5	10	8	7.5	6			Pennsylvania
77	*73*	*59.5*	*57*	*45*	*37*	*33.5*	*21.5*	*16*	*13*	*12*	*9.5*			
48.8	46	37.5	36	28.5	23.5	21.5	14	10.5	8.5	8	6.5	0.5		Cold Ashton
77.5	*73.5*	*60*	*57.5*	*45.5*	*37.5*	*34*	*22*	*16.5*	*13.5*	*12.5*	*10*	*0.5*		
58.5	56	47.5	46	38.5	33.5	31.5	24	20.5	18.5	18	16.5	10.5	10	Bath
93.5	*89.5*	*76*	*73.5*	*61.5*	*53.5*	*50*	*38*	*32.5*	*29.5*	*28.5*	*26*	*16.5*	*16*	

TRAILBLAZER TITLE LIST

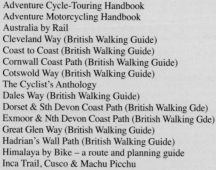

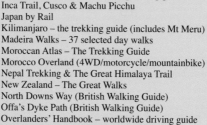

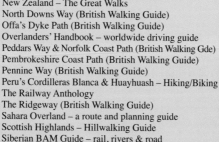

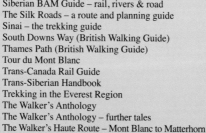

For more information about Trailblazer and our
expanding range of guides, for guidebook updates or
for credit card mail order sales visit our website:

www.trailblazer-guides.com

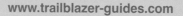

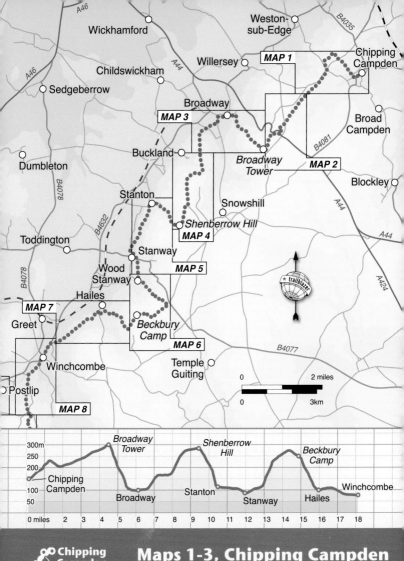

Maps 1-3, Chipping Campden to Broadway 6 miles/9.6km – 2¾-3¼hrs

Maps 3-8, Broadway to Winchcombe
12 miles/19.3km – 5½-6½hrs
NOTE: Add 20-30% to these times to allow for stops

Bath

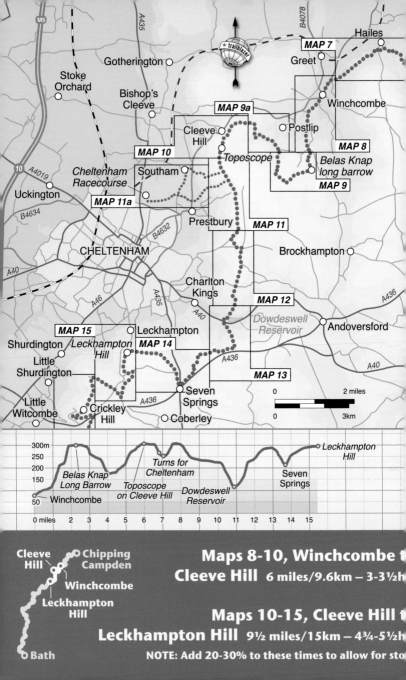

MAP 7

Hailes

Greet

Gotherington

Stoke
Orchard

Bishop's
Cleeve

Winchcombe

MAP 9a

Cleeve
Hill

Postlip

MAP 10

Toposcope

MAP 8

Belas Knap
long barrow

Cheltenham
Racecourse

Southam

MAP 9

Uckington

MAP 11a

Prestbury

MAP 11

CHELTENHAM

Brockhampton

Charlton
Kings

MAP 12

Dowdeswell
Reservoir

Andoversford

MAP 15

Leckhampton

Shurdington

Leckhampton
Hill

MAP 14

Little
Shurdington

Seven
Springs

MAP 13

Little
Witcombe

Crickley
Hill

Coberley

0   2 miles

0   3km

300m
250
200
150
50

Leckhampton
Hill

Belas Knap
Long Barrow

Turns for
Cheltenham

Seven
Springs

Winchcombe

Toposcope
on Cleeve Hill

Dowdeswell
Reservoir

0 miles   1   2   3   4   5   6   7   8   9   10   11   12   13   14   15

Cleeve
Hill

Chipping
Campden

Winchcombe

Leckhampton
Hill

Bath

Maps 8-10, Winchcombe t
Cleeve Hill 6 miles/9.6km – 3-3½h

Maps 10-15, Cleeve Hill t
Leckhampton Hill 9½ miles/15km – 4¾-5½h

NOTE: Add 20-30% to these times to allow for sto

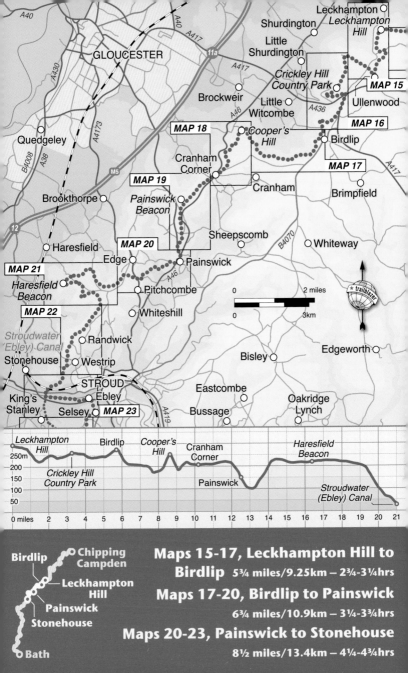

Leckhampton Hill
Shurdington
Little Shurdington
Leckhampton Hill
Leckhampton

A40
A417
A417
11a
A417

GLOUCESTER

A430
A40

A4173

Quedgeley

B4008
A38

M5

Brockthorpe

12

Haresfield

MAP 21
Haresfield Beacon

MAP 22

Stroudwater (Ebley) Canal

Stonehouse

King's Stanley

Selsey

Brockweir

Little Witcombe

Crickley Hill Country Park

Birdlip

MAP 15

Ullenwood

MAP 16

A436

Cooper's Hill

MAP 18

Cranham Corner

MAP 17

Cranham

Brimpfield

A417

MAP 19

Painswick Beacon

MAP 20

Edge

Painswick

Pitchcombe

Whiteshill

Sheepscomb

Whiteway

B4070

A46

Randwick

Westrip

STROUD

Ebley

MAP 23

A419

Bisley

Edgeworth

Eastcombe

Bussage

Oakridge Lynch

0   2 miles
0   3km

★ trailblazer

Leckhampton Hill
250m
200
150
100
50

Birdlip

Cooper's Hill

Cranham Corner

Crickley Hill Country Park

Painswick

Haresfield Beacon

Stroudwater (Ebley) Canal

0 miles 2 3 4 5 6 7 8 9 10 11 12 13 14 15 16 17 18 19 20 21

Birdlip
Chipping Campden
Leckhampton Hill
Painswick
Stonehouse
Bath

Maps 15-17, Leckhampton Hill to Birdlip 5¾ miles/9.25km – 2¾-3¼hrs

Maps 17-20, Birdlip to Painswick 6¾ miles/10.9km – 3¼-3¾hrs

Maps 20-23, Painswick to Stonehouse 8½ miles/13.4km – 4¼-4¾hrs

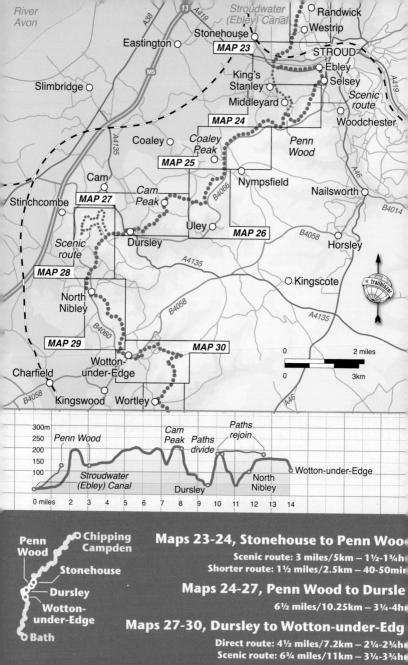

River Avon

A38
13 A419

Stroudwater (Ebley) Canal

Randwick

Westrip

Stonehouse

MAP 23

Eastington

M5

STROUD

Ebley

Selsey

King's Stanley

MAP 24

Middleyard

Scenic route

A419

Slimbridge

Woodchester

A4135

Coaley

Coaley Peak

MAP 25

Penn Wood

Nailsworth

B4014

Cam

B4066

Nympsfield

A46

Stinchcombe

MAP 27

Cam Peak

B4058

Horsley

Uley

MAP 26

MAP 28

Dursley

A4135

Scenic route

North Nibley

Kingscote

A4135

B4058

B4060

MAP 29

MAP 30

Wotton-under-Edge

Charfield

Kingswood

Wortley

A46

★ trailblazer

0   2 miles

0   3km

300m
250
200
150
100

Penn Wood

Cam Peak

Paths divide

Paths rejoin

Stroudwater (Ebley) Canal

Dursley

North Nibley

Wotton-under-Edge

0 miles   2   3   4   5   6   7   8   9   10   11   12   13   14

Penn Wood

Chipping Campden

Stonehouse

Dursley

Wotton-under-Edge

Bath

Maps 23-24, Stonehouse to Penn Wood

Scenic route: 3 miles/5km – 1½-1¾h
Shorter route: 1½ miles/2.5km – 40-50min

Maps 24-27, Penn Wood to Dursley

6½ miles/10.25km – 3¼-4h

Maps 27-30, Dursley to Wotton-under-Edge

Direct route: 4½ miles/7.2km – 2¼-2¾h
Scenic route: 6¾ miles/11km – 3¼-3¾h

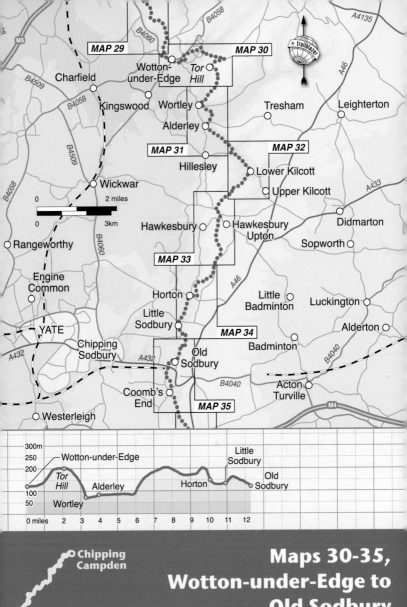

MAP 29

MAP 30

Wotton-under-Edge

Tor Hill

A4135

A46

B4058

B4060

Charfield

Kingswood

Wortley

Tresham

Leighterton

B4509

B4058

Alderley

MAP 31

MAP 32

Hillesley

Lower Kilcott

A433

Wickwar

Upper Kilcott

Didmarton

0   2 miles

0   3km

Hawkesbury

Hawkesbury Upton

Sopworth

Rangeworthy

MAP 33

B4060

A46

Engine Common

Horton

Little Badminton

Luckington

YATE

Little Sodbury

MAP 34

Alderton

A432

Chipping Sodbury

A432

Old Sodbury

Badminton

B4040

Coomb's End

B4040

MAP 35

Acton Turville

Westerleigh

M4

300m
250
200   Wotton-under-Edge
                                          Little
                                          Sodbury
Tor Hill   Old
                Alderley   Horton   Sodbury
150
100
50   Wortley

0 miles   2   3   4   5   6   7   8   9   10   11   12

Chipping Campden

Wotton-under-Edge

Old Sodbury

Bath

Maps 30-35, Wotton-under-Edge to Old Sodbury

12¼ miles/19.7km — 6-6¾hrs

NOTE: Add 20-30% to these times to allow for stops

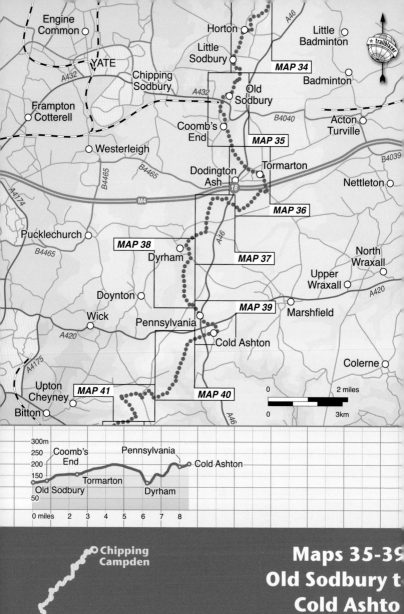

MAP 34

MAP 35

MAP 36

MAP 38

MAP 37

MAP 39

MAP 41

MAP 40

0   2 miles

0   3km

300m
250
200
150
50

Coomb's
End

Pennsylvania

Cold Ashton

Tormarton

Old Sodbury

Dyrham

0 miles   2   3   4   5   6   7   8

Chipping
Campden

Old Sodbury
Cold Ashton
Bath

Maps 35-39
Old Sodbury t
Cold Ashto

8½ miles/13.7km – 4¼-4¾h

NOTE: Add 20-30% to these times to allow for sto

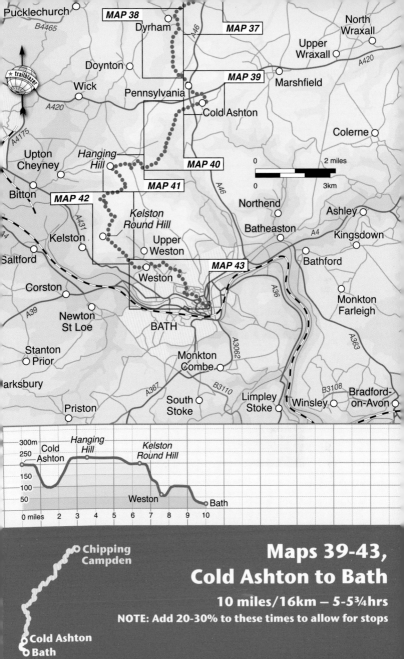

Maps 39-43,
Cold Ashton to Bath

10 miles/16km — 5-5¾hrs
NOTE: Add 20-30% to these times to allow for stops

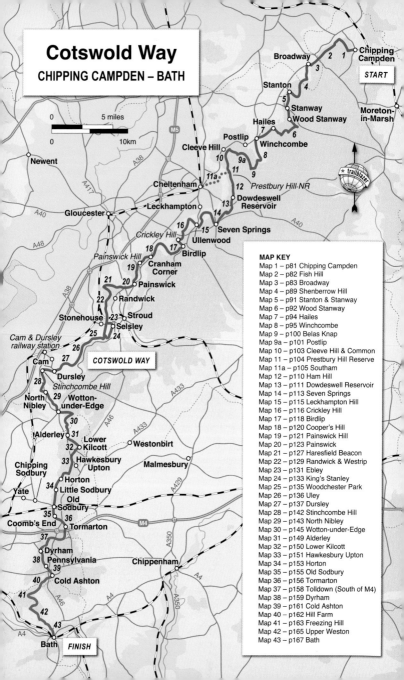

Cotswold Way

CHIPPING CAMPDEN – BATH

START

Moreton-in-Marsh

Chipping Campden

1
2
Broadway
3
Stanton
4
5
Stanway
Wood Stanway
6
Hailes
7
Postlip
Winchcombe
Cleeve Hill
8
10
9a
9
11
Prestbury Hill-NR
11a
12
Cheltenham
Dowdeswell Reservoir
Leckhampton
13
14
Newent
Seven Springs
15
16
Crickley Hill
17
Ullenwood
18
Birdlip
Painswick Hill
19
Cranham Corner
Gloucester
21
20
Painswick
22
Randwick
Stonehouse
23
Stroud
25
Selsley
24
Cam & Dursley railway station
26
Cam
27
Dursley
28
Stinchcombe Hill
North Nibley
29
Wotton-under-Edge
30
Alderley
31
Lower Kilcott
32
33
Hawkesbury Upton
Chipping Sodbury
34
Horton
Little Sodbury
Old Sodbury
Yate
35
36
Coomb's End
Tormarton
37
Dyrham
38
Pennsylvania
39
40
Cold Ashton
41
42
43
Bath
FINISH

Westonbirt
Malmesbury
Chippenham

COTSWOLD WAY

trailblazer

0   5 miles
0   10km

MAP KEY
Map 1 – p81 Chipping Campden
Map 2 – p82 Fish Hill
Map 3 – p83 Broadway
Map 4 – p89 Shenberrow Hill
Map 5 – p91 Stanton & Stanway
Map 6 – p92 Wood Stanway
Map 7 – p94 Hailes
Map 8 – p95 Winchcombe
Map 9 – p100 Belas Knap
Map 9a – p101 Postlip
Map 10 – p103 Cleeve Hill & Common
Map 11 – p104 Prestbury Hill Reserve
Map 11a – p105 Southam
Map 12 – p110 Ham Hill
Map 13 – p111 Dowdeswell Reservoir
Map 14 – p113 Seven Springs
Map 15 – p115 Leckhampton Hill
Map 16 – p116 Crickley Hill
Map 17 – p118 Birdlip
Map 18 – p120 Cooper's Hill
Map 19 – p121 Painswick Hill
Map 20 – p123 Painswick
Map 21 – p127 Haresfield Beacon
Map 22 – p129 Randwick & Westrip
Map 23 – p131 Ebley
Map 24 – p133 King's Stanley
Map 25 – p135 Woodchester Park
Map 26 – p136 Uley
Map 27 – p137 Dursley
Map 28 – p142 Stinchcombe Hill
Map 29 – p143 North Nibley
Map 30 – p145 Wotton-under-Edge
Map 31 – p149 Alderley
Map 32 – p150 Lower Kilcott
Map 33 – p151 Hawkesbury Upton
Map 34 – p153 Horton
Map 35 – p155 Old Sodbury
Map 36 – p156 Tormarton
Map 37 – p158 Tolldown (South of M4)
Map 38 – p159 Dyrham
Map 39 – p161 Cold Ashton
Map 40 – p162 Hill Farm
Map 41 – p163 Freezing Hill
Map 42 – p165 Upper Weston
Map 43 – p167 Bath